HOW TO GROW AS AN ARTIST

HOW TO *Grow* AS AN *Artist*

DANIEL GRANT

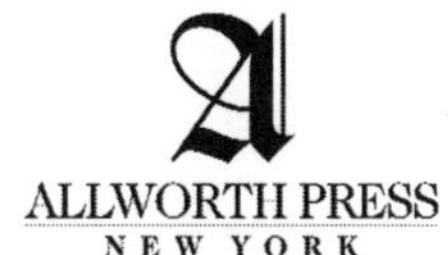

07 06 05 04 03 6 5 4 3 2

Published by Allworth Press
An imprint of Allworth Communications
10 East 23rd Street, New York, NY 10010

Cover design by Annemarie Redmond

Page composition/typography by Integra Software Services Pvt. Ltd., Pondicherry, India

An earlier edition of this book was previously published under the title *How to Start and Succeed as an Artist.*

Library of Congress Cataloging-in-Publication Data
Grant, Daniel.
How to grow as an artist / Daniel Grant.
p. cm.
Includes bibliographical references and index.

ISBN 1–58115–244–2
1. Art—Vocational guidance. I. Title.
N8350 .G743 2002

2002009120

Printed in Canada

Contents

Introduction

During the 1960s and 1970s, it was commonly said in the higher echelons of the art world that "painting is dead." "I'm merely making the last painting which anyone can make," Ad Reinhardt said in a 1966 interview about one of his many black-on-black paintings. Formalist tendencies brought to their extreme had made traditional painting—with its emphasis on brushwork, the mix of colors, and the idea of the picture as a window to the world—seem tedious and irrelevant, and many painters themselves began to look to other media, such as photography, film, video, and performance, which weren't so weighed down by history. The idea that painting was a pleasure in its own right didn't seem relevant.

The realist painter Fairfield Porter was told by critic Clement Greenberg: "You can't paint like that anymore." At least, the reason for Porter's low regard in the art world was made explicit to him. Greenberg's view that the train of art moves only one way on one track, and Reinhardt's opinion that his painting was where the train comes to a stop, reflect a hierarchical system in which only relatively few artists, holding certain rarified beliefs, could be considered worth looking at—all others are anachronistic daubers.

Many things stop people from making art: It could be the never-ending chores around the house, or the job, or raising children, or fear of not being capable enough, or fear of art itself. "Art" and "artist" are such loaded words that some people prefer to just keep their distance. Clearly, the art world itself has not always been helpful in this regard, denigrating as amateurs those artists who do not pursue certain ideas and art-making practices. The "pluralism" of the 1970s and postmodern eclecticism of the 1980s, 1990s, and 2000s have enlarged the scope of permissible styles, media, and subject matter, yet it is easy for artists to find themselves wide of acceptance by the art world. The much lauded "outsider" art of the past decade refers not to artists whose work had been overlooked by the major art publications and institutions but to untrained artists whose work bears a similarity to anthropological finds. Of course, artists need to maintain an awareness of new ideas and styles in their field by attending exhibitions and by reading critiques, essays, and books—less to be told what to do or how to do it than to keep their own art fresh by periodically challenging their own work.

What distinguishes art from almost every other pursuit—vocation or avocation—is that the credentials of the artist are of no particular importance to the creation of art. Certainly, art schools will rarely hire teachers without masters' degrees in fine arts, but the only degrees earned by Henri Matisse and Wassily Kandinsky were in the law. Matisse was twenty-one, a clerk in a law office in 1890, when he took his first art class, and Kandinsky was thirty in 1896, when he moved to Munich, Germany, in order to study painting, turning down the post of professor of law at the University of Tartu in Estonia, which had just been offered to him.

Artists are people who have defined themselves as such; those who believe in their own artwork have as much right to call themselves artists as the most celebrated figures whose works are displayed in galleries and museums. Art's greatest strength is that it is not the sole domain of specialists and technicians, that it follows no laws or doctrines. In fact, most art movements since Impressionism have made a point of defying "rules" and traditions. Art will remain alive as long as there are people interested in making it.

There are no right and wrong ways to develop one's artistic skills or exhibit and sell one's artwork, only approaches that may be better suited to certain artists than to others. While some people prefer to go it alone, others may join an art club or society, for example, in order to meet fellow artists working in the same medium with whom they can talk about art or socialize. Yet other artists choose to make those kinds of associations in an art class, joining a society primarily in order to exhibit with an established group. There are societies and classes for every purpose.

As much as artists are producers, they also are consumers—of art materials, art societies and other groups, of art classes and workshops, of services to the field and of books like this one—who need to be aware of the choices available to them as well as the benefits and (potential) drawbacks of each.

By its nature, art is a very private activity; yet, because art is a form of expression and communication, it is also by nature intended to be made public. It is in works of art that we are able to discover what an artist has been feeling and thinking, and it is through the process of creating that an artist is generally able to find a "voice." In developing one's artistic potential, one is able to make this voice more clear and distinct, better equipped to put a wider range of ideas into visual form. Certainly, the more adept or mature an artist becomes, the more prepared he or she is to present artwork to the outside world.

PART ONE

The Education of an Artist

CHAPTER ONE

Developing One's Skills with Others

Art, like everything else, takes practice. For many nonprofessionals, that frequently involves taking classes, working in a studio alongside other students engaged in their own or a common project under the supervision of an experienced teacher.

In decades past, the opportunities for art instruction were quite limited—adult education classes at a community center, for amateurs, and college and art-school degree programs for the professionally minded, with a rare exception, such as New York's Art Students League, somewhere in between. Nowadays, the possibilities for art classes are varied indeed, with programs offered at museums, the burgeoning number of non–degree-granting art schools, as well as art workshops (sponsored by inns, travel agencies, and artists themselves) and courses for nondegree students at degree-granting colleges and art schools. The hierarchy also is no longer so clear, as amateurs and professionals often find themselves in the same classes, pursuing new or improved skills for the same or different reasons.

For instance, approximately half of the students enrolled in the MFA in Visual Art program at Vermont College of the Union Institute (see chapter 2), a degree program in which students pursue self-designed independent study at home and spend only ten days per year on the campus meeting with faculty, already earn a living as art teachers while the rest work in other, varied fields. According to Jessica Lutz, director of the program, many of the students who are art teachers want the MFA degree for reasons of career advancement in teaching, and a host of professional, or purely personal, goals bring the others to the program. The common denominators for all these students are, first, that they seek the level of instruction of an art school but may not be in a position to leave their homes and jobs for two years in order to obtain it, and, second, the high level of their artwork. "To be accepted into the MFA program, they must produce work worthy of being in the program," Lutz said.

Continuing Education

Other art schools have instituted a range of alternative course options for nontraditional students, which attract amateur and professional artists. In these classes, one may often find professionals seeking to learn new media and techniques, those in other fields considering a career change, as well as individuals who simply desire instruction at a high level. The Minneapolis College of Art & Design, for example, has a continuing education program (one offered course is a month-long art workshop in Florence,

Italy), a two-year part-time post-baccalaureate certificate program for students with a bachelor's degree but not a BFA, and online courses (featuring chat rooms and posted questions and answers) with a workload equal to what is expected of a normal studio class. The School of the Museum of Fine Arts in Boston also offers daytime and evening art classes through continuing education, a one-year, full-time post-baccalaureate program, and a four-year diploma program for students who already hold bachelors' degrees and do not need the liberal arts component of the BFA.

The post-baccalaureate program is popping up at a number of schools, pursued by students who are considering enrolling in an MFA program but who need to bring their artwork up to a higher level. The certificate program of the Corcoran College of Art and Design in Washington, D.C., is actually titled an Associate of Fine Arts Degree Program, designed for part-time students (many of the classes are scheduled in the evenings and on weekends) and allowing students six years to complete the course of study. Frequently, certificate students are enrolled in the same classes as full-time students pursuing baccalaureate or masters' degrees, and they are graded along with everyone else based on identical expectations. (Continuing-education courses, on the other hand, do not assign grades or offer course credits, and the instructors may or may not be the same as in degree programs.)

More on the career-change side is the Cleveland Institute of Art, whose continuing education department offers two certificate programs—in digital multimedia and desktop publishing. The Art Institute of Boston at Lesley University also offers diploma and certificate programs, including a two-year studio-intensive Advanced Professional Certificate program in either graphic design or illustration, created for students who already received their bachelors' degrees and are looking to develop professional career skills. These classes are held during the day, and one pays normal full-time tuition.

Many art schools have certificate programs in specific fields—the School of the Art Institute of Chicago has just one in drawing, while the Rhode Island School of Design offers seven in the applied arts (advertising and print design, art appraisal, computer graphics, decorative painting, interior design, new media, natural-science illustration, and Web design)—while the Maryland Institute College of Art and the Philadelphia Academy of Fine Arts more generally provide certificates in fine arts.

Certificate programs vary greatly from one school to another, in the number of classes required and the length of time one may take to complete the program. The certificate program of the Lyme Academy of Art in Old Lyme, Connecticut, for instance, is comparable to Boston's diploma program in terms of the number of required classes and the length of time expected to complete the course of study. "Our certificate is much more of a professional program," said admissions counselor Chris Rose, a fact that may be true but, in terms of a credential or a line on a résumé, will not offer any greater weight. The résumé value of a certificate is questionable, and students who have graduated these programs may need to content themselves solely with what they learned. "We used to offer the certificate degree," said Amy Miguel, spokeswoman for Massachusetts Communications College in Boston, which focuses on commercial art training, "but we discontinued it, because we weren't placing any of our graduates."

While all degree students apply for acceptance into the school through the admissions department—which requires a portfolio review, recommendations or letters of reference, submission of an application, perhaps an interview and college-board or graduate-record exam scores—certificate programs may or may not involve admissions. Additionally, the same course at Otis College of Art & Design in Los Angeles may be priced differently for different students, depending upon their intentions. An enrolled baccalaureate student at Otis would pay $630 per credit for a three-credit class, while another student in a certificate program pays $395, and yet a third student, who is not taking the course for credit, is charged $360. The differences are chalked up to administrative expenses of recording the grade and credit for a transcript. Of course, if noncredit students decide that they want a certificate or higher degree from the school, they would not be able to apply the class to a degree program retroactively but would have to take the course again.

Art Classes

Before the Second World War, choices for art classes were either extremely limited or nonexistent for most people, which was the main reason that those seriously interested in studying art were faced with the decision of moving to some major city (such as Chicago, New York, or Paris) in order to obtain high-level instruction. Nowadays, with professional artists teaching in art departments at colleges and universities around the country and the emergence of regional art markets, the opportunities have increased exponentially. One can take art classes through adult-education programs at high schools and community (or senior citizen) centers, from artists in their studios and at arts centers, at museums, art associations, and degree-granting institutions.

Adult education programs tend to be the least intensive, providing basic information for beginners, while classes offered at arts centers and museums allow more time to work in a studio with more rigorous standards set by peers as well as the instructor. Community college, college, and university art classes, which frequently are open to non–degree-seeking students when not filled by regular students, offer the largest blocks of studio time. These latter classes are often taught with greater formality than those at high schools and arts centers, and may include specific assignments, homework, and serious critiques.

This hierarchy doesn't always hold true, however, as many of the same instructors at the college level also teach at museums, arts centers, and in adult-education programs. As a survey of the variety of art classes offered in Fairfield County, Connecticut, and the Boca Raton–West Palm Beach area of Florida reveals, the teachers may alter their approach and requirements depending upon the venue, but not always. Kevin Thomas, who teaches courses at the Silvermine Art Guild in New Canaan, Connecticut, and Northern Westchester Center for the Arts (in Westchester County, New York), as well as in the art department of New York University, noted that at all three institutions he finds "intelligent, extremely motivated students." However, there is a far greater range in skill levels at community art schools—"from the complete beginner to people who are almost ready to be out on their own"—than at a university, where all of the students were probably the art stars in their high schools. Also, whereas his NYU students are "looking for a lot of instruction and have class goals that they have to meet," students at Silvermine and (to a lesser extent) Northern Westchester Center for the Arts "want some technical know-how so they can do what they came there to do. They're too headstrong for the kind of teaching I do at NYU." These adult students are less interested in being trained from scratch and are less likely to take an assignment. "To a degree, my job is to circumvent their lack of skills to help them get what they came for. At a college, there are requirements to go through before you gain your freedom, but students at Silvermine don't want to wait that long."

Similarly, Rick Yasko, a drawing instructor at both Florida Atlantic University in Boca Raton, Florida, and the Boca Raton Museum of Art, said that "my classes are definitely more relaxed when I'm teaching at the museum than at the university. I'm more demanding of students in the university, because I am supposed to be providing an academic training for students who are going on to pursue graduate programs in art, or to find a job, and need a professional-looking portfolio. At the museum, there are no grades, and, if I give an assignment, it usually can be completed by the time the class is over."

A number of his students at the museum also take his courses at the university on a nondegree basis. The nondegree people, he has found, are "sometimes more dedicated to their art than the regular students, because they're not interested in a grade or a degree." As it is not uncommon for these students to take the same course again and again, Yasko tries "to gear things differently each time the course is given, in order to let them try new media"—such as silverpoint and pastels—"and new ideas about drawing."

Other differences between taking a class at the university and at the museum are the cost and the amount of time involved. Florida Atlantic University charges $76.50 per credit to Florida residents for its three- or four-credit fourteen-week classes ($250 per credit to non-Florida residents). The Boca Raton Museum of Art, on the other hand, requires $120 for its once-a-week (for six weeks) class. Again, the differences may not be so sharp since, according to the museum's art school registrar Lois Prochlik, "we have a number of people who take two or three classes. They spend the whole day here." The difference in price is also considerable between New York University, where classes are $820 per credit, and Silvermine, where semester-long (twelve weeks), once-a-week, three-hour classes "are in the $300 range," according to the school's director, Cindy Claire. "There may be an additional model fee."

If classes at a museum are less stressful than at a university or college, those taught at arts centers are often even more easy going. Jak Kovatch, who has taught for decades at both Silvermine and the University of Bridgeport, as well as night school classes at a high school and even correspondence classes through Famous Artists, described community art classes as a "nonthreatening environment. You are permitted to experiment, blue-sky, without fear of being chastised for doing something wrong." Barbara Wasserman, a Boca Raton painter who teaches at both the Boca Raton Museum of Art and at the Armory Art Center in West Palm Beach, also noted that "an art center is a more family-like institution. Universities can sometimes treat you like a number, and museums are more focused on the needs of the museum than on painting students. An art center, on the other hand, is focused on its students because the students are its reason for being."

Eight-week, three-hour classes at the Armory Art Center, which was set up in 1987 after the Norton Gallery of Art in West Palm Beach closed its teaching facility, cost $120. With the overlap of a number of instructors at both the Armory Art Center and the Boca Raton Museum, and the fact that many of the students take classes at both, the level of teaching between the two institutions is not significantly different. However, several of the teachers indicated that more classes at the museum have specific assignments, such as painting from a model or learning color values, than at the art center, which has more of a do-your-own-thing approach.

Wasserman noted, for instance, that some of the students in her classes at the Armory paint in a highly realistic style, while "others are very abstract. The challenge for me is to be able to work with each one of them, in a manner geared to their interests and to their level of skill." Another instructor at the Armory, watercolorist Lynn Thurmond, also teaches at the private Everglades Club in West Palm Beach, where the range of skill and devotion to developing one's craft among students is wider. "There are some people at the Everglades Club who are very serious about their work and really want me to give them any advice I can," she stated. "There are other people who just have the time to do something, and art is relaxing and a sociable experience. A lot of them don't want as much guidance and instruction and are pretty adamant about having their way about it. There's nothing wrong with that, but, at the Armory, almost everyone wants to get their money's worth out of me."

Other than these kinds of art classes, one may locate adult-education or night-school programs, classes offered by artist associations, and workshops offered at an artist's own studio. These frequently are less expensive, because students do not have to pay as much for overhead expenses (rent, utilities, security, custodial services), and frequently go further along the road of informality.

There are various sources of information on art classes, starting with a local or state arts agency, since many institutions offering art instruction apply for governmental funding. High schools and community centers, arts centers and organizations, museums, and colleges all may provide classes or refer inquirers to those that do. R. R. Bowker's *American Art Directory,* which costs $195 but is available at many public libraries, lists art schools and college art departments as well as art associations around the United States (by state and city) and the world.

Those wanting to take a class should decide in advance what they are looking for, such as a class exclusively for beginners or one with a mix of different levels of skill. Adult-education classes, which may be taught by high school art instructors or someone in the community, generally last two hours a weeknight for six to eight weeks, while those offered by colleges may meet for four-hour stretches lasting an entire semester. Some classes have live models, others don't. Some classes provide specific activities or assignments, while others allow students to work on whatever they choose. Some schools have fixed time periods for classes, others allow those wishing to take a class to walk in any time. Some teachers take a very proactive role, assuming their students want considerable instruction and even homework, and others may just wander around students' work areas from time to time, offering only the slightest commentary. Some teachers emphasize detailed critiques of student work, while others prefer to work on the level of suggestion. Some teachers may spend the entire class working on their own projects, while letting students with questions approach them, and some classes do without instructors completely.

Usually, it is the presence of a particular teacher that makes more of a difference than the specific school, and potential students might want to sit in on a class to see if they like what other students are doing and what the teacher is saying. This may be especially useful when one is taking a class at a college, as the content of the course may be difficult to comprehend by the language used in the syllabus but easier to understand in practice. At other times, the instruction may seem too basic or not rigorous enough. Robert Hertz, who currently teaches drawing and portraiture at both the Armory Art Center and the Boca Raton Museum of Art, remembered an art class he sat in on, in which the instructor "showed you a picture and asked you to copy it. After you had completed the assignment, he looked at it and said, 'Very nice.'"

It is not uncommon for students who have enjoyed an artist's instruction at a class to also study with the artist at his or her studio. "If you find a good instructor," Rick Yasko, who has held occasional one-day workshops at his studio (charging between $25 and $50 per person), said, "you follow them around continuously." It may or may not matter to certain students that their instructor is a full-time artist who happens to teach, as opposed to a full-time teacher who also creates art. Yasko, for instance, teaches not only at Florida Atlantic University and the Boca Raton Museum of Art, but at Barry University (at Miami Shores), Broward Community College in Davey, and Palm Beach Community College. Art instructors are always expected to be artists first, but teaching positions are generally so rare and so poorly paid that artists must get two, three, or four jobs in order to support themselves and their art, which they no longer have much time to pursue. All that running around may, for some, also prove detrimental to their art and lessen their interest in teaching.

"The difference between me and someone who only teaches for a living is enthusiasm," said Sharon Koskoff, a self-supporting artist in Delray Beach, Florida, who also teaches painting and drawing at the Armory Art Center. "I never feel that I'm really working unless I'm creating art, so I can bring some of that enthusiasm to my students."

The Benefits of Taking an Art Workshop

There are a lot of ways to learn how to create art or improve one's artistic skills. Trial and error on one's own is the most common. Many people also look for help from other, skilled artists, which increases the cost of that learning but may speed it up and give it new direction. Art schools, art classes, correspondence-course art schools, instructional videotapes, art instruction books, and art workshops are among the main choices in this category.

Each type of instruction requires something a little different from the would-be student. Degree-granting art schools often require the greatest commitment of time and money; students leave these programs not only with studio art training but with in-depth knowledge of art history and theory. Art classes and correspondence art courses, on the other hand, require less time and money but cannot provide the intensity and individual attention of the art-school experience. Instructional videotapes and art-instruction books cost even less, and make no specific demands on one's scheduling, but are the most impersonal.

Art workshops are something in-between: They provide an intense art experience, but for a relatively short period of time—three days or a week, maybe two—that may be easier for busy people to schedule; their cost ranges widely, from $200 to $2,800, depending upon the length of the workshop, the renown of the artist-teacher, and whether or not one needs to travel to the workshop site, paying for accommodations and food as well as transportation.

A potential advantage of workshops over art classes is that, in a workshop, participants study with a professional working artist; not all art class instructors are full-time artists. Workshops also generally include demonstrations by the artist—art classes and schools rarely if ever do—which enables students to see every step in the creative process, from how to put paint on a palette and clean brushes afterwards to how to capture a certain quality of light on a canvas.

In many workshops, full-time, self-supporting artists can be found among the students. They add a degree of seriousness of purpose for the less advanced, and afford themselves the opportunity to expand their thinking and techniques in directions they hadn't tried before or perhaps felt they couldn't move in on their own.

Some workshops focus on particular media, such as pastels, watercolors, oil paints, acrylics, printmaking, and sculpture, while others concentrate on specific subject matter—such as the figure, landscape, portraiture, or seascapes. Some artists hold workshops in their own studios, while others are hired by hotel owners and workshop sponsors at a university or vacation setting to teach over a five- or six-day period, and still other artists hold classes on cruise ships or lead groups to foreign countries in order to paint there.

Hundreds of these art workshops are offered each year, advertised in the classified sections of *American Artist* and *The Artist's Magazine* as well as other art publications, and knowing how to choose the right one can be daunting. Actually, the sheer volume of workshops is an indication in itself. As one looks over the promotional materials for a variety of workshops in different locations, many of the same instructors' names frequently come up. These artists are often invited back to the same workshop site year after year, and it is safe to assume that they have established a good reputation for their teaching, critiques, demonstrations, and ability to get along with their students. It is the artists who are not as capable in those areas whose names drop out of sight after a period of time.

Almost all workshop teachers or sponsors will answer questions over the telephone and, perhaps more useful, mail a brochure or some other information about the artist that shows his or her work (seeing examples of artwork will help the more experienced prospective student determine the artist's own level of quality) and may also indicate how the workshop will be conducted. Not all brochures are equally informative. Artists' own brochures are more likely to use color reproductions of their work and provide some sense of their artistic approach, for instance, whereas the material provided by hotel owner/workshop sponsors is more frequently in black-and-white and more explicit about the accommodations and area attractions than about what happens during the workshop.

A number of the same artists who lead workshops have also written art-instruction books or created videocassettes of their methods, which provide a sense of their approach to teaching. For instance, portrait artist Daniel Greene, who leads approximately twenty week-long workshops a year, is the author of two books, *Pastel* and *The Art of Pastel,* and has two videos of himself at work on a portrait. Zoltan Szabo and Frank Webb, who both hold watercolor workshops, are represented by instructional videocassettes and eight books (six for Szabo, two for Webb). A small investment in a book or videocassette may help one decide whether or not to make the larger investment in a week-long workshop. In addition, many artists either have written for art magazines or have been profiled in them. There is a lot of information available about those who lead workshops, and prospective students shouldn't be shy about asking.

The majority of workshop participants are women, middle-aged and older. Chris Unwin, a watercolorist who organizes cruise-ship workshops and sometimes leads them herself, noted that "male artists attract more men to workshops. Frank Webb, for instance, attracted an incredibly high percentage of men to his workshop, probably a third." Between one-quarter and one-half of the workshops of certain prominent artists are attended by people who have been there before, and prospective students can ask the artist for references from past students. From these people (who are likely to speak favorably about the artist and the workshop), one can inquire about the kind of individual attention each student receives, whether or not there are demonstrations and critiques (and what these demonstrations and critiques consist of), the number of models used (or other kinds of assignments given), the level of ability of most workshop participants, the amount of studio space, the number of students in the group, how participants interact inside and outside of class, and whether the week felt like a vacation or serious, intense study. Word-of-mouth is usually the best guide one way or another.

There are a number of areas for which prospective students may do troubleshooting: Some workshop instructors lecture too long, providing more information and advice than students can hold at one time, and, by the time participants are allowed to start working, they have lost some of their energy. Some instructors seem to be "on an ego trip," Chris Unwin said. "They'll say, 'Anyone who wants to paint may do so but I'll be over here, painting for anyone who wants to watch.' Well, who wouldn't watch the artist instead of painting oneself, but that defeats the purpose of the workshop."

All of the students in a given workshop deserve and expect individual attention, and some may attempt to dominate the workshop leader's time, but good instructors know how to give everyone equal time and consideration, taking each student at his or her own level. Everyone in the class also expects that critiques and comments on their work will come from the instructor, who was the reason students signed up in the first place, and may resent instead hearing the teacher ask the other workshop participants for their opinions. There is also the question of personal style. Some instructors are naturally enthusiastic, encouraging students to get excited about their work, while others are more relaxed and low-key in their approach. There are followers of both types of instructors and all the various types in-between, more often depending upon what ideas and techniques the artist has to teach.

Of course, not everyone cares as much about the artist-teacher's own work and how the workshop is structured as they do about the opportunity for a vacation-with-art. "Actually, I don't like the way Gerald Brommer paints, but he's a very nice person and a good teacher," said Floridian Marjorie Johnson who has taken watercolor and sketching workshops with Brommer in Maui, Hawaii, and Oaxaca, Mexico, that were arranged by Artists Workshop Tours Agency of Chula Vista, California. Johnson and her husband both took these trips (she painted while he pursued sightseeing) because "we both have always wanted to go to these places." She added that the two of them haven't just gone on their own because "I might not have found the same spots to paint in. It might not be as comfortable to just paint by myself, and I like the company. There is a lot of camaraderie."

For other students, the skill of the teacher is of paramount importance. Peter Seltzer of Bethlehem, Connecticut, who claimed to have always been interested in art but never pursued it, stated that, back in 1984, "the owner of an art shop was showing me someone's drawings; it was someone whose work I had seen before, and I noticed an enormous improvement in that person's work. I commented about that change, and the shop owner mentioned that this person had studied with Daniel Greene. I spent five summers studying with Dan after that."

The intensity of the workshop experience is frequently left to the participant to decide. Some students who have traveled a distance to an area they've never seen before may choose to paint in the morning and sightsee during the afternoon, rejoining the group in the evening for a meal and a critique by the instructor. "Some of our beginners may get carried away by being on a cruise—they decide that they want to go scuba diving," Chris Unwin said. "We encourage that by scheduling free time." Bernice Taplitz, who lives on Long Island, New York, and who has taken painting workshops with several different instructors, noted the vacation atmosphere of these events, pointing out that "you may not learn anything, but enjoy the weekend."

Other workshops demand full-time attention to one's artwork, which may mean traveling to an attractive place but spending the entire time staring at a model or learning about color, composition, design, and values. "I work the hell out of them," Jack Beal stated. "No one plays here. I've asked some of the students what other workshops are like, and a number of them have said, 'No one has ever worked me this hard.' That's the way I want it."

Workshops for Beginners, Intermediate, and Advanced Artists

Workshops come in all varieties. Some are oriented toward beginners, others are for those with some art-making experience, and still others are for people with considerable art training, or even professional artists, and many accept a mix of all three. The workshops that accept potential students on a first-come, first-served basis are more likely to have students with a wide range of experience than those in which a selection based on one's level of skill takes place.

Most art workshops are filled on a first-come, first-served basis, but not the ones offered by husband-and-wife painters Jack Beal and Songra Freckelton. Those who attend the workshops they teach must first submit an application and slides of their work; then applicants must describe their expectations for the workshop, the areas in which they feel they need improvement, and their "general attitude about making art," Freckelton said. Why all the questions?

"We don't want raw beginners," she said. "We don't want people who expect they're just coming for a vacation. We don't teach fundamentals here, how to draw, how to do composition, how to mix colors. They have to know how to do that before they come here."

As a result, the Beal-Freckelton workshops are described as for "intermediate and advanced" students, and some professional artists come as well. Beal and Freckelton look over the applications they receive to weed out the inexperienced.

The application form painter Tony Van Hasselt sends out to those interested in taking his workshop has even more questions—additionally inquiring about the individual's drawing ability (pick one: "OK," "fair," and "[need] help"), medium, exhibition history, where studied art previously and the level of art expertise (beginner, intermediate, advanced, or professional)—and applicants must also submit slides or photographs of their work in order that Van Hasselt may determine for himself their skill at "composition and how they handle the medium." Similar to Jack Beal and Sondra Freckelton, Van Hasselt usually limits his workshops to intermediate and advanced students, and he checks to make sure beginners aren't putting themselves up a notch.

"The terms—beginner, intermediate, and advanced—are awfully hard to define," he said. "People who apply may think they are advanced, because they have painted for a number of years, but I may look at their work and think they are beginners." He added that he often advises beginners to take a class or two where they live, in order to improve their skills, because otherwise "it's too frustrating for them and for me" when they take his workshop.

Hard-and-fast definitions of ability are not easily come by. Certainly, the art world is filled with a number of highly charged terms. An "artist," for instance, should refer to a person who makes art, but it tends to be a quite value-laden word that may indicate someone's lifestyle, occupation, or level of seriousness. One is far less likely to be accused of pretentiousness for calling oneself a "painter." The word "amateur" also has a number of objective and pejorative meanings, from "A person who engages in any art, science, study, or athletic activity as a pastime rather than as a profession" (*American Heritage Dictionary*) to "superficial or unskillful" (*The American College Dictionary*). Mostly, it is a negative designation: An "amateur psychologist" means a "busybody," and an amateur artist suggests a "dabbler," someone untrained and ungood. Art workshops further crowd the art field with terms that are similarly subjective in their definitions. What are beginner, intermediate, and advanced artists? Is a beginner someone who has never held a paintbrush before, or simply new to a particular medium? Does advanced mean "at a professional level" or just "experienced in the medium"?

Few workshop instructors themselves can formulate definitions, and they are not always strict in adhering to their guidelines. "I don't like to turn anyone down," said painter Barbara Savage. "We accept most of our applicants," Freckelton said, and many others who jury their applicants acknowledged the same.

Who gets in and who doesn't can seem a bit serendipitous. In some cases, instructors admit students to their workshops solely on the basis of a recommendation from a colleague, or they may choose not to accept an applicant based on the kind of art the individual pursues, regardless of that person's level of experience—certainly, there needs to be a reasonable fit between what the instructor has to offer and what a student requires. Painter Wolf Kahn noted that he pointedly "tries to make a group every time. I take every man, because there're always more women than men, and I try to get a sufficient number of young people, because otherwise you're stuck with a lot of people just talking about their ailments. Besides that, it's totally pot luck."

In general, art workshops that are organized by a third-party sponsor, such as an inn or travel agency, are less likely to sort students by level of skill, while artists who run workshops out of their own studios are more apt to ask for information about applicants. Janet Walsh, who teaches watercolor workshops, said that she doesn't have "much to do with putting a group together" when the event is organized by a sponsor, but will "cull through" applications for classes taught at her own Lloyd Harbor, New York, studio. However, the process of selecting those students rests on her "intuition" and the desire of someone to take one of her workshops: "Someone who has really pushed to get in, who has called a number of times and clearly wants it, I'll take that person," she said.

The purpose of designating a workshop for a higher level of skills may be twofold: The first is to attract a certain type of student who might be bored by a class whose members primarily need to focus on fundamentals; the second is to help would-be students select the most appropriate instruction—presumably, beginners would know to shy away from a class called "intensive monotype" when they have never done any kind of printmaking before. The detailed descriptions of a workshop, written up by the instructor or sponsor, would reveal the degree of skill and experience assumed.

Distinctions, however, can become blurred very easily. William Herring, a painting instructor, looks for intermediate and advanced students and requires all applicants to submit slides and a letter stating what they hope to achieve through the workshop in order to be accepted, but he is more interested in "heart than in skill, because skill can come later," said Sara Chambers, who arranges Herring's workshops. Pat Deadman, another painting instructor, also identifies her programs as structured for intermediate and advanced students, but that refers not to who may take the class but "to the level of my teaching. I don't talk about the kind of paper to use or how to mix colors. Of course, if somebody asks me about those things, I will answer the questions. But that uses up a lot of time that takes away from my teaching."

According to Larry Blovits, a landscape artist and workshop instructor, most people take an art workshop because they are "dissatisfied with the level of work they are doing. They've hit their self-taught wall and want to do what you're doing."

Beginners, he claimed, often lack basic skills—understanding of color, composition, depth, light, and volume—and "don't know how to draw. But, if you offer a drawing workshop, that's the one they don't take. Too many students put the cart before the horse—they want to do advanced painting before they know how to draw and, as a result, they come to a class looking for shortcuts and easy answers." In the open-to-all workshops Blovits has led, he continually has found himself "hammering in the basic fundamentals."

Painter and workshop instructor Ann Templeton also said that "I don't take beginners at all," noting that beginners require so much attention when they are starting out that she cannot assist other students equally. "I prefer intermediate and advanced students, and I try to make that clear in the brochure I send out."

Some classes simply lend themselves to more experienced students by their very nature. Daniel Greene, who leads portrait workshops, stated that his students generally already understand many of the fundamentals of painting and are looking to "learn how to paint people—for instance, friends, children, or grandchildren—because that's an area in which they are lacking." On occasion, Greene has taught master classes, for which applicants were required to submit a portfolio of their work; however, most of his workshops have been filled on a first-come, first-served basis.

Because he and most other workshop instructors accept all comers, the potential for more advanced students to be bored by slower students, or beginners to feel overwhelmed by a level of teaching that assumes students understand the basics, is ever present. Instructors need to be able to switch gears rapidly and easily, conveying information in a manner that appeals to everyone and making every student feel appreciated and helped at his or her level—no easy feat. "My preference is for people who are advanced, because we get to deal with much more esoteric areas of instruction, which can be more fun," Greene said. "But it is also rewarding to see beginning students develop their skills." Many open-to-all-level workshops are balancing acts for teachers. Some instructors attempt to accomplish this by giving equal time to every single student, while Wolf Kahn claims that he speaks to all students "on a high spiritual, intellectual level, and they respond to that. From the rawest beginner to the professional, they all want technical tricks, but once you tell them that this isn't important they believe you and try to create work that is personal and meaningful."

Prospective workshop applicants should ask for the names of past students to inquire how attentive the instructor was to each person and whether or not boredom or confusion were ever problems for group members. Chris Unwin noted that teachers of beginner classes not only attempt to help students understand fundamentals of artmaking but seek to direct them to where their strengths and interests are in art. "These workshops help students figure out who they are," she said. On the other hand, the more complicated teaching in classes directed to advanced students are "not at all about finding yourself" but to learn "technical things."

The composition of students in a workshop is difficult to predetermine, even when certain levels of artistic skill are identified, and yet it may be as important as the instructor, because group members learn almost as much from each other as from the teacher. Where there is a mix of skill levels, beginners may learn from more experienced students. Kahn noted that a drawback of master classes and others directed toward advanced students is "a dog-eat-dog atmosphere when everybody thinks he's a hotshot." Similarly, painter and occasional workshop instructor Janet Fish said that "someone who has sold some work in his lifetime may have a high opinion of himself and not be as open to criticism," whereas "someone who is totally untrained may be really ready to learn." For that reason, Carmen Layden, who runs Valdes Art Workshops in Santa Fe, New Mexico, primarily organizes for beginners "because you don't have to unlearn them of bad habits that more experienced students may have developed over years." The major frustrations for teachers are "people who think they know something but really don't." Other instructors also complained about experienced students who are "hard-headed" and "set in their ways" and who "can't handle the critique."

The expectations of students in a juried workshop are likely to be higher than in first-come-first-served classes, because of their prior experience in art or the particular medium (such as watercolor) or the specific subject matter (for instance, landscape). The students look for instruction on a higher level, such as a particular technique to create certain effects, or a design viewpoint, or a discussion of conceptual and theoretical issues, perhaps just the critique of a master artist. Mixed-level classes sometimes lead to frustration for both the instructor and advanced students who want to maintain a dialogue on a conceptual level, and for the beginner who is trying to keep up. When his workshops include a wide range of skills, Van Hasselt noted that he may schedule a 4:00 critique, "but I'll have the beginners in my class come in at 3:30. Otherwise, it puts the more advanced people to sleep." Daniel Greene stated that some of his regular students just keep working while he explains fundamentals to his beginning students, "and they'll stop and tune in when I get to something at a more advanced level."

Workshops on all levels tend to be intense experiences, because students continually are being challenged by new techniques and ideas, but the intensity may be greatest for those with more advanced skills. For one thing, the critiques may be tougher (or just tougher to withstand) for more experienced students. Additionally, the teaching approach is likely to be more demanding. "I push the envelope with more advanced people," said Jeremiah Patterson, a painting workshop instructor. "I talk about sophisticated concepts that I think about, but it wouldn't be fair to talk about those things with beginners, because they wouldn't understand."

Thousands of workshops are offered throughout the year and around the country, for artists of most media and all levels of skill. Many are arranged by the instructors themselves, while inns and schools hold most of the others. The March issues of *American Artist* magazine and *The Artist's Magazine* provide substantial listings of who is offering what where and when. Another source of information is Art Workshop Directory (*www.artworkshopdirectory.com*), which provides a periodically updated list of workshops categorized by location.

Artists Workshops Sponsors

Below are a number of the largest workshop sponsors (rather than workshops offered by individual artists), where one may write for information.

In the United States

Alabama

American Society of Portrait Painters
P.O. Box 230216
2781 Zelda Road
Montgomery, AL 36123
(800) 622–7672
www.asopa.org

Arizona

Scottsdale Artists' School, Inc.
P.O. Box 8527
Scottsdale, AZ 85252
(408) 990–1422 or (800) 333–5707
www.scottsdaleartschool.org

Sedona Arts Center
P.O. Box 569
Sedona, AZ 86339
(502) 282–3809
www.sedonaartscenter.com

California

Artist Workshop
2230 Pennsylvania Avenue
Fairfield, CA 94533
(707) 425–1560

Artist Travel
5455 Sylmar Avenue
Sherman Oaks, CA 91401
(818) 994–2402
E-mail: *galitaly@aol.com*
www.artistravel.com

Artists Workshop Tours Agency
606 Myra Avenue
Chula Vista, CA 91910
(619) 585–8071

Cambria Pines Lodge Workshops
2905 Burton Drive
Cambria, CA 93428
(805) 927–4200

Central Coast Studio Workshops
Suite C
365 Quintana Road
Morro Bay, CA 93442
(805) 772–4198

CSU Summer Arts
Humboldt State University
Arcata, CA 95521
(707) 826–5401

D'Pharr Painting Workshops
8527 MacDuff Court
Stockton, CA 95209
(209) 477–1562

Hillcrest Art Center
800 Hillcrest
Cambria, CA 93428
(805) 927–1537

Ladybug Art Gallery & Workshop Studio
462 Rose Street
Bishop, CA 93514
(619) 873–3600

Lighthouse Art Center Workshops
575 Highway U.S. 101 South
Crescent City, CA 95531
(707) 464–4137

Mendocino Art Center
P.O. Box 765
Mendocino, CA 95460
(707) 937–5818

Merced College Watercolor Workshop
3600 M Street
Merced, CA 95348
(209) 384–6223

Pacific Academy of Fine Arts
6821 Laguna Park Way
Sebastopol, CA 95472
(707) 823–2179
www.pacacad.com

Palos Verdes Art Center Master Series Workshops
5504 West Crestridge Road
Rancho Palos Verdes,
CA 90274
(310) 541–2479

Redwood Coast Art Workshops
Lighthouse Art Center
575 U.S. Highway 101 South
Crescent City, CA 95531
(707) 464–4137

San Diego Artists' School Workshops
P.O. Box 803
Jamul, CA 91935
(619) 697–9114

Colorado

Anderson Ranch Arts Center
Workshops
P.O. Box 5598
Snowmass Village, CO 81615
(970) 923–3181
www.andersonranch.org

Art in the Aspens
1340 Dallas Street
Aurora, CO 80010
(303) 343–9789

Artists of the Rockies Workshops
Westcliffe Centre for the Arts
P.O. Box 930
Westcliffe, CO 81252
(719) 783–2296

Blackhawk Mountain School of Art
Box 5324
Estes Park, CO 80517
(800) 477–2272

Colorado Watercolor Workshops
3305 Brenner Place
Colorado Springs, CO 80917
(719) 591–0380

Higher Elevations Artists Workshop
P.O. Box 457
Lake City, CO 81235
(212) 246–4405

Loveland Academy of Fine Arts
205 12th Street, S.W.
Loveland, CO 80537
(800) 762–5232

Schalew Corporation Workshops
346 South Karval Drive
Pueblo West, CO 81007
(719) 547–0329

Upper Edge Gallery Workshops
303 East Main
Aspen, CO 81611
(303) 544–0803

Connecticut

Brookfield Craft Center
Workshops
P.O. Box 122
Brookfield, CT 06804
(203) 775–4526
www.brookfieldcraftcenter.org

Mystic Art Association
9 Water Street
Mystic, CT 06355
(860) 536–7601
www.mystic-art.org

Rudman Watercolor Workshops
274 Quarry Road
Stamford, CT 06903
(203) 322–1448

Delaware

Rehoboth Art League
12 Dodds Lane
Henlopen Acres
Rehoboth Beach, DE 19971
(302) 227–8408

Florida

Armory Arts Center Master Artist Workshops
1703 South Lake Avenue
West Palm Beach, FL 33401
(561) 832–1776

Art Center for Sarasota
707 North Tamiami Trail
Sarasota, FL 34236
(941) 365–2032
www.artsarasota.org

Gainesville Fine Arts Association
P.O. Box 4323
Gainesville, FL 32613

Gallery on Fifth
950 Third Avenue North
Camples, FL 34102
(941) 435–7377

Hilton Leech Studio Watercolor
Workshops
P.O. Box 15766
Sarasota, FL 34277
(941) 924–5770

Palm Beach Photographic Workshops
600 Fairway Drive
Deerfield Beach, FL 33432
(407) 391–7557

Portrait Society of America
P.O. Box 11272
Tallahassee, FL 32302
(877) 772–4321
www.portraitsociety.org

Katherine Rowland Workshops
P.O. Box 35187
Sarasota, FL 34242
(813) 349–1714

Visual Arts Center of Northwest
Florida Workshops
19 East 4th Street
Panama City, FL 32401
(904) 769–4451

Georgia

Atlanta College of Art Workshops
1280 Peachtree Street, N.E.
Atlanta, GA 30309
(404) 898–1169

Hawaii

Hui No'Eau Visual Arts Center
2841 Baldwin Avenue
Makawao, HI 96768
(808) 572–6560
www.maui.net/hui

Illinois

Artists Book Works Workshops
1422 West Irving Park Road
Chicago, IL 60613
(312) 348–4469

Indiana

Art Barn
695 North 400 East
Valparaiso, IN 46383
(219) 462–8520

Louisiana

New Orleans Watercolor Workshops
8809 Tanglewild Place
New Orleans, LA 70123
(504) 737–5281

Maine

Eastport Arts Center
P.O. Box 153
Eastport, ME 04631
(207) 853–2955

Maine Coast Art Workshops
2 Park Street
Rockland, ME 40841
(207) 594–2300

Sebasco Art Workshops
Rock Gardens Inn
P.O. Box 178
Sebasco Estates, ME 04565
(207) 389–1339
www.rockgardensinn.com

Round Top Center for the Arts
Box 1316, Business Route 1
Damariscotta, ME 04543
(207) 563–1507

Maryland

Haystack Mountain Workshops
408 Washington Street
Cumberland, MD 21502
(301) 777–0003
(800) 286–9718

Massachusetts

Cape Cod School of Art
P.O. Box 948
Provincetown, MA 02657
(508) 487–0101
www.capecod.ned/artschool

Copley Society of Boston
158 Newbury Street
Boston, MA 02116
(617) 536–5049
www.copleysociety.org

Creative Arts Center
154 Cromwell Road
Chatham, MA 02633
(508) 945–3583
www.creativeartscenter.org

North Shore Arts Association
197 Rear East Main Street
Gloucester, MA 01930
(508) 283–1857

Patuxent Art Workshops
12220 Shadetree Lane
Laurel, MD 20708
(301) 725–0386
(Workshops take place on Cape Cod, Massachusetts)

Rockport Art Association
The Old Tavern on Main Street
Rockport, MA 01966
(978) 546–6604

Seaward Inn Painting Holidays
Seaward Inn
Marmion Way
Rockport, MA 01966
(508) 546–3471

Michigan

Creative Art Workshops
6850 Brookeshire Drive
West Bloomfield, MI 48322
(313) 669–4736
(800) 750–7010
www.creativeartworkshops.com

The Depot Watercolor Workshops
420 Rail Street
Negaunee, MI 49866
(906) 475–4067

Helga's Palette
P.O. Box 736
Sault Ste. Marie, MI 49783
(906) 632–3437
(941) 983–0119

Kalamazoo Institute of Arts
314 South Park Street
Kalamazoo, MI 49007
(616) 349–7775

Northern Michigan Art Workshops
720 South Elmwood Suite 3
Traverse City, MI 49684
(231) 941–9488
(231) 941–5873

Minnesota

Atelier North School of Classical Realism
1066 Highway 61 East
Two Harbors, MN 55616
(218) 834–2059

Bloomington Art Center
10206 Penn Avenue South
Bloomington, MN 55431
(612) 948–8746

Grand Marais Art Colony
P.O. Box 626
Grand Marais, MN 55604
(800) 385–9585

Minnesota River School
190 South River Ridge Circle
Burnsville, MN 55337
(800) 205–2489

Missouri

Artists Unlimited Fourth Annual Workshop
Contact: Sandra Luck
9804 East 76th Terrace
Raytown, MO 64138
(816) 353–1422

Montana

Beartooth School of Wildlife Art
Box 103
Big Timber, MT 59011
(406) 932–5228

Phantom Spring Ranch Art Workshops
P.O. Box 487
Canyon Creek, MT 59633
(406) 368–2347

Nebraska

Art Workshops
6741 Kansas Avenue
Omaha, NE 68104
(402) 571–6299

Autumn Art Workshops
Route 2
Box 79
Oshkosh, NE 69154
(308) 772–4365

New Jersey

Cinnaminson Art Workshops
1316 Sylvania Avenue
Cinnaminson, NJ 08077
(609) 829–3485

New Mexico

Artisan Santa Fe School of Fine Art
717 Canyon Road
Santa Fe, NM 87501
(505) 988–2179
www.artisan-santafe.com

Carrizo Art School
Drawer A
Ruidoso, NM 88345
(800) 687–2787

Casa Feliz Workshops
137 Bent Street
Taos, NM 87571
(505) 758–9790

Cloudcroft Summer Workshops
213 East Fir Avenue
Muleshoe, TX 79347
(806) 272–3889
(Workshops take place in Cloudcroft, New Mexico)

Fechin Institute Art Workshops
P.O. Box 220
San Cristobal, NM 87564
(505) 776–2622
www.fechin.com

Flyfishing and Painting Workshop
P.O. Box 574
Santa Fe, NM 87504
(888) 833–3383

Mountain Majesty Workshops
P.O. Box 66
High Rolls, NM 88325
(800) 682–2547

New Mexico Artists' Association
2801 Rodeo Road
Suite 239B
Santa Fe, NM 87505
(505) 982–5639

Plein-Air Painters of America
P.O. Box 32270
Santa Fe, NM 87954
(505) 982–6379
www.p-a-p.com

Plum Tree Workshops
Box A–1
Pilar, NM 87531
(800) 373–6028

Rio Grande Artes Workshops
Holy Cross Retreat
P.O. Box 158
Mesilla Park, NM 88047
(505) 524–3688

Taos Institute of Arts
P.O. Box 1389
Taos, NM 87571
(505) 758–2793

Trillium Workshops
31 Walmer Road Unit 1
Toronto, Ontario M5R 2W7
Canada
(800) 263–1505
(Workshops take place in Santa Fe, New Mexico)

Valdes Santa Fe Art Workshops
1006 Marquez Place
Santa Fe, NM 87501
(505) 982–0017
E-mail: *valdes@sfol.com*

New York

Arts Guild of Old Forge, Inc.
Arts Center, Rte. 28 at Whistle Creek
Old Forge, NY 13420
(315) 369–6411

Drawing Academy of the Atlantic
180 Varick Street
New York, NY 10014
(212) 206–7444

Fabrizio Art Studios
1556 Third Avenue
New York, NY 10128
(212) 289–1466

Hudson River Valley Art Workshop
Greenville Arms
P.O. Box 659
Greenville, NY 12083
(518) 966–5219
(888) 665–0044
www.artworkshops.com

Manhattan Graphics Center
476 Broadway
New York, NY 10013
(212) 219–8783

New York Academy of Art
419 Lafayette Street
New York, NY 10003
(212) 505–5300

Omega Institute
RD 2, Box 377
Rhinebeck, NY 12572
(914) 338–6030

Pastel Society of America
15 Gramercy Park South
New York, NY 10003
(212) 533–6931

Pearl Art & Craft Workshops
2411 Hempstead Turnpike
East Meadow, NY 11554
(516) 731–3700

R & F Encaustics
110 Prince Street
Kingston,
NY 12401
(800) 206–8088

Skidmore College Summer Six
Art Program
Saratoga Springs, NY 12866
(518) 581–5000, ext. 2372

Woodstock School of Art
P.O. Box 338
Woodstock, NY 12498
(845) 679–2388, ext. 51

North Carolina

Penland School Summer Workshops
Penland, NC 28765
(704) 765–2359

Willow Wisp Farm Studios
1615 Charlotte Highway
Fairview, NC 28730
(828) 628–0401
www.willowwispfarmstudios.com

North Dakota

International Music Camp Summer
School of Art
1725 11th Street, S.W.
Minot, ND 58701
(701) 263–4211

Ohio

Artist's Studio Workshops
North Light Art School, 1507 Dana Avenue
Cincinnati, OH 45207
(800) 825–0963

Ohio Institute of Photography Workshops
2029 Edgefield Road
Dayton, OH 45439
(513) 294–6155

Six Steps to Success
Color Q, Inc.
2710 Dryden Road
Dayton, OH 45439
(800) 999–1007

Valley Art Center Workshops
155 Bell Street
Chagrin Falls, OH 44022
(440) 247–7507

Oklahoma

Bartlesville Art Association Workshops
P.O. Box 3211
Bartlesville, OK 74006
(918) 333–4134

Oklahoma Art Workshops
6953 South 66th East Avenue
Tulsa, OK 74133
(918) 492–8863

Oregon

A.I.M. Workshops & Painting Trips
P.O. Box 279
Jacksonville, OR 97530
(541) 899–1179

Art in the Mountains Workshops
P.O. Box 845
Bend, OR 97709
(541) 318–1423
E-mail: *art@empnet.com*
www.artinthemountains.com

Joseph Art School
P.O. Box 106
Joseph, OR 97846
(800) 459–3605

Oregon School of Arts and Crafts
8245 Southwest Barnes Road
Portland, OR 97225
(503) 297–5544

Pennsylvania

Handcrafter Gallery and Studio
112 School Lane
Telford, PA 18969
(215) 721–9505

Pine Knob Inn
Box 275
Canadensis, PA 18325
(717) 595–2532

Pocono Pines Gallery and Workshops
Pocono Pines, PA 18350
(717) 646–3937

South Carolina

Hilton Head Art League Workshops
P.O. Box 7753
Hilton Head Island, SC 29938
(800) 995–4068

Tennessee

Farmhouse Artist, Inc.
P.O. Box 6
Walland, TN 37886
(615) 982–7479

Texas

Artists and Craftsmen Associated
2917 Swiss Avenue
Dallas, TX 75204
(214) 368–5829

Bayou Oaks Artist Colony
Contact: Judy Courtwright
Rte. 1, Box 211
Angleton, TX 77515
(409) 848–1888

Cowboy Artists of America Museum
P.O. Box 1716
Kerrville, TX 78029
(210) 896–2553

Fredericksburg Artists' School
1212 Bush Crossing
Fredericksburg, TX 78624
(830) 997–0515
www.fbgartschool.com

Hill Country Arts Foundation
Jeaneane B. Duncan–Edith McAshan Visual Arts Center
P.O. Box 176
Ingram, TX 78025
(210) 367–5120

Mossy Brake Workshops
Mossy Brake Art Gallery
Route 2, Box 66B
Uncertain, TX 75661
(903) 789–3288

Prude Ranch School of Art Workshops
Box 3451
Ruidoso, NM 88345
(Workshops take place in Ft. Davis, Texas)

Vermont

Art Workshops of Vermont
Box 57
Chittenden, VT 05737
(800) 445–2100

Pine Mountain Studio
Rte. 313
Battenkill Road
Arlington, VT 05250
(802) 375–6038

Sketch Vermont Art Workshops
Gallery on the Green
One The Green
Woodstock, VT 05091
(800) 9-ARTIST

Virginia

American Academy of Equine Art
P.O. Box 1315
Middleburg, VA 22117
(864) 486–4667

Art Farm Workshops
Rt. 5, Box 85
Lexington, VA 24450
(703) 463–7961

Art League
105 North Union Street
Alexandria VA 22314
(703) 683–2323

Shenandoah Valley Art Center
P.O. Box 907
Waynesboro VA 22980
(703) 949–7662

Thistledown Farm Workshops
Rte. 2, Box 259
Hot Springs, VA 24445
(703) 962–1801

Webster's World
6644 Barrett Road
Falls Church, VA 22042
(703) 698–1920

Washington
Academy of Realist Art
5004 Sixth Avenue, N.W.
Suite B
Seattle, WA 98107
(206) 784–4268

Coupeville Arts Center
Palettes Plus II Workshops
P.O. Box 171
Coupeville, WA 98239
(360) 678–3396

Creative Colored Pencil
Workshops
1620 Melrose
Seattle, WA 98122
(206) 622–8661

Santa Fe Intensive Drawing & Pastel
Workshop
c/o The Academy of Realist Art
5004 Sixth Avenue, N.W.
Suite B
Seattle, WA 98107
(206) 784–4268

Seattle Academy of Fine Arts
University Heights Center
5031 University Way, N.E.
Seattle, WA 98105
(206) 526-ARTS

Wisconsin
Dillman's Creative Arts Foundation, Inc.
Dillman's Sand Lake Lodge, Inc.
P.O. Box 98F
Lac du Flambeau, WI 54538
(877) 878–8949
www.dillmans.com

Peninsula Art School Workshops
Box 304
Fish Creek, WI 54212
(414) 868–3455

Abroad

Bermuda
Hudson River Valley Art Workshops
P.O. Box 659
Greenville, NY 12083
(518) 966–5219
(888) 665–0044
www.artworkshops.com
A seven-day workshop in the
Bermuda Islands

Canada
John Abott College
P.O. Box C.P. 2000
Ste. Anne de Bellevue
Quebec H9X 3L9
Canada
(514) 457–3063

Federation of Canadian Artists
952 Richards
Vancouver, British Columbia V6B 3C1
Canada
(604) 274–2838

Arts Mont-Tremblant
C.P./ P.O. Box 448
Mont-Tremblant
Quebec J0T 1Z0
Canada
(613) 345–6058

Holland College Centre of Creative Arts
50 Burns Avenue
Charlotte, Prince Edward Island C1E 1H7
Canada
(902) 566–9310

Island Lake Lodge
Box 3023
Collingwood, Ontario L9Y 3Z2
Canada
(705) 444–2331

Island Mountain Arts Workshops
Box 65
Wells, British Columbia V0K 2R0
Canada
(800) 442–2787
(250) 994–3466
www.imarts.com

Metchosin International Summer School of the Arts
3505 Richmond Road
Victoria, British Columbia V8P 4P7
Canada
(604) 598–1695

Strathgartney Country Inn
Bonshaw RR 3
Prince Edward Island C0A 1C0
Canada
(902) 675–4711

Trillium Workshops
92 Lakeshore Road East
Unit B2
Mississauga, Ontario L5G 1E3
Canada
(800) 263–1505

White Rock Summer School of the Arts
Box 150
White Rock,
British Columbia V4A 6E7, Canada
(604) 536–1122

England

Academy of Realist Art
5004 Sixth Avenue, N.W.
Seattle, WA 98107
(206) 784–4268

Mounts Bay Art Centre
Trevatha, Faugan Lane
Newlyn, Penzance,
Cornwall TR18 5DJ
England
(44) 736–66284

Summer School of Painting & Drawing
Henlian Mill, Llangynyw
Welshpool, Powys
Wales SY21 8EN
Great Britain
(44) 938–810269
(44) 702–617900

France

A.I.M. Workshops & Painting Trips
P.O. Box 271
Jacksonville, OR 97530
(541) 899–1179

Art Trek
P.O. Box 1103
Bolinas, CA 94924
(415) 868–9558

En Plain Air School of Painting
12 Rue d'Orchampt
75018 Paris
(33) 142–541035
(301) 961–1062
www.epatours.com

South of France Painting Workshops
24 Rue de la Ville
34320 Fontas
France
(33) 67–25–20–76

Greece

Aegean Workshops, Artists International, Inc.
148 Black Point Road
Niantic,
CT 06357
(860) 739–0378

Apelles Art International Workshops
P.O. Box 99537
Raleigh, NC 27624
(800) 274–2544

Art School of the Aegean
P.O. Box 1375
Sarasota, FL 34230
(941) 351–5597

Guatemala

Art Workshops in La Antigua
Guatemala 4758
Lundale Avenue South
Minneapolis, MN 55409
(612) 825–0747
www.artguat.org

Italy

Artsmart
41 Lincoln Terrace
Harrington Park, NJ 07640
(201) 768–1151

Art Workshop International
463 West Street
New York, NY 10014
(800) 835–7454
www.artworkshopintl.com

Brentwood Art Center
13031 Montana Avenue
Los Angeles, CA 90049
(310) 451–5657
www.brentwoodart.com

Florence Academy of Art
Via delle Casine, 21/r
50122 Florence
Italy
(39) 55–234–3701
www.florenceacademyofart.com

International School of Art
06057 Montecastello di Vibio PG
Perugia
Italy
(39) 75–878–0223
(212) 386–2705
www.giotto.org

Grand Marais Art Colony Workshops
P.O. Box 626
Grand Marais MN 55604
(800) 385–9585

La Romita School of Art, Inc.
1712 Old Town, N.W.
Albuquerque, NM 87104
(800) 519–2297
www.laromita.org

Paint in Italy
Studio 309
41 Union Square
New York, NY 10003
(212) 486–1462

Voyagers International
P.O. Box 915
Ithaca, NY 14851
(607) 273–4321
(800) 633–0299
www.voyagers.com

Mexico

Acapulco Art Workshops
2882 West Long Circle
Littleton, CO 80120
(303) 738–8824

Puerto Rico

Tropical Workshops in Puerto Rico
c/o Galleria San Juan
204 Boulevarde Del Valle
San Juan, PR 00901
(809) 722–1808

Tour Booking Agencies

Art/Tours, Inc.
2293 Venetia Place
Indialantic, FL 32903
(321) 777–7761
www.artistworkshops.com

Artists Workshop Tours Agency
606 Myra Avenue
Chula Vista, CA 92010
(619) 585–8071

Creative Art Workshops
6850 Brookeshire Drive
West Bloomfield, MI 48322
(248) 669–4736
(800) 750–7010
www.creativeartworkshops.com

Friends of the Arts & Sciences
Leech Studio
4433 Riverwood Avenue
P.O. Box 15766
Sarasota, FL 34277
(813) 923–3031

Webster's World
P.O. Box 2057
Falls Church, VA 22042
(800) 952–9641
www.webstersworld.net

CHAPTER TWO

Learning to Make Art Alone

Art instruction comes in many forms, from the structured curriculum at most degree-granting art schools to more free-form classes at arts centers, adult-education programs, art workshops, and private lessons at an artist's studio. Quite varied in their own way, all of these types make certain demands on students—for instance, they must all regularly transport themselves to some place where the instruction will take place at specific times—which may prove to be a larger burden for some students than others. Parents with small children may not be able to get away for a class, and those living in rural areas might find the commute too long. Those with full-time jobs or those who are incapacitated, are also at a disadvantage in selecting a convenient way to develop and improve their artistic skills.

For many people, learning to create art at home is the only (and best) solution. A number of options exist for this type of learning, including correspondence art classes, instructional videotapes, online art courses, and limited or low-residency programs at art schools.

Correspondence Art Courses

Home study may also solve the problem of shyness—students who tend not to speak up much or who generally sit in the back—and it has an equalizing aspect: One's looks, the sound of one's voice, and meekness in the face of other students who do all the talking are eliminated, and one is judged solely on the basis of one's artwork. Instruction is primarily one-on-one, mediated only by the written word. Additionally, a home-study course, many graduates of these programs claim, teaches independent thinking, because one is away from the direct influence of instructors and fellow students.

These courses may also be a younger person's first exposure to art. Lee Anne Miller, former dean of the art school at Cooper Union in New York City, and commercial illustrator Robert Heindel took lessons from the Art Instruction Schools (in Minneapolis, Minnesota) and Famous Artists School (in Westport, Connecticut), respectively, when she was thirteen and he sixteen years old. However, the students tend to be older, retired, and predominantly female at both the Art Instruction Schools in Minneapolis and the Master Class Studios in Cincinnati, Ohio. "The kids are gone, and they have time to try their hand at art," said Charles Berger, director of instruction at Master Class Studios. "They still may not want to do much traveling, and they also want to learn the absolute fundamentals, which you may not get at many art schools and classes because they tend to assume you know a lot of that by now."

Correspondence-course schools frequently set certain time limits for the completion of their lesson programs in order to receive a certificate or diploma (which only indicate that the student has finished the program and are usually not accepted toward actual degree programs in colleges or universities), but these time allotments are generous. The fees for these programs of home study range widely, from $220 at the Gordon School of Art in Green Bay, Wisconsin, for each of twelve year-long levels of instruction, to $2,300 for the two-year, twenty-seven-lesson art course offered by Art Instruction Schools. For their money, students are provided with textbooks (that describe and provide illustrations for every step in the process of drawing and painting) and, except for Master Class Studios, most or all of the art materials one needs to complete the assignments. The schools pay for the shipping of these items.

Correspondence schools generally provide workbooks that contain lesson plans for students. The difference between these step-by-step workbooks and general art instruction books that one could purchase in a book store or art shop has less to do with the information provided (although the workbooks are likely to have a more abbreviated presentation) than the somewhat more impersonal style of writing. Anyone who buys Tony Couch's *Watercolors: You Can Do It!* is probably as much interested in how Tony Couch does it as it is in how the reader can learn to become a watercolorist him- or herself, and one approaches this book looking for Couch's particular methods and secrets.

The workbooks, more than art instructional guides, also aim to approximate what one learns in a regular art class (if one were attending an art school) as well as the way a student is taught. Famous Artists School's *How to Draw the Human Figure* workbook begins with a section on the materials used (pencils, pastels, charcoal, drawing board, eraser, paper) and soon has one drawing: at first, gestures, then configuring the body as a series of cylinders, moving on to contour drawing, and, later, an analysis of anatomy. Photographs of male and female models in various poses, partially or completely nude, are also included in the workbook. Students pay the postage for completed assignments sent back to the schools to be evaluated. The art instructors who look over each student's work may be on staff or on call, but students cannot be assured of having the same teacher twice, except at the Gordon School of Art where John Gordon is the only teacher. There are four instructors at Master Class Studios, and ten at Art Instruction Schools. "Students benefit from a variety of opinions," Don Jardine, former director of education at Art Instruction Schools, said. "They get the expertise of each instructor." Those evaluations or critiques vary in the degree of personal attention. Some may be fully handwritten, while others are preprinted sheets with various boxes (such as "Needs work in color" or "Needs work in line") checked off, with far fewer individual comments noted.

As some students are less interested in purchasing an instructional video or attending a large art class precisely because of the lack of feedback and individual attention, this may be a great point of consumer interest for them. Charles Berger noted that prospective students should "ask the schools you are interested in for a copy of the kinds of things you get in critiques. If you end up taking the course and you get something that doesn't correspond with what you were told or shown, you have a cause for complaint."

Another concern that potential students should keep in mind is whether or not the school's particular lesson plan fits their goals. Most of these schools began with a commercial art emphasis, focusing on cartooning, advertising design, illustration, and other purely marketable skills, and some of their current courses still carry that flavor. That may not appeal to every prospective student. Don Jardine noted that sales representatives for the Art Instruction Schools tell people in their presentations, "You can be successful. You can earn a living at something you would ordinarily do for fun," while other schools do not push moneymaking in their promotion. Since it is an accredited institution, the certificate of completion and grades for each lesson area received from Art Instruction Schools may be transferred to other colleges, although the specific number of credits differ from one college to another. "We provide a certificate of completion, because a lot of people who take our courses want a piece of paper saying they completed the course," noted Charles Berger, adding that the certificates have no other, higher value. Learning and having accomplished a set of assigned tasks are their own reward.

Even the old-style correspondence school can learn some new tricks, particularly through the World Wide Web. The Brooklyn, New York–based Interactive Art School (*www.interactiveartschool.com*) offers a "virtual" correspondence course in which all teaching and interactions between the school—consisting of one instructor, Barry Waldman—and the student take place on the Web. There is but one course, and students are supplied with ten textbooks, some art supplies, and a digital camera (unless they already have one) as part of their signing up for the ten-lesson course. When they complete each lesson assignment, students photograph their work and e-mail digital images to the school as e-mail attachments. Waldman then posts a written and drawn (or painted) individual lesson critique to the student's personal Web folder on the school's Web site. At the end of the course, students are sent a compact disk with all ten critiques, a letter suggesting next steps, and a Certificate of Completion. The cost of the full ten-lesson course is $995 ($845 if the student does not need to be supplied with a digital camera), or $255 per lesson ($110 without the camera).

Although not as popular as they had been in the past, there are still a number of correspondence-course art schools these days, which are listed in the Resources section at the end of this chapter.

In its heyday during the 1950s and 1960s, Famous Artists School had 40,000 enrolled students; now, Famous Artists School no longer accepts students but continues to sell its supply of workbooks and other instructional materials. A number of other schools have simply closed. The reasons for the decline are manifold: There are more opportunities nowadays for art instruction in classrooms, with adult-education programs at high schools, community colleges, and large universities, even in the most rural locations of the country. In addition, the videocassettes sold by individual artists and video production companies provide quite graphic depictions of everything from the most basic problems of which tool to use and how to mix colors to technical problems of perspective and the creation of certain visual effects; others also focus on particular genres, such as portraiture or landscape painting. The cost for these videos is also less than for full correspondence courses, ranging from $29 to $59 for a two- to four-hour videocassette.

"The books that a correspondence school sends out can tell you all the same things, and even more, that are on a video, but it's still on a printed page," said Charles Reid, a painter who had first studied art through the Famous Artists School but now teaches art through workshops and several videotapes. "Even if the picture in the book is in color, you still don't see the thing actually being done, as with a video."

Correspondence art courses, which are usually advertised in art magazines such as *American Artist* and *The Artist's Magazine*, still make sense to a number of people. The local art instructor may not be to every student's taste; timing and distance still can be troublesome with art classes. Videos, of course, cannot comment on one's work or answer specific questions.

Art Instruction Books and Videocassettes

Deciding whether or not to learn artmaking (or to improve one's artistic skills) through reading or watching is a matter of personal choice, depending upon how the individual best learns. "Reading books and attending workshops are great aids to learning; they're the most direct route to your goal," Tony Couch writes in his book *Watercolor: You Can Do It!* However, Couch's teaching is also available on several videocassettes. Presumably, he believes that videos are at least a relatively direct route.

Frequently, the same artists are represented by both books and videocassettes that feature their work and method; for people who are interested in the particular artist, it may be wise to collect both, because either one or the other will be lacking something. Reading about how an artist works is never as good as seeing that person at work, and a fifty- or sixty-minute video can only provide so much information. In Charles Reid's "Flowers in Watercolor," for instance, one hears the artist discussing his technique, but one also watches in silence as Reid mixes colors and applies his brush to paper. Reid is also author of six art instruction books and, in *Painting by Design*, one learns how to approach a subject analytically, largely as an abstract form: "It's my aim to get you to see any subject you choose as a set of very definite shapes composed of color, light, and shadow. Forget what your subject represents . . . . Concentrate instead on what it *is*, a piece of a puzzle or part of a pattern that's meant to be arranged in some compelling way with other shapes."

There may be good reason for purchasing both books and videocassettes: Teaching (in any field of endeavor) usually involves explaining how something is done and then demonstrating it. Books tend to be preferable for explanations, while videos provide the show-how; ideally, students would want to refer to both forms of instruction, offering them much of the benefits of taking an actual studio art class (minus, of course, the teacher who could offer specific pointers). If one cannot afford to purchase both the video and the book, however, the decision depends on which method may prove most instructive to the potential buyer. Of course, books tend to cost less than videocassettes.

"I always tell people that if they have enough money for just one thing, get the book," Tony Couch said. "A book has more information, and it covers everything. The video is more limited; it looks at only one part of what you have in the book. I think some people can learn from just a book, while I doubt anyone can start painting by just watching a video." On the other hand, Frank Webb, author of *Watercolor Energies* and *Webb on Watercolor* and the subject of a video, believes that videocassettes are preferable for beginners. "Books presuppose a certain acquaintance with art terms, while videos assume absolutely nothing," he said. He added that the written text is "sequential," moving logically from one idea to the next, while "film has an all-at-once quality in which one can apprehend across the field. You have the sound, the gestures in video; it's equal to being in the artist's studio."

One never can be exactly sure what to expect from any specific type of art instruction—book or videocassette—until it has been tried. A particular teacher may not be rigorous enough, or a book too wordy, the video image too grainy, or the correspondence school instructor not personal enough, for one's individual tastes. However, there are usually ways to cut one's losses if a specific program doesn't work out. Schools frequently allow students to drop courses with just minimal penalties, and the sponsors of art classes usually require payment only for the classes one has attended.

With art instruction books and videocassettes, however, the situation is a bit more complicated. One cannot "sit in on" a video as one can at an art class or school, and most art instruction books are not available in libraries for browsing. Some books, of course, are sold in bookstores and art supply shops, and one may thumb through or study them as long as the store manager or sales help will tolerate it. Of course, there are also television art instruction programs, such as those offered by the late Bob Ross, Michael Ringer, and Gary Jenkins, which cost the viewer nothing and offer the opportunity to determine whether or not one could learn to paint through watching TV.

More commonly, those who are interested in learning or developing their artistic skills in art find out about art instruction books and videocassettes through advertisements in the back pages of art magazines, where the cost of advertising limits the amount of information about them. What's more, most art instruction books and videos have similar titles—*Make Your Watercolors Sing* and *Making Color Sing* (published by North Light Books and Watson-Guptill, respectively)—that make ferreting out differences somewhat difficult.

How does one find out about and choose among them? There are many questions that prospective buyers should ask. Does the book feature a variety of illustrations (by a number of different artists or by one artist?) or just a few pictures and a lot of text? Is there enough information in the video for repeated viewings? Is the writing clear, the author's philosophy a help rather than a hindrance? Are the chapters set up as self-contained lessons or is the book divided according to various themes? Does the video offer step-by-step instruction on selecting a subject, choosing colors and mixing them, using brushes and other materials, building up layers, and, finally, creating an image, or does it more specifically highlight a particular artist at work? Is the book or video geared to the level of the student?

There is a book or video for every aspiring artist, but each person must determine what he or she wants or needs, then formulate questions for the publishers of these materials. Most publishers, video production companies, or artists selling their books and videocassettes will provide a brochure or some written information about their products, which may include critical reviews in art magazines, testimonials from satisfied customers, a biography of the author or artist, and a sample illustration as well as some idea of what is featured in the book or video. Many of these same companies and artists will also answer questions over the telephone (some have toll-free numbers, while others return calls left on their answering machines). North Light Book Club sends out a catalog to club members fourteen times per year, and this offers a range of information about each listed book. However, customers find that "there's not a lot of information available when buying over the phone," according to Libby Fellerhoff, editor of the Book Club. "There are just orders."

Prospective buyers would want to know the type of medium used, and whether the book or video is intended for beginners or artists with intermediate or advanced skills.

The five videos sold by How Great Thou Art, all of which feature demonstrations and commentary by the company's president Barry Stebbing, focus exclusively on the beginner, offering a step-by-step approach to solving basic artistic problems, starting at the level of "how to hold a pencil, how to draw lips." George Labadie's five instructional videocassettes on painting the figure, which are sold directly at (877) 662–3412, or *www.gslabadie-aws.com*, are directed at the intermediate and advanced students, although that information is not specifically noted anywhere on the videotape nor on the box it comes in. What makes his teaching most appropriate for experienced artists, he noted, is the fact that "I don't talk about what paints, paper, or brushes to use. You can find that kind of thing out anywhere."

Tony Couch's ten videos, on the other hand, which are also sold directly—(800) 491–7870, *www.tonycouch.com*—are designed for what he described as a "more generalized audience," and his commentary includes a mix of basic and more sophisticated information. However, his video series breaks down into more basic (the first three cassettes), specific demonstrations (the next three), one cassette on design ("everyone is deficient there," he said), and drawing (the remaining three). There are a number of art instructional video production companies (listed below), but many artists have become major producers and distributors of their own videocassettes. Terry Madden leads the pack with twenty-four videos on watercolor painting, sold by subscription in two year-long courses in which students purchase one video per month for twelve months at a cost of $25 apiece—contact Terry Madden's Watercolor Workshop, (800) 321–8088, *www.watercolorworkshop.com.* Along with the videos comes a workbook and binder (for notes). Viewers watch demonstrations, and assignments are given in each of the videos, although they are not to be sent to Madden—they are solely for the student's own benefit. However, one may e-mail questions to Madden, and he will answer them on the Q&A section of his Web site. Madden identified his audience as "some absolute beginners and others who have tried watercolors, but were frustrated and want to try again." Those who purchase all twelve videos in a course receive a certificate of completion with the last videotape in the series.

When the specific level of reader or viewer is not indicated, the book or video is probably intended for the more experienced artist. Prospective buyers, especially those who are gaining their first serious exposure to artmaking, would certainly want to know whether or not there is a description of the tools used (airbrush, brushes, palette knives, pencils, for instance) and discussion and definition of such concerns as shape, space, edges, contrast, color temperature, color mixing, color intensity, perspective, composition, content, foreground and background, texture, line, grids, surface, and how they all relate to each other. Book buyers of all levels of skill and experience would also be interested in knowing if different styles are represented (abstract, impressionist, realist, for example) as well as a variety of subjects (water, landscape, the figure) and ways of working (from a photograph, a model, in the studio, outdoors).

With a videocassette, one expects to see the particular artist at work and only that artist's finished work, while in general, art instruction books offer a wider range of artistic styles and choices, but not always.

No promotional brochure or selected reviews can answer all of one's questions, and other concerns may only be discovered after the book or video is purchased. Are the color reproductions in the book of a suitably high quality, and does the artist in the video appear comfortable in front of a camera? Books should provide a detailed discussion of the topics or artistic problems at hand while, in a video, the commentary should be subordinate to the image—no one wants an hour of a talking head.

There may be other problems that a student of art has with the manner of teaching in the book or video that have nothing to do with technical deficiencies in the product. One's ability to learn from any given teacher is quite personal, and it is no different when the teacher is a book or videocassette. However, as opposed to a teacher in an art class with whom the "chemistry" doesn't quite work, one cannot simply leave and not pay for any more, as books and videos must be purchased in advance. A final question to ask the publisher, video production company, distributor, or artist is about the returns policy.

There are no federal (or state) mandates that customers have to be completely satisfied with products they purchase. The Federal Trade Commission or state attorney general may bring action on false claims ("Guaranteed to Teach Anyone to Paint a Million-Dollar, Museum-Quality Masterpiece in One Week") or misrepresentations in advertisements. However, many claims that seem misleading, such as "Learn How to Paint," are not specific enough to warrant state or federal inquiry if a customer is not satisfied. According to Bonnie Janson, an attorney for the Federal Trade Commission, "it would be extremely difficult to win a complaint if you didn't learn to paint, because it's a subjective problem—you may be stupid. In this realm, any claim may be true or not true, because we're dealing with judgment and ability. Who can say which are the correct tips to learning how to paint?"

There are also inherent limitations in learning solely through books or videocassettes, which should be taken into account. One advertisement for a $29.95 video from the Quinten Gregory Studio in Boise, Idaho, for example, claims to show "how professional artists paint to sell! How to create your own scenes, use the value scale and avoid amateurish habits. The keys to professional work with drawing, oil, and watercolor demos. 1 hour." That is a rather tall order for a sixty-minute presentation, regardless of how experienced the student may be, and buyers who take the advertisement at face value may find themselves set up for failure. Expectations need to be appropriately lowered, befitting the manner and length of instruction. A better reason for purchasing this video than discovering how "professional artists" paint is that one is familiar with the work of Quinten Gregory or interested in painting in a similar manner.

Potential buyers should be equally aware that not everything can be taught in a book or videocassette. Had someone thought to make a film of the highly influential artist and teacher Hans Hofmann instructing his students, and selling it to other artists, the result might have proven an exercise in futility. Hofmann's importance to a generation of artists is traced to the interactive, personal give-and-take that occurred in his class, which would not have translated well into an hour-long segment in which technique, color selection, choosing the right brushes, and picking a subject all might have to be included.

Learning good techniques is important, but art is also a matter of self-discovery. Any lesson program, in a book or on a video, that only stresses technique—how to paint a tree or a cloud (in effect, visual cliches), how to blend colors or use a fan brush for certain effects—may be destructive to one's inherent originality. Potential book or video buyers would want the instruction to strengthen their technical skills while offering ways to more fully realize their individual talents.

Art instruction books and videocassettes may stand alone as a complete form of learning—Tony Couch, for instance, attempts in his ten videos to teach a top-to-bottom course in drawing, design, perspective, color theory, art materials, and painting—although they are likely to be more effective as an addition to direct contact with an art teacher. One may open the book or pop the video into the VCR any time to read or hear some piece of information again, whereas the art class instructor is not likely to be as amenable to repeating him- or herself. Those who are reading an instructional book or watching a video while taking an art class may find different approaches to the same visual problems confusing, although Terry Madden believes that such an arrangement has its good side: "I may be telling people something that's totally different than what another teacher says, but that makes people question, and that's good."

Some companies do have return policies, but their provisions vary widely, as each company makes its own rules, determining its own period of time for returns or refunds, and determining which reasons it considers valid. Watson-Guptill Publications allows buyers to exchange one book for another, if they are not satisfied and provided that the book has not been damaged, but does not make full refunds. North Light Book Club, on the other hand, will allow buyers to make an exchange or to receive a full refund. If a North Light customer receives a book that he or she did not order, the company will send out a mailing label within ten business days so that the book could be sent back postage-free. Signilar Art, which produces and distributes art instruction videos, also agrees to take tapes back in exchange or for full refunds, according to the company's president, Teresa Spinner. "There are people who decide that a video just isn't for them. You can't penalize them for that."

Many marketers of videocassettes fear the potential for illegal copies and, in order to protect themselves, have established returns policies that are only exchange policies—they will exchange a defective video for one that is free of defects—without the possibility of a refund. Terry Madden's Watercolor Workshop, on the other hand, will refund a dissatisfied customer's money, less shipping costs and a 15 percent "reshelving fee." Tony Couch noted that he permits "a thirty-day money-back guarantee," adding that he has had "very few returns, generally because something is wrong with the tape, for instance the tape broke." On some of his videos, Couch has placed anti-piracy technology that, if someone attempted to make a copy, would result in a poor-quality reproduction, which has resulted in some returns. "One guy actually told me, 'Something's wrong here. I tried to copy it, and it didn't work,'" he said.

James Godwin Scott, a watercolorist who distributes his own series of videocassettes, provided a refund to one dissatisfied customer "who had a pretty flimsy excuse: He thought it was in oils. It is very difficult to discern whether or not someone has made a copy." In general, however, it is wisest to assume that, when a company or individual makes no specific mention of a return or refund policy, none probably exists. Efforts to satisfy customers with complaints may range quite widely, which is why finding out in advance as much as possible about the books or videocassettes offered is so important.

Some companies may not have a written policy about the products they offer, but will provide detailed information about their books or cassettes as well as offer a money-back guarantee over the telephone. As noted previously, some of them are quite happy to discuss their products with potential buyers by phone, allowing them to gauge the callers' level of understanding and answer specific questions. To be on the safe side, one should write down what is said about the particular book or videocassette as well as about the returns or refunds policy and the name of the person with whom one spoke. If any misrepresentation is made, such as the description of a money-back refund if one is unhappy for any reason, then one may make a formal complaint to one's state consumer protection office, the state attorney general, or the Federal Trade Commission (one's state consumer protection office will likely advise which route to take).

One way in which those interested in trying out videocassettes, short of buying them, is by renting, from Video Learning Library—5777 Azalea Drive, Grants Pass, OR 97526, (541) 479–7140—for $6 per week (payable by credit card). Most public libraries, however, do not carry these videos. One Web site, Art Talk (*www.arttalk.com/LearnShops/BookStore/bookstore.htm*), includes a sizeable listing of art instruction books, sorted by artistic media, which have been reviewed by others who have already purchased them.

Art instruction books, of course, are not the only sources for printed information and advice on how to create art. Magazines and journals for artists, such as *American Artist* and *The Artist's Magazine,* also contain technical columns, offering specific suggestions in a variety of media. These same publications also frequently review instructional books and videos in the field.

The back pages of *The Artists' Magazine*, *American Artist*, *Sunshine Artists*, and several other art periodicals have advertisements for videos by well- and lesser-known artists working in a variety of fields. In many instances, these are professionally made home movies, sold by the artists themselves; some artists seem to have as large a product line as General Motors. It isn't necessarily wiser to purchase from a publisher or distributor than from the artist, as it is the particular artist and his or her technique that is reason for buying the videocassette in the first place.

Online Art Courses

"There are people who believe that online courses are just a high-tech version of correspondence courses," said Stephen Anspacher, associate provost for distance learning at Parsons School of Design in New York City. "I believe they are wrong." He has a point. Studying art through the Internet requires a real degree of comfort with computers (weeding out those with little experience of chat rooms and who don't own scanners) and, since all but one of the online art classes currently available are offered through degree-granting institutions and taught by regular faculty, the classes tend to be more rigorous and intensive than the comparatively relaxed correspondence courses. There is also the issue of class participation, which does not exist in the correspondence world. Still, assignments are made by a teacher in a remote location, worked on by a student at home, and then sent back to the teacher electronically (usually) or by mail (occasionally).

Computer technology permits a number of students working at home to communicate with each other, and a faculty member to communicate with all of them. A major benefit of an actual art class—a multiplicity of ideas and techniques shared among class members—is combined with the convenience of working at home and avoiding a commute. "The actual making of the work is still done in a traditional way," said Tom Hyatt, vice-president for technology at the Maryland Institute College of Art in Baltimore. "Putting work on the Web lets everyone in the class see it. The technology allows for a genuine critique."

Most online art instruction courses are in the area of graphic design, often involving computer applications, such as Web design and the use of specific software for advertising illustration; the courses do not teach the basic operation of the software—students may be directed to tutorials that will allow them to gain familiarity with PhotoShop, or Illustrator, or other relevant computer programs. Many of the design classes are taken by people already in the field who look to learn new skills, or by others seeking a career change. However, there are online classes in traditional fine art media, such as drawing, painting, sculpture, and printmaking, at many of the same institutions. An online orientation is generally offered to help students understand how they could take the course.

All of the online art instruction classes operate in the same basic manner. The instructor writes a prepared lesson that is posted on the Web "classroom" (chat room) and consists of a summary of the ideas to be pursued throughout the course and in the next assignment. At the Art Institute Online, the online creation of the Art Institute of Pittsburgh, one may either read the lesson or, by clicking on the menu, hear a professional narrator (not the actual instructor) read it to you. It has been already well established that no one reads lengthy treatises on a computer screen, and faculty often receive extensive weeks-long training in how to communicate briefly, as well as how to encourage group participation and maintain direction when teaching students who show up only as e-mail messages. Art instructors usually do not lecture anyway, and long-windedness simply would not work in an online class.

The instructor makes an assignment with a specific due date, and students usually photograph their finished work, scanning it into the computer and transmitting it to the online classroom or mailing the work in. The online classroom participation consists of offering an evaluation, or critique, of other students' work, and a defense, or discussion, of one's own, as well as responding to other students' remarks and to questions posed by the instructor. The quality of one's classroom participation and the artwork itself are the basis of any grades or credit offered.

Mike Lawsky, curriculum development director at Art Institute Online, noted that most students submit their work and discussion group comments between the hours of 11 P.M. and 3 A.M. East Coast time, which may indicate that they are getting to their classwork after a long day of doing something else, or that they live all over the United States (in different time zones) and around the world. The World Wide Web has allowed artists, as everyone else, greater opportunity to find the resources and programs that meet their cost and scheduling needs rather than simply settling for whatever is closest. Clearly, no instructor can be expected to man the online classroom at all hours of the day or night, and most distance learning programs are designed to be "asynchronous"—not taking place at any one time.

However, some online classes do have "real time" class periods once a week, in which students are expected to participate—again, through e-mail messages. "The instructor bears the burden of juggling conversations, answering questions from this person, asking a question of that person," Tom Hyatt said. "You do have to be a pretty fast typist." With fifteen to twenty students per class in most online courses, that can be a lot of conversations and questions all at one time. Hyatt added that one of the distance learning instructors in his program is "not a good typist. We had to bring someone in to do the actual typing for him."

While the Art Institute Online does not permit students and faculty to communicate by telephone "for reasons of logistics," according to Lawsky, such communication is allowed elsewhere. Rebecca Alm, former chairman of the fine art department at the Minneapolis College of Art & Design and now the senior developer of the college's distance learning initiative, said that students have access to each other and to faculty by "telephone connections, and it's not uncommon that people do dial up one another. It's kind of fun to actually hear their voices. I want to touch them." However, she added that it is valuable for everyone involved to "get to know each other through the work and not based on how they look or sound."

A number of schools with online or distance learning programs offer a free sample of a class, such as touring an online classroom where an instructor's comments, students' responses, and artwork are posted. Since the same faculty generally teach online and actual classes, customary methods of evaluating a school—collegiate guides, school rankings—may also help prospective students select the most appropriate programs. Just as in regular classes in a school, online students may decide to drop a course for any reason and receive a prorated refund.

The cost of an online course at an art school or college is likely to be the same as for a traditional studio class, although the number of weeks in the course are often fewer, reflecting the fact that distance learning is a more intensive form of instruction, taking place throughout the week and not limited to specific class times. "Students are required to interact with the faculty five days out of every seven, and attendance is taken," Lawsky said. At the Minneapolis College of Art & Design, both the online and traditional studio one-credit courses are $505 ($318 for students not seeking the college credit) and $1,515 for three-credit courses ($953 noncredit). Similarly, at Parsons School of Design, online and traditional studio classes cost $660 per credit for students seeking course credit, while noncredit or certificate students pay a set price of between $350 and $600 for the class. While the traditional and online classes at Parsons tend to start at the same time, Anspacher stated, the online courses usually end several weeks sooner.

Distance learning, which is available on the graduate degree level and for noncredit students, is not yet envisioned as replacing an undergraduate degree education. "The social aspects of education are equal to, or more important than, the intellectual elements of it," Anspacher said. "Undergraduates need to be physically present at the school." That view was seconded by William Barrett, director of the San Francisco–based Association of Independent Colleges of Art and Design, who noted that online art instruction is "hard to do well, and it costs a lot to develop." He added that, "with the rapid development of community colleges in the country, it's not so difficult anymore to find good, inexpensive courses where you can actually go to a class and talk to somebody."

Online courses for artists aren't limited to studio classes. Art Marketing Workshops (*www.artmarketingworkshops.com*) provides a series of four-week classes in marketing, fundraising, and selling artwork, while Parsons offers a five-week course titled "Presenting Your Artwork to Galleries," in which twenty lessons are intermittently posted by a New York City nonprofit art center director Chana Benjamin. She also teaches the same basic material in a regular classroom at Parsons, "but I don't mind not seeing" the online students "in person. In class, people's attention fades in and out, and they keep asking the same questions, and I keep repeating the same answers. When I'm teaching online, I can just tell someone, 'Refer to Lesson Two.'"

Limited Residency Programs

Despite all the alternatives to attending an art school, art academies and university art departments continue to attract the nontraditional (older, employed, retired) art student for the rigor of the instruction and, for some, the degree. Thoughts of attending art school, however, quickly seem like daydreams: How could I just up and leave my job, my home, my family? A number of art schools have developed their own solutions to this problem—limited or low residency programs—that only require students to be on campus a certain number of days or weeks per year and pursue their independent study coursework from their homes. Vermont College of the Union Institute, for example, requires students in its MFA in Visual Arts program to be at the college for ten days twice a year, during which time they attend seminars, meet with faculty, and present their work. For the remainder of this two-year program, students work at home independently, researching and writing papers (some long, mostly short), creating art and meeting periodically with an artist mentor in their area who will guide them in the development of their work. (The college has a list of potential mentors all over the United States, although students in the program may select a different artist to fulfill this role, subject to approval.) The cost of this program is $5,643 per six-month semester, plus $495 for a residency on campus each semester.

In a somewhat different version of the same idea, Antioch University McGregor's (in Yellow Springs, Ohio) Masters of Art program allows students five years to complete their degree program, which includes a four-day residency on the campus twice a year, regular meetings with a mentor in their area (Antioch arranges to find this person), and certain college-level course work that may be completed at any school with the credits counted toward the Antioch degree (requiring a B average or better). The cost of this program is $2,291 per quarter, plus a $75 "technology fee."

Low or limited residency doesn't mean low tuition. The $18,360 per year tuition for the Maine College of Art's two-year MFA program, which is only offered as a limited residency, is the same as the annual tuition for students in the on-campus BFA program. The primary benefit for students in a self-directed program is that they can pursue a degree and their artwork in their own way without having to uproot their lives.

Students in these programs tend to be older than the customary twenty-something MFA student—thirty-five is the average age at Maine College of Art, forty at Vermont College of the Union Institute—and "the majority have been out of school for some time," said Margaret Harmon, codirector of the MFA in Visual Arts Program at Vermont College. "Some are looking to teach at the college level and need an MFA for that, while others want a way to focus on their own art."

Not being physically around fellow students hasn't "made much of a difference at all" for Timothy Jones, a second-year student in Maine College of Art's limited residency program, whose artwork includes video, installations, and performance. "I'm already part of a community of artists in San Antonio, which is very strong." Before selecting Maine College of Art, Jones, who received a Bachelor of Fine Arts in painting in 1989 from the Rhode Island School of Design, noted that he had investigated other graduate programs, discovering that "most of the time, graduate students work on their own anyway. At Yale, faculty may come over once or twice a semester to see what you're doing." By telephone (occasionally) and through e-mails (mostly), Jones maintains contact with other students in his program, transmitting images and just "keeping in touch."

RESOURCES

Correspondence Art Schools

Art Instruction Schools
3309 Broadway Street, N.E.
Minneapolis,
MN 55415
(612) 362–5060
www.artists-ais.com

Cartoonerama
Box 248
Chalfont, PA 18914
(215) 822–9158
www.cartooncrossroads.com

Famous Artists Schools
19 Newtown Turnpike
Westport, CT 06880
(203) 845–2333
NB: Only sells workbooks

Gordon School of Art
P.O. Box 28208
Green Bay, WI 54324
(800) 210–1220
www.newmasters.com

Master Class Studios
6628 Afton Avenue
Cincinnati, OH 45213
(877) 627–6101
www.masterclassstudios.com

For more information on these and other correspondence course schools, contact the Distance Education and Training Council (1601 18th Avenue N.W., Washington, DC 20009, (202) 332–1386. *www.detc.org*).

Art Instruction Videotape Publishers and Distributors

Artists InterActive Video
5722 Huntington Avenue
Richmond,
CA 94804
(510) 526–4604
www.aivideo.com

U.S. Artquest, Inc.
7800 Ann Arbor Road
Grass Lake, MI 49240
(800) 200-RT4U
www.usartquest.com

Art Video Productions, Inc.
P.O. Box 941
Woodland Hills, CA 91365
(818) 884–6278
(888) 513–2187
www.artvideostore.com

Discover Art with Sandra, Inc.
P.O. Box 262424
San Diego, CA 92196
(858) 578–6005
(888) 327–9278
www.discoverartwithsandra.com

The Draw Squad
Darrell Wright Video Productions
9360 Activity Road
San Diego, CA 92126
(888) 288–4336
www.drawsquad.com

How Great Thou Art
Publications
Box 48 WP01
McFarlan, NC 28108
(800) 982–3729
www.howgreatthouart.com

Liliedahl Fine Art Studio
808 South Broadway Street
La Porte, TX 77571
(877) 867–0324
www.old-master-art.com

North Light Book Club
P.O. Box 9274
Central Islip, NY 11722
(877) 889–6290
(800) 289–0963

Signilar, Inc.
P.O. Box 278
Sanbornton, NH 03269
(603) 934–3222
(800) 205–4904
www.signilar.com

Watson-Guptill Publications
770 Broadway
New York, NY 10003
(800) ART-TIPS

Online Art Programs

The Art Institute Online
420 Boulevard of the Allies
Pittsburgh, PA 15219
(877) 872–8869
(412) 291–5100
www.aionline.edu

Maryland Institute College of Art
1300 West Mt. Royal Avenue
Baltimore, MD 21217
(410) 225–2255
www.mica.edu

Minneapolis College of Art and Design
2501 Stevens Avenue South
Minneapolis, MN 55404
(800) 874-MCAD
www.mcad.edu

Open Learning Agency
4355 Mathissi Place
Burnaby, British Columbia V5G 4S8
Canada
(604) 431–3000
(800) 663–1663 (within Canada)
www.ola.ca

Parsons School of Design
New School for Social Research
66 Fifth Avenue
New York, NY 10011
(212) 229–5880
www.newschool.edu

Limited Residency Master's-Level Programs for Studio Artists

Antioch University McGregor
800 Livermore Street
Yellow Springs, OH 45387
(937) 769–1800
www.mcgregor.edu

Art Institute of Boston at Leslie University
700 Beacon Street
Boston, MA 02215
(617) 585–6600
(800) 773–0494
www.aiboston.edu

Maine College of Art
97 Spring Street
Portland, ME 04101
(800) 639–4808
www.meca.edu

Syracuse University
Graduate School
Suite 303, Browne Hall
Syracuse, NY 13244
(315) 443–1525
www.syr.edu/program/courses/distance/isdp

University of the Arts
Summer MFA Program
320 South Broad Street
Philadelphia, PA 19102
(215) 717–6106/6489
(800) 616–2787
www.uarts.edu

Vermont College of the Union Institute
36 College Street
Montpelier, VT 05602
(800) 336–6794
www.tui.edu/vermontcollege

CHAPTER THREE

New Beginnings, Beginning Anew

The art world never seems to run out of enthusiasm for the latest twenty-something-year-old creating the art of the moment. At age twenty-one, however, Arnold Kolb had no time for art: He was busy figuring out ways to process uranium as part of the Manhattan Project in America's race to develop the atomic bomb during the Second World War. Art, in fact, would have to wait until he took early retirement from Dow Corning in 1982 at the age of fifty-nine.

Returning to the Art World Later in Life

Art frequently must wait until children are grown, or a nest egg has been established, or until just the fear of the word "artist" has been overcome. Sometimes, being older and wiser helps, for instance, in knowing not to personalize rejection or in understanding how to promote and market a product (in this case, art). Self-expression requires an understanding of oneself, which isn't always found in twenty-year-olds, and it may take time for ideas to percolate. Certain levels of skill also come to people at different rates. After decades of research spent developing and then helping younger people to understand electron microscopy, Kolb "had learned how to talk to a variety of people and get them interested in what I'm doing. It takes years to know how to select information and put it forward in a certain way."

At other times, being older works against a new artist. "Normally, I look for people who can be said to have potential—that is, they're young," said New York City art dealer Nohra Haime. Chicago art dealer Douglas Lydon echoed that sentiment, noting, "In most cases, you lose money on artists in the first few years in the hope that they will develop over twenty years. The joy of taking on artists is watching them come into fruition. Do you get the same rewards with artists who are near the end of their lives?" Another New York dealer, Nancy Hoffman, claimed that she "never looks at anyone's age on a resume—I just look at the work," but pointed the finger at collectors "who are always looking for a young, hot, new person."

Many art dealers, when they first open their galleries, look for artists their own age. Clearly, that wasn't the case when "Grandma" Moses had her first art show at New York City's Galerie St. Etienne in 1941 at the age of eighty-one, but her career was anomalous in a number of ways. Retirees cannot look to a world of retirement-age art dealers but must seek the acceptance of gallery owners who are often half their age.

Having more experience and a stronger sense of their own worth than when they were in their twenties may also require a psychological adjustment for older people refashioning themselves as artists. They may not be satisfied with low prices for their work, having valued themselves in a different way for so long. They may be anxious to make up for lost time and expect great things all at once. Artists' advisor Katharine T. Carter, who has worked with a number of retirees entering the art market as artists, noted that some older artists "anticipate the moon. They want a one-person exhibit at a New York gallery and reviews in the *New York Times*. They believe that miraculous things will happen overnight." When reality sets in, she added, the result is considerable disappointment.

Moving from success in one career to square one in another may also require a few deep breaths. "I was spoiled working for Leo Burnett," said Ron Condon of Winnetka, Illinois, a full-time painter now who was a group creative director and senior vice-president at the Chicago-based advertising company until he left in 1998 after thirty-eight years, at the age of sixty. "I was very well respected and used to getting my way. Then, I went around to art dealers who don't even look at my work or pay any attention to me. They can be so snooty. I wanted to say, 'Hey, buddy, I've made four or five times your salary,' but I didn't, because you don't want to burn your bridges—you might need these people some day. Still, it was very hard to humble myself."

But humble himself he did, not only when Condon began showing his work to dealers but, before that, when he enrolled as a full-time student-at-large at the School of the Art Institute of Chicago, taking courses with people "who were one-third my age. And some of them were a lot better than me." During his years at Leo Burnett, Condon had painted watercolors now and again, but he went to school in order to learn to paint in oils, which he had never done in his life. "I felt I really had to cram, to make up for lost time."

Starting at the Top

At age sixty-one, Phil Joanou similarly decided that, after thirty-five years in the advertising industry, he wanted to devote the remainder of his life to painting. In 1994, he left the Dailey & Associates agency in Los Angeles, where he was chairman of the board and chief executive officer, to move with his wife to New York City. There, he enrolled at the New York Academy of Art (earning a master's degree in 1996) and rented a studio in the Tribeca section of downtown Manhattan. "For two years, I shut myself up in my studio in order to get a body of work," he said. "I wanted to have something to show dealers, and I wanted to start out in New York with a one-person show. With all the years of business under my belt, I knew that you have only one time to make a first impression.

"The advice I received over and over again," he added, "was to go to art openings, hang out, see if your work would look good there, get friendly with dealers and artists, and maybe eventually someone would ask to see your work and show it. That's reasonable if you're younger and inclined to do that. If I were right out of art school, I would go to openings with a pack of other people, so we could all give each other courage. But, at this point of my life, I don't have thirty years to make a career. If I were a dealer, and some old fool like me came sauntering up at an opening and tried to kiss my butt, I'd tell him to get lost. I knew I had to start at the top."

Joanou's approach to the art world had all the makings of a failure—with no art career credentials (no history of exhibits, no experience of collectors buying his work, and no reviews by critics), why would any New York City gallery give this person a show? Katharine T. Carter, whom he sought to set this plan in motion, regularly cautions artists not to set their sights too high. "It's easier to sell dealers on someone with an active exhibition record," she said. "If someone was not quite active in creating art and showing it in the course of a career, that person's expectations of what is doable may not be realistic."

In these cases, she prefers to try to place an artist's work in nonprofit spaces, smaller galleries and museums, often not in the art hothouse of New York City but in smaller cities and towns, in order to build an exhibition track record. "They have to start at the bottom, as though they're twenty again. To shoot for things that are too high is ridiculous. I look for smaller spaces that welcome artists who are more mature, and I try to get the artist to help pay for a lot of the costs, such as shipping and promotion. Many older people have a mindset from fifty years ago, when dealers did a lot more for artists, such as shipping and insuring work and paying for all the advertising. I tell these artists, 'dealers don't do that anymore—you can't wait for someone to do this for you; you need to think about creating a partnership with dealers, which makes you much more attractive to them.'"

As it turned out, they both got what they wanted. Joanou's work was exhibited at the Walter Wickiser Gallery in New York in June 1999, and Joanou picked up a lot of the costs. Besides underwriting magazine and newspaper advertisements, providing the gallery with a mailing list, and paying for the printing and mailing of invitations, Joanou also sent out personal invitations to people he knew well. As a result, two pieces sold from that show, one for $4,000 and another for $20,000.

A clear advantage that the more mature artist has over someone younger is a wider circle of acquaintances—professional colleagues, clients, personal friends, parents of their children's friends, members of clubs and associations to which they have belonged—who are likewise older and apt to have larger incomes. Ron Condon notified many of the people in his personal and professional address book of his February 2000 show—his first exhibition of art ever—at Lydon Fine Arts in Chicago and sold twenty of the twenty-two paintings on display. ("Sometimes," Douglas Lydon said, "you stop worrying about how old the artist is and just get bowled over by the quality of the work.")

Not only business connections but business experience helped Norman Mercer of East Hampton, New York, who in 1976, at the age of sixty, retired from the company he founded (English Town Cutlery of Freehold, New Jersey, which produces plastic-handled stainless steel tableware) in order to be a full-time sculptor. "I think I have been more logical and commercial in approaching galleries than I might have been in my twenties," he said.

Pricing is particularly an area in which Mercer had strong opinions: "I was anxious to price my work for distribution, but my business experience showed me that lower-priced pieces are viewed as decorative, whereas higher-priced items were viewed more as art. Someone might buy a $2,000 piece with no questions, but with a $29,000 work they will want a big discount. It's more work to negotiate over a discount, but it is because that $29,000 work is more desirable to people." Similarly, in order to "capitalize on my age" and keep prices high, he has not produced a large edition of sculptures but only one at a time.

Certainly, this type of thinking goes against accepted art world wisdom. "A lot of older artists cannot accept low prices for their work—it's kind of a psychological barrier they can't cross," said New York art dealer Stephen Rosenberg. "Their skill level may be equal to, or better than, many younger artists, but younger artists are more willing to start at the bottom, which you have to do if you lack name recognition."

Katharine Carter noted that many dealers "just can't deal with difficult, cantankerous, older artists," but sometimes mature artists bring knowledge and intuition about buying and selling that art dealers may lack. Of course, artists who have shored up their financial base and are not dependent on sales in order to eat may feel less need to take a dealer or advisor's advice.

Beginning Again

Another mature painter without previous art world credentials but with name recognition in the world of business, Herb Murrie, sold out his first show at Lydon Fine Arts in 1998. At his second show the following year, twelve works were purchased, averaging $6,500 apiece. Murrie had semi-retired as chairman of MLR Design in Chicago at the age of fifty-nine in 1995 in order to "lighten my load and devote the rest of my life to painting."

Unlike Kolb, Joanou, and Condon, Murrie had a background in painting—he received a bachelor's of fine arts degree in painting from the University of Illinois in 1957 and was even offered an assistant professorship there—but chose to pursue commercial design, developing corporate marks and brand images over the years for such clients as Bristol-Myers, Coca-Cola, Kraft Foods, Nestle, Proctor & Gamble, and Quaker Oats. "Every so often, I would get back into painting for a time, but business would always pull me away from it," he said. "I always felt that some part of me belonged in the painting world. Sometimes, I would wonder what might have happened if I had taken that assistant professorship and devoted the rest of my life to painting. That idea flitted in and out of my mind, but not for long. There was work to be done and no sense to wasting time on what might have been."

However, unlike Joanou and Condon, Murrie was willing to start his painting career from scratch, entering art competitions around the United States. At some of these, he won awards, such as an honorable mention at the annual show of the Navarro Council for the Arts in Corsicana, Texas, an artist showcase award at Manhattan Arts International, and the top prize at the Baker Art Center in Liberal, Kansas. "Entering these contests, I thought, would give me some exposure," he noted. "If you can get some juried awards that have nothing to do with selling work, I thought I might convince gallery owners that my work was worth showing."

A second reason that Murrie was interested in entering competitions is that it involved mailing slides of his work to people rather than actually walking into a gallery and meeting someone. Confidence in one field of endeavor doesn't always translate into others. In fact, he mailed slides to Lydon Fine Arts, rather than delivering them in person, in part "because no one knows how old I am from my slides." A feeling that the art world belongs to the young and that, at their age, they should not expose themselves to ridicule may hinder many older artists from pursuing their dreams. "A lot of mature artists ask me, 'Am I too old for this?' and I reassure them that they are never too old," said Caroll Michels, a career advisor to artists. "Dealers who believe that an artist's age matters are limited in their thinking, and artists have to stand up against this nonsense." However, there is probably no profession that exposes an individual's vulnerability—at any age—more than artist, and older artists are likely to see themselves as having more to lose than gain. Murrie stated that, frequently, "I say to myself, I'm successful. People have acknowledged that the work I do is good. But, in the art world, you wear your heart on your sleeve. Mailing slides out keeps me from being too hurt when people look at my work and say, 'Oh, it's very interesting.'"

To some of their friends and colleagues, this late-in-life dedication to art seems to come out of left field, but it was often just waiting for the right time to emerge. Condon, for instance, studied commercial art (layout and design) in Cincinnati, because "my father said he wouldn't pay for me to study fine art." Karen Nangle of Savannah, Georgia, was an observer of the art world for decades before finally making the plunge as a painter of abstract landscapes in the late 1990s. A graduate of Vassar College in 1959, majoring in art history, she worked for a time as a librarian at the Museum of Modern Art and, after getting married, commuted from Darien, Connecticut, to New York City to work as a picture researcher at a stock photography agency, taking time off to be a full-time mother. "All those years, looking out car and train windows, internalizing the landscape, feeling more and more frustrated that I never had time to paint until I was ready to burst," she said. "Finally, when I moved with my husband down to Savannah in 1993, I decided that I'm not just going to get another job. I'm going to paint."

Switching Professions

Louise Sennesh's husband "couldn't understand how I ended up in medicine," because she always wanted to paint. Her mother was an artist, making portraits, teaching art, and creating courtroom sketches for newspapers and television stations, and much of Sennesh's childhood was spent working with one art material or another. However, she also had a strong interest in science and found that, by college, there was a need to choose between the two. In 1986, her mother died, "and, sometimes, when someone close to you dies, you take on their identity." Two years later, she quit her work as a child psychiatrist, and both Sennesh and her husband thought she had made a good choice, but not everyone was so convinced. A resident of McLean, Virginia, she thought for a time about combining her artistic and scientific interests to pursue medical illustration ("I did anatomical drawings in med school") and called Johns Hopkins University in Maryland, which has a well-established medical illustration degree program. "I called up, and a woman there said to me over the phone, 'How can you do this? You're a doctor, and now you want to be an artist? I'm not even going to take your name.'"

Like Joanou and Concon, Sennesh looked for retraining and went to George Washington University, where she received an MFA in painting in 1997. There were a number of older, returning students in her program, and just immersing herself in an art environment made the decision to be a full-time artist seem more tangible and less self-indulgent. "I put child development theory to the test," she said. "You are always developing, we tell people, and now it was my turn." A medical career, of course, has a predetermined pathway, starting with medical school itself, then two years of hospital residency, another year of internship and psychiatric residency, leading then to very specific, advertised jobs. After receiving her degree, she "bounced around among a number of things," including landscapes, portrait, and floral commissions. "I scouted around for a gallery and received a lot of rejection. I would feel terrible. There were some days I just said, 'I don't need another character-building experience.'"

Eventually, Sennesh contacted Caroll Michels, who began organizing her search for places to show and sell her work. A significant percentage of Michels's clients are older artists, who may or may not have had formal art training but are looking to treat their interest in art in a more professional manner. "Many of these artists have worked in business, so they are familiar with the concepts of marketing and building product-recognition," Michels noted. "I simply need to direct them in ways in which they can use their business skills to start selling art."

Going Back to Art School

In 1992, Anna Joelsdottir's last child left home and she had some choices to make. A resident of Iceland, she was moving to Chicago with her second husband, a United States citizen. She thought about obtaining a teaching license in Illinois, since she had taught elementary school children before. Instead, she went to art school in order to pursue painting, taking classes at the School of the Art Institute of Chicago and eventually entering as a full-time student in the Master of Fine Arts program at the age of fifty-three.

She is part of a growing trend of older people who are developing their artistic skills within a degree program at an art school. "There is a changing demographics of students at art schools," said Samuel Hope, executive director of the National Association of Schools of Art and Design in Reston, Virginia. "Where once you only had the eighteen-to-twenty-two age cohort, now you see people in their thirties, forties, fifties, and even sixties." Many of these older artists are nonmatriculated students-at-large or enrolled in continuing education courses. Almost half of the students at the non–degree-granting Art Students League in New York City are fifty years of age or older; in the continuing education program at the Rhode Island School of Design, students over fifty account for 20 percent.

"Most of our students are between thirty and forty-nine," said Pat Thornton, associate director of continuing education at RISD, adding that these students are taking courses primarily for career changes. Among the most popular classes are computer graphics and interior design.

There are a variety of ways for older people to enter an art program, starting with continuing education courses (nondegree, generally held in the evenings); taking classes as a student-at-large (daytime courses along with degree students); pursuing a bachelor or master of fine arts degree; and working toward a diploma in studio art (fulfilling all the requirements of a bachelor's degree without the liberal arts curriculum).

Returning to school as a full-time student is clearly not an option for every older artist, because of the commitment of time and money. People with active careers and ties to a community are not likely to have the freedom of many eighteen-year-olds to find a fine art program they like somewhere around the country. Because of this, the percentage of full-time students fifty years of age or older in art schools tends to be small. Some schools, however, have larger numbers than others. While only two percent of the students at the Massachusetts College of Art in Boston are over fifty, 17 percent of the students who entered the degree program at the nearby School of the Museum of Fine Arts in the Fall of 1999 are in that age range. The Savannah College of Art and Design in Georgia averages between 10 and 15 percent annually.

Going back to school was "hard" for Joelsdottir, because she "had been out in the world for a long time and I was seen as a professional. But I had to humble myself to come here." She might have saved some pride and the tuition by simply working steadily in her studio, "but it might have taken years longer to reach the same point. Going to school speeds up the process." She added that "I needed the feedback, to have someone else's eyes look at my work."

Returning to school was "tough" for James Barnhill, seventy-eight, because, as a public speaking teacher and head of the theater department at Brown University in Providence, Rhode Island for thirty-three years, "I was used to handing out grades, not receiving them." His workload at Brown had always been too full to indulge an interest in sculpture, and, immediately after retiring, he enrolled as a full-time student at RISD. Instead of maintaining a pedagogical distance from the eighteen-to-twenty-two-year-olds, Barnhill was now an equal in the classroom with them, sometimes not even their equal. It was also "tough" to discover that "I was not the best. I was certainly a B student, but some students were spectacular. I found that I didn't have the kind of vision and large-scale viewing of the problem that some others had. That was indeed a very new position for me to be in."

Art is itself a realm of self-discovery, and art school may prove the same for students whose self-image and understanding of the world had been formed long before. Pursuing art in one's later years, according to a number of psychological studies, may also give one a healthier and longer life. Dean Keith Simonton, professor of psychology at the University of California at Davis who has spent years researching creativity in older people, said that when people start over in something new, like art, "it's almost as though they are young again. It's exciting, like first love: You think, at age fifty or sixty, that you know who you are; then you try something else and, whammo, you learn a lot of new things about yourself. You peak at a time when other people are drying up. That allows you to express things you may have repressed for twenty or thirty years, and that helps you mentally and physically."

Don Howard, sixty-eight, who retired in 1993 after almost thirty years as a management consultant and immediately began a four-year degree program at the School of the Museum of Fine Arts in Boston, noted that "it added twenty years to my life to have twenty-year-olds all around me. I learned to stop thinking like a sixty-year-old and started thinking like I was, maybe, thirty or forty: I gained a much younger point of view. I started to think, I can make a ten-foot-tall sculpture, I can make an enormous collage. I gained a can-do way of life."

A number of his retired friends, he added, "who had very successful careers have had very unsuccessful retirements. I've seen a lot of drinking, marriages breaking up, people going around glassy-eyed wondering what to do."

Another who has felt a rejuvenation through studying artmaking full-time, Sarah Hollis Perry, received a diploma in studio art at the age of sixty-five from the School of the Museum of Fine Arts in 1999. She had raised five children and worked for thirty-seven years in the field of photographic research, first for Polaroid and later for the Rowland Institute for Sciences in Cambridge. She had taken some continuing education classes off and on since 1981, but they did not strike her as being at a high enough level. "It seemed as though the other students didn't take themselves seriously, or the teachers didn't take the students seriously, so I was never completely satisfied," she said. In 1994, she decided to cut back her hours at the Rowland Institute and enter the museum school full-time, and the difference was enormous. "For me, what I was doing in school was not about making money," she said. "You go from doing everything that my parents wanted, as a good girl should do (and I was a good girl), to getting married and doing what a good wife and mother should do, and having a job and doing what I am expected to do for an employer. Then, in art school, I began to do something just for me. It's so thrilling, so exciting. Suddenly, it's just like being born."

A school, of course, is more than just classes; it is a community of students learning together. As the majority of the students in the bachelor's programs are still right out of high school, their social interests (dating) and intellectual realm may strike older students as limited. ("They haven't lived life out of school," Joelsdottir said. "In some ways, that's a handicap.") Many older students noted that their young classmates were frequently prone to fads, focusing on whatever was in the latest issue of *Artforum* or *Art in America.* Ruth Kristoff, who received an MFA in sculpture from the University of Massachusetts in 2000 at the age of fifty-one, occasionally found the extreme political and theoretical stances of her fellow students abrasive. "I'm a strong feminist—I believe in what I can do—but I'm not in-your-face," she said. "Sometimes, it seemed in school that art that wasn't in-your-face wasn't really art."

Art school culture may emphasize taking strong (and perhaps arbitrary) stands, heightened individuality, and sometimes just oddity, as students attempt to separate themselves from others and try to remake themselves into what they believe an artist is supposed to be. "Students at RISD recognized that they were very different than the students at Brown, and they gloried in it," Barnhill said. "You see kids with various hair colors. There was a girl with a lot of tattoos, and she gave a speech on her tattoos. I couldn't get into that."

As a result, many older students take a more business-like approach to art school, taking courses, discussing technical and professional concerns with their instructors, and then going home to work, leaving the culture of art school behind. "I had social interactions with other students during lunch or on field trips," Howard said. "These relationships never lasted very far from school. It's just easier for me to bond with people closer to my own age."

Older students are likely to find, Samuel Hope said, that their maturity, perspective, and experience will keep them grounded amidst the swirl of artistic conceits: "Many older students putting themselves through art school are there because they want to get the knowledge and know what getting the knowledge is. Younger students are often there because they want to be like someone else."

PART TWO

The Artist's Studio

CHAPTER FOUR

Studio Practices

For an artist, getting down to work requires a studio in which to create. The more this space can be limited to artmaking—as opposed to sharing the living room or kitchen—the better for maintaining one's artistic concentration, ensuring the health of other family members (especially children), and obtaining a studio insurance policy. Getting down to work also means having the right materials; knowing which are the right ones involves research and some trial and error.

The Home Studio

When the architect Charles Gwathmey designed a two-story house in Southampton, New York, for his father, the renowned painter Robert Gwathmey, half of the downstairs was the artist's studio. "Painting was such a big part of his life," the architect said, "not just his work, that it didn't seem right to separate where he lived and where he worked."

Consigning such a large portion of one's living space to artmaking may not satisfy every family. However, where the studio should be—at home or somewhere else—is a question that most artists (professional and hobbyist alike) have to confront. For some, the distractions of home require that they pursue their art elsewhere, perhaps renting a studio downtown. "I had a studio in the attic once," said painter Gregory Gillespie. "It was cramped, cold, dirty; it had poor light, and you could hear everything going on in the house. Now, my studio isn't far from the house, maybe a hundred yards, but it is a significant psychological distance."

Others, however, find that working at home makes the most sense. The reasons may be young children at home, the cost of renting a studio elsewhere, or just the inconvenience of traveling. "For a while, I rented a studio in a factory building in Boston," said Jane Smaldone, a painter who lives and now makes art at home in Roslyndale, Massachusetts. "I like working at night, but I didn't feel safe going there at night, especially since I didn't have a car and took public transit."

She arrived at a solution by converting the attic of her house into a studio, at a cost of between $4,000 and $5,000, not including her husband's labor. Considering the fact that the rent for her downtown studio was $400 per month, the cost of the conversion (the largest expense of which was supplying heat to the room) was recouped in one year.

What artists need in a studio is as individual as the artists themselves are, and converting a room into a studio will likely be as elaborate or simple as the artists are able to afford. Traditionally, artists require a window (preferably with a northern exposure, as that offers a relatively unvarying source of light during daylight hours) and a sink (for clean-up). The cost of adding a sink frequently convinces artists to do without additional plumbing and take their brushes to an existing bathroom. An attic or bedroom that receives little natural light may be helped by skylights, which cost between $200 and $300 (not including labor for installation), although many artists may prefer to exercise greater control over the light in their studios by using lamps or floodlights. Artists with jobs or small children, who are only able to work on their art at night or early morning, may especially rely on artificial light.

Garages, spare bedrooms, basements and attics, sometimes kitchens and living rooms, may be taken over by the artist of the family when home studio space is required. Each has its advantages and drawbacks. In a kitchen, everything would have to be cleaned up thoroughly after each artmaking session before any food touches the same kitchen surfaces, and art could only be created between meals. In such a public room, there is also a problem of privacy, as many artists would not want everyone passing through to see (and comment upon) the latest work in progress. When a studio is situated in a well-traveled area, the likelihood of passers-by getting paint on their clothes also increases substantially. Basements and attics have less traffic, but moisture in one and cold in the other as well as a lack of light in both might prove challenging without extensive remodeling.

For instance, Josie Lawrence, a painter in Hanover, Massachusetts, who works at the Kennedy Library in Boston, uses a space heater for warmth in the attic of her house, which she uses as a studio. "The cold makes oil paints harder and less pliable," she said, "and I have to put the heater on for a while in order to soften up the paints before I can go up to work."

David Deutsch, a painter who spends half the year in Boca Raton, Florida, and the other half in Manhasset, New York, has encountered mild problems in both of his home studios. In Florida, the studio is the garage, and the natural light is sufficient when he keeps the garage door open during the day. When he has tried to paint at night, however, "I have to turn on artificial lights, which attracts bugs, and there are just so many of them down here that I can't stand it and give up," he said. In Long Island, the studio is a guest bedroom on the second floor, and the solvents he uses for his oil paints create an odor that pervades the entire upstairs of the house. "I use odorless solvents, but my wife says there still is a smell."

Certain kinds of artwork, such as printmaking (which uses strong, toxic solvents) and sculpture (which often employs noisy, heavy machinery and creates extensive amounts of dust) may simply prove incompatible with a private home or neighborhood. Ventilation systems, exhaust fans, and even permission from the municipality to use certain kinds of equipment in a residential community may be required (see chapter 5).

The benefits of having a studio at home are also the hazards. Susan Baker, a painter in North Truro, Massachusetts, noted that having a studio in the front room of her house means that she is "there when things happen. I can answer the telephone and watch my son. Having a studio somewhere else sounds like a pain to me." On the other hand, Beverly Ferguson-Deevy, a pastel artist in Plainville, Massachusetts, whose studio is the family garage, said that "sometimes, I can be getting pretty deep into my work, and hours go by—I don't even notice. All of a sudden, I hear a tiny 'Mommy' from one of my children, and a whole train of thought is blown away.

Everything goes blank, like when the computer crashes, and I'll have to start again another day."

Young children are a common reason that many artists (especially women artists) prefer to work at home, yet they need to be instructed that Mom's (or Dad's) art studio is not *their* studio. "My children do not enter my studio, under pain of death," Ferguson-Deevy said. "All in all, they've been pretty good at respecting that rule."

The artist-parent, too, must learn to tune out household noises in order to concentrate. Smaldone, who has a one-and-a-half-year-old daughter, hired a baby-sitter for sixteen hours a week in order that she may work undisturbed in her studio. "Sometimes, I hear the baby screaming," she noted. "Basically, I have just trained myself to ignore it."

Similarly, Jon Imber, a painter who lives with his family in a loft (a wall separates the living space from the studio) in Somerville, Massachusetts, stated that he loves not having to travel to work and to be able to work all the time, if he wants. "I set up my life so that I can work where I live," he said, "but now that I have a family, I'm not sure it's such a good thing. It's very distracting when you can hear your own kid, or your wife, on the other side of the wall. There is a wall but, psychologically, it's as though the wall isn't there."

A studio is not just one more room in the house but a space in which one is allowed to be messy, and it may never be entirely cleaned: A different set of standards applies to a studio than to the rest of the house, and sometimes there are different clothes. David Deutsch noted that one problem he has with an at-home studio is that occasionally "I forget to take off my painting shoes and track paint through the house." Other artists find that they do not take their own time in the studio as seriously when they are working at home, preferring to make art somewhere else. "I like to go to work, like other people," said John Shahn, a sculptor who lives in Roosevelt, New Jersey, and rents a studio space in the same town. Jody Mussoff, an artist in Riverdale, Maryland, who works in the library at the Hirshhorn Museum in Washington, D.C., noted that when doing her art at home she is "always conscious of something that needs to be done around the house. I can hear the bathroom calling, 'Clean me, clean me.'"

"The problem of having a studio in your home is having a studio in your home," said Edwin Ahlstrom, a painter in Monrovia, Maryland, who teaches art at Montgomery College in Rockville. "With a studio somewhere else, you may only get two or three times a week, but you will pick up where you left off and it's your time completely, without the constant pull of whatever is going on inside the home."

An additional problem cited by a number of painters whose studios are in their homes is that, by working at home, they become isolated, not meeting other artists who can offer informed ideas, or even camaraderie.

Jennifer Gilbert, a Boston art dealer, noted that the where-to-have-the-studio issue is a "two-sided coin, but you often find that women like the idea of a studio at home, because the studio gives credibility to the work they do at home, while men in general prefer a studio away from home and accept a studio at home only as a matter of keeping costs down." Some artists find that the best way to make art at home is to build an addition to their house that becomes the studio. Ahlstrom, who has used his home basement ("it can be distracting when you hear the kids are running around upstairs") as a studio and rented space in office buildings ("traveling back and forth late at night is not ideal"), created a $20,000 addition to his house for a twenty-two-by-twenty-eight-foot studio with a twelve-foot ceiling. He wanted the large space, in part because he shares the studio with his wife, Judith, a portrait painter, and also because "you need to be able to step back, fifteen feet or so, to see your work at a distance."

Judy Shahn, a painter in South Truro, Massachusetts, whose twenty-four-by-twenty-six-foot studio was built attached to her house in 1978, found that in the days when her studio was in a small, upstairs bedroom, her work had gotten smaller and smaller. After the addition, the scale of her paintings grew significantly. For her, the primary benefit of working at home is that "it is wonderful to start working in the morning, before you even get dressed. It's frustrating not to be able to get to work when you're snowed in and your studio is somewhere else."

On a smaller scale, a twelve-by-twelve-foot studio with a cement floor, metal siding, high ceiling, picture window, and a skylight was built in 1992 for Jody Mussoff by her partner. She, too, had the experience of setting up a studio in her apartment ("one-half would be the studio and the other half would be everything else, and the smell of oil paints and solvents pervaded everything") and renting space in factory buildings ("it was a funky neighborhood that could be dangerous at night"). "In some ways, it's the best of both worlds," she said. "It's handy to be at home, and it's not a big outing to go to the studio. But, when I'm in my studio, I can't hear the phone or see that the bathroom needs to be cleaned, so I can really concentrate on my work."

Selecting Art Materials

These days, almost everything that can be marketed is sold through mail-order catalogues: appliances, books, clothing, food, flowers and plants, furniture, guns, "kit" cars and sailboats, sports equipment, tools, and even artwork are offered by the hundreds of companies that sell items through catalogues. It should be no surprise, then, that art supplies may also be purchased from catalogue companies, and for the same reasons for which all of the other items are marketed through the mail. Many people live at a distance from the retail outlets that would have precisely the supplies they want, and local stores may not offer abundant variety or competitive prices. In combination with the items that are sold in local shops, mail-order art supply companies offer artists a wide range of products, prices, and quality. Even the wait for the mail may be shortened, if one wishes to pay for overnight delivery.

Buying through the mail, however, may also cause artists a high degree of nervousness and uncertainty. Products that cannot be examined and tested, salespeople who cannot offer detailed information, brands that are unknown to the prospective buyer, and items that will only be sold in large quantity can easily unsettle artists and hobbyists who must make their decisions based on short descriptions and (usually) black-and-white photographs in a catalogue. Like dealing with the art market itself, buying art materials through the mail requires one part knowledge, one part faith.

Practically anything that a painter, printmaker, sculptor, or commercial artist needs is available in the many art supply catalogues—from brushes, canvases, inks, paints, pigments, overhead projectors, and papers, to drafting tables, chisels, clays, easels, frames, mats and sketchbooks, and a lot more than that. Frequently, the products listed in these catalogues—for example, Winsor & Newton paints—are well known and could be found (and, thereby, tested) at major art supply shops. Other products, such as Daniel Smith Finest Oil Colors or Nova Color Artists' Acrylic Paint, bear the name of the mail-order company—they cannot be found elsewhere and tested, which requires potential buyers to read the catalogue descriptions closely as well as to ask for additional information. Highly detailed information may not be easily obtainable if the mail-order company is not the product's manufacturer. Many companies buy paints from manufacturers and affix their own proprietary names on them, similar to supermarket brands of food items. The art product may be quite good, selling at an attractive price, but the people working at the mail-order company are unlikely to have much information on the permanence, light-fastness, ingredients, and precise color index number of pigment, for example.

There are, for example, more than a dozen Hansa Yellows on the market, varying from the very fugitive to the permanent, according to Mark David Gottsegen, chairman of the committee on artists' paints and related materials of the Philadelphia-based American Society for Testing and Materials. Without knowing the color index number, a buyer will not know how the pigment holds up in combination with other pigments or over time.

"You don't want to buy some paint based on the name Hunt's Red or Joe Blow's Roast Beef Red, because you don't really know what color you're getting," Gottsegen said. "If the mail-order company isn't the manufacturer, go to the manufacturer and ask them what's in it."

Himself a buyer of watercolor paints and papers from mail-order companies, Gottsegen recommended that artists obtain the respective ASTM standard specifications for oil paints, acrylics, and watercolors in order to have a precise description of pigments as well as the composition and durability of paints. These specifications cost $10 apiece, and one should write to American Society for Testing and Materials, 100 Barr Harbor Drive, West Conshohocken, PA 19428, (610) 832–9500.

There aren't similar standards for other art supplies, and one must rely on obtaining good answers to questions. In addition to more personal preferences, for instance, sculptors and potters would want to know the firing color range and grog of clays as well as whether or not they are pre-pugged and wedged; painters would be interested in the type (bristle, sable, or synthetic), softness, ability to maintain a point and length of hairs on brushes as well as the length of the handles; printmakers and watercolorists would need to know the acidity, quantity, rag content, size, and sizing of papers. Daniel Smith (located in Seattle, Washington) attempts to ease potential paper buyers' concerns by offering sample packets of papers—an $8 sampler containing one sheet of every paper it sells in four-by-five size, as well as a printmaking paper packet and a watercolor paper sampler in regular size sheets, priced between $30 and $40 for each.

Since 1989, federal law (the Labeling of Hazardous Art Materials Act) also requires all art product labels to include a conformance statement ("conforms to

ASTM D–4236"), the name and address of the manufacturers or other responsible party and a telephone number at which further information about chronic toxicity can be answered, and a list of the names of any chronically hazardous ingredients and appropriate hazard warnings. In fact, it is now illegal to sell any art material without these items on the label (see chapter 5). The federal Occupational Safety and Health Administration demands that manufacturers provide Material Safety Data Sheets for their products that contain oxides or quantities of toxic elements. The law requires that these sheets be made available to employers whose employees use the product. Although manufacturers and importers are not required (except in a few states) to supply these sheets to individual consumers, artists should only buy from companies that do supply them. Most reputable companies that have nothing to hide are willing to supply them. Artists might want to ask the mail-order companies to send those sheets in advance of purchasing a particular item and certainly when the product is bought.

Sometimes, more information can prove confusing. Dick Blick Company (located in Galesburg, Illinois), like many other companies, uses the "AP Nontoxic," "CP Nontoxic," and "Health Label" seals of the Boston-based Arts and Creative Materials Institute on the labels of their paints. Both "AP" and "CP" indicate that the Institute certifies the products are safe even for children ("AP" specifically refers to nontoxicity, while "CP" includes both nontoxicity and performance requirements), and "Health Label" signifies that the warning label on the product has been certified by an ACMI toxicologist and, if hazards are found, appropriate warnings are printed on the label. The same paints, however, may be sold by other mail-order companies but without the ACMI emblems to indicate their safety.

Daniel Smith, on the other hand, provides the lightfastness rating for many of the paints that company sells, paints that are also sold by other companies. One shouldn't assume, therefore, that the same paints are less toxic when purchased through Dick Blick or more durable when bought from Daniel Smith, only that Dick Blick considers product safety a strong selling point in its promotion of these products, while Daniel Smith emphasizes longevity. Customers would still want to buy at the best price, all other things being equal.

Obtaining detailed information on art supplies is never easy, either from catalogues or even from many art shops. Customer service representatives are likely to have basic information about products and can answer some questions. If they don't have the immediate answer, the representatives will generally attempt to get the information from someone at the company or from the manufacturer, calling back the person who made the inquiry. Some mail-order suppliers provide ongoing training seminars for their representatives, which may consist of listening to a talk about certain products by salesmen of the manufacturers or watching a promotional video supplied by the manufacturer. Other companies hire people with art backgrounds for customer service jobs, who will still be provided some training, because they are likely to be asked lots of questions over time.

Problems are not unheard-of between mail-order companies and their buyers, regardless of the kind of merchandise sold, such as receiving the wrong item, receiving damaged goods, or an incorrect credit card billing. Many companies have time limits on returns, which may vary greatly; others may require explanation. Other mail-order art supply companies simply refer to a "reasonable period of time" as acceptable for returns. According to a customer service employee at Arthur Brown in Maspeth, New York, the company has no time limits for returns of pens, providing that they haven't been used, although there may be a restocking fee for other items if returned within a "reasonable amount of time, for instance, not more than three months." The employee did not indicate the amount of the restocking fee.

A number of companies make blanket statements of guaranteed satisfaction in their catalogues, promising to accept all returns for whatever reason in exchange for another item or one's money back. In order to save yourself and a mail-order company some headaches, it is wisest to obtain as much advance information as possible about the products that may be purchased.

However, if a buyer believes that he or she is a victim of mail fraud (being duped by a misleading or false advertisement made in a catalogue) or consumer fraud (for instance, money is not refunded, or some advertised "handmade" papers were actually created by machines), that person should complain to one of the following agencies. The Federal Trade Commission, which regulates sales through the mail, can found at Pennsylvania Avenue at Sixth Street N.W., Washington, DC 20580. For matters regarding out-of-state sellers, one should notify the Postmaster General, at 475 L'Enfant Plaza S.W., Washington, DC 20260; this office will investigate and turn over its findings to the U.S. Attorney, who may indict. If the seller is in the the buyer's home state, the buyer's State Attorney General's office can help, as can the nearest office of the Better Business Bureau—contact information can be found by writing to the Council of Better Business Bureaus, Inc., 4200 Wilson Boulevard, Arlington, VA 22203. Finally, if the seller is a local dealer, the local Department of Consumer Affairs can be of service. There are jurisdictional differences between each of these offices, and some have more power than others.

Many companies that sell products through the mail also belong to various associations, which one may contact in order to resolve disputes with their members as well as find out which companies are members in advance of making a purchase. Becoming a member of an association does not ensure the quality of an art product, but the organizations do maintain standards to which member companies must adhere. Among these organizations are the Advertising Mail Marketing Association, at 1333 F Street N.W., Washington, DC 20004, (202) 347–0055; Direct Marketing Association, at 1120 Avenue of the Americas, New York, NY 10036, (212) 768–7277, or at 1111 19th Street N.W., Washington, DC 20036, (202) 955–5030, *www.thedma.org*; National Art Education Association, at 1916 Association Drive, Reston, VA 22091, (703) 860–8000, *www.naea-reston.org;* and National Art Materials Trade Association, at 10115 Kincey Avenue, Huntersville, NC 28078, (704) 948–5554, *www.namta.org*.

Most catalogues are free, although some cost up to five dollars (that amount is refundable with one's actual order of art supplies). Despite the fact that these are mail-order companies, buyers increasingly place orders over the phone, sometimes with a fax, or by e-mail. Some companies have toll-free numbers, while others require buyers to make long distance calls, and yet others provide no telephone number at all, ensuring that business is wholly conducted through the mail. The price of the telephone call may not always help determine from which company to order products. Co-op Artists' Materials (headquartered in Atlanta, Georgia), for instance, has a toll-free number, yet the company requires a minimum purchase of $35 for telephone orders whereas there is no minimum for orders that are mailed in. Jerry's Artarama (located in New Hyde Park, New York), which also has a toll-free telephone number, requires a minimum order of $50 if one is ordering by phone, and $20 if by mail.

In general, prices for products in mail-order catalogues compare favorably with the same or similar items in smaller art supply stores, and they may be equal to or a bit higher than those items in larger stores of major cities. Sales taxes will not be applied unless one buys from a mail-order company in one's own state. Beyond the prices of the items in the catalogues are shipping and handling charges, which, of course, will not exist for supplies bought directly at a store. Shipping costs are determined based on a percentage of the dollar value of the purchase, and one receives a better break with larger orders. It may also be impossible to purchase just a small amount of some item, in order to try it out, as companies often require orders in bulk. That bulk rate keeps the overall price low, but consumers may feel reluctant to buy a lot of a product they have not sampled.

Montgomery Ward developed the mail-order business in the 1870s as a way of bringing store-quality supplies to people in outlying areas, but buying through the mail is no longer the exclusive domain of those in rural regions. Artists in suburbs and cities are currently the predominant buyers from art catalogues. The tremendous volume of art products on the market would overwhelm most stores but not necessarily a five-hundred-page catalogue. One cannot completely get away from relying on written or oral descriptions of products and old-fashioned trial and error, but artists who know what they need and can formulate the right questions minimize their risks.

The ability to purchase art materials through the mail has grown dramatically over the past two decades, aided more recently by the Internet, which has allowed art-supply stores to expand their reach. Pearl Paint started out as a store on Canal Street in New York City in 1933, for instance, and it is still there to this day. However, there are now twenty-four other Pearl Paint outlets around the country where many of the same art supplies are available, and one may also purchase these products through mail order, telephone order, and the Internet. The differences between exclusively mail-order companies and stores that also sell art supplies by mail have been blurred, but the result has been more options for purchasing the materials that artists need, and the same consumer protection laws apply to mail-order operations, regardless of how large a percentage of their business is actually transacted through the mail. See the Resources section of this chapter for a listing of the largest companies selling mail-order merchandise for artists.

Artist-Made Supplies

Given the abundant offerings in art stores and mail-order art supply catalogues, most artists' supply needs are easily satisfied. What image to put on the canvas, paper, or negative, or to shape into a sculpture, is the more immediate concern. Some artists, however, find that they cannot create the images they want because of something lacking in the materials they are using. Perhaps they cannot find the right color of pastel, or they want a thicker paper with more linen content, or the color of the paint loses its intensity when mixed with white, or they want to make art in a way that is currently not done, or the quality of the material has declined while the cost has increased.

Various artists experiment with their materials, making their own paper or mixing various substances in with their paints, for instance, some having more success than others. The venerable art supply manufacturer Winsor & Newton was founded in 1832 by two artists, William Winsor and Henry Charles Newton, who both had an interest in chemistry—Winsor was in charge of oil paints, while Newton handled watercolors. Even today, some painters have gone back to original sources in order to make their own paints, free of the fillers and additives that commercial manufacturers use to extend the life, decrease the drying time, and increase the consistency of the pigments. A small but growing number of artists, who have become proficient in making their own materials in quantity, have created specialized lines of art supplies for other artists. Frequently, these supplies are less expensive by weight than those produced by large manufacturers, and the quality is as high or better.

"Years ago, there were two really good artist paints to buy, both made in Holland—Old Holland Paint and Bloxx," painter Bill Jensen said. "But then, Old Holland was sold to someone, and old man Bloxx died, and the quality really fell off, in some cases below student grade. If Carl ever stopped making paint, I would have to get a paint machine and make it myself." That Carl is Carl Plansky, a painter who, since 1984, has operated Williamsburg Art Supply in Brooklyn, New York. He sells paint to many of the most renowned contemporary artists, including Jensen, Brice Marden, Joan Mitchell, and Susan Rothenberg. There are more than sixty colors in Plansky's line of oil paints, which he calls "handmade oils," as opposed to paints created from a set recipe. "Any company with enough scientists can work out a formula," he stated. "They machine-grind the pigments, which may make them lose some luminosity, and then the pigments are treated with fillers and additives to give the paint shelf life and an even consistency. I keep experimenting: I work with every batch of raw pigment I receive to grind it to its maximum luminosity and soak it in oil for the right amount of time. I can also manufacture one pint of paint for what the big companies charge for a one-ounce tube, and I pass those savings on to my customers."

Many of the artists making art supplies for other artists refer to the "handmade" quality of their products, in contrast to the more generic nature of mass-produced items. Plansky noted that his paints are "the equivalent of health food." Stefan Watson, who started Watson Paper Company in Albuquerque, New Mexico, in 1979, producing handmade papers for artists, said that "if mass marketing had its way, everyone would use the same products. Who says that all paper has to be white, that it has only a standardized thickness?"

Gail Spiegel, a painter and owner of Vasari Classic Artists' Oil Colors in New York City, noted that "people are dissatisfied with mass-produced paints, with the fillers in their colors, the way pigments are extended, and the paint dries on you. When you mass-produce paint, you cut corners and the quality suffers. Artists have told me that they have tried my paints and have gotten excited again about painting."

Keith Lebenzon of Portland, Oregon, a craftsman making calligraphy and watercolor brushes, claimed that the difference between his brushes and those manufactured by larger companies is that "mine are made by hand, which makes all the difference in the world. No two brushes are alike. Every one has a personality. People have told me that these brushes have changed their lives." Another difference between his brushes and those of his competitors, Lebenzon stated, is the use of hairs from the Roosevelt elk (which only lives in the Pacific Northwest and is on the national list of endangered species) and the silver fox for several models.

Artists involved in creating art materials for artists also frequently stress their aim of providing these products at affordable prices, recognizing that art is not a high-paying profession for most. "I look out for the needs of painters," said Robert Gamblin, a Portland, Oregon, painter who spent ten years researching how to make paints before offering them for sale in 1980. "Painters need to have raw materials of high quality at affordable prices. I don't take economies inside the tube, such as adding fillers, but I will take them outside the tube. I have no distributors, no marketing people, no sales reps—that adds up to 22 percent to the cost of doing business."

Art Guerra, a painter who has operated Guerra Paint & Pigments in New York City since 1983, is another who claims to "look out for" artists. Selling over 250 dry pigments and water-based urethanes as well as a variety of antifoam, thickeners, dispersing and texturizing agents (allowing artists to mix up their own acrylic paints to desired levels of strength and thickness), Guerra says that he charges "one-quarter of the price of the big manufacturers, and you're using better materials, too."

He considers himself "not only a business but an information source," offering prospective pigment buyers a booklet that lists (among other things) the exact color, durability, weatherability, and alkali-resistance of the pigments as well as what these terms mean. Guerra also sells, packaged in jars, oil paints of his own making.

In addition to his own creations, Guerra sells tubes of oil paint produced by William & Arthur of Brooklyn—Bill Rabinowitz and Art Graham, both of whom paint (although Rabinowitz is primarily a chemist) and both of whom worked for years at Grumbacher artist paints. Just like Bill Jensen, both Graham and Rabinowitz express disappointment at artist paint "companies that are taken over by people who are only in it for making money," Graham stated, "who don't really care whether they're selling oil paints or candy wrappers or gum. You need to have a moral position with regard to art materials, and you have to love the product, love making the product, and love what the product is used for."

Whereas the high prices and diminishing quality of commercially available paints had originally pushed Robert Gamblin, Art Guerra, Carl Plansky, Art Graham, and Bill Rabinowitz to make their own, Suzanna Starr and Ladd Foresline of Cochecton, New York, invented oil sticks in 1984 because, Starr said, "I wanted to draw rather than use a brush, but I also wanted the thing I drew with to feel more like oil paint. There was nothing like that on the market, so we created these oil sticks." At first, the two sold these sticks to artists who heard of them by word of mouth, bypassing retail stores, "but that proved impossible," Foresline stated. "We're artists—that's why we got into making these things in the first place—and not manufacturers. It's a lot of work to do all of this, and I think we both gained respect for manufacturers because of all the work involved." In 1991, Winsor & Newton bought the product, and the two artists have returned to their art as well as to researching new art products.

In a similar vein, Diane Townsend began creating her own pastels in 1971 because she "couldn't find what I was looking for. The colors I observed in nature weren't made commercially, and I also didn't like the consistency of what I was buying. The colors and consistency seemed to get in my way." Many artists would assume that, if they had trouble with consistency, the problem is with them and their technique, but Townsend noted that "I'm arrogant and hardheaded. I secretly think I'm right and everybody else is wrong." Among her past and current customers are Chuck Close, Jim Dine, and Elizabeth Murray ("They're great pastels," Murray said). Townsend currently produces pastels in 130 colors (three tones each, three sizes each) two or three days a week—they are sold through New York Central Art Supply in Manhattan—devoting the rest of the time to her art.

Other artists have come to make their own art materials, not because they wanted something new, but rather as a result of recreating techniques that are centuries-old and even forgotten. Eric and Roger Rieger, brothers and painters living in Denver, Colorado, founded Lapis Arts in 1987 in order to sell oil paints made in the same manner since the Italian Renaissance. "I couldn't get the glazing effects with the umbers I was buying," Eric Rieger said. "They were coming out very chalky, so I started mixing my own paints." He spent a number of years researching how paint was made, traveling in Europe to study with alchemists, and, finally, in association with his brother, produced a line of oil paints that suited their purposes.

Richard Frumess of Rifton, New York, on the other hand, became interested in hot wax or encaustic painting, a technique that dates back to ancient Greece where it was a common process for both easel painters and muralists. Painting with wax—usually white refined beeswax combined with dry pigments and some resin—is a somewhat cumbersome activity and was eventually supplanted by the use of tempera and oil painting. Interest in encaustic painting has revived over the past two hundred years, in part due to the fact that it is "the most durable of all paint," Frumess said. "It won't rot or yellow with age as paint made with linseed oil does. I like painting with encaustics because of the enamel-like finish, the jewel-like effect. Texturally, you also get a large range of effects—you can build it up and carve into it."

He formed R&F Encaustics in 1982 (the only source of encaustic paints in the country), adding a line of oil sticks in fifty-two colors in 1990. "There is a lot to be said for artists making a product as opposed to a big company making it," Frumess stated. "Artists are basically making it for themselves, so it is a labor of love. Making encaustics is also very labor intensive and expensive, a process that big companies don't want to deal with, because they want to mass-produce things quickly to make as big a profit as they can." The labor intensiveness, however, has proven to be a problem for him, as "I haven't painted in a couple of years now because of the work of producing encaustics."

As noted above, more and more artists have come to make their own materials as well as experiment with the products they use. One cautionary note is that experimentation needs to be based on research and an understanding of the chemistry of substances that are combined. Art Graham noted that some artists "work up some homemade color, but they don't really know how to make paint. They get very strange ideas from their late-night readings, and, if they don't do things right, it will fall right off the canvas."

As with anything else they might buy, artists should ask questions in advance in order to ensure that what they purchase meets their expectations. Howard Wolfe, executive director of the Huntersville, North Carolina–based National Art Materials Trade Association, noted three areas of concern when buying paints: The first is consistent quality, that "within a certain tolerance, different tubes of the same paint will be exactly the same." The second is knowing to what standards the paints are manufactured, and whether or not they have been subjected to color- and lightfastness as well as permanency tests, such as those developed by the American Society of Testing and Materials. A third question is whether the people making the art supplies are actually creating them from scratch or if some or all of the product has been made by someone else. "Anyone can go to a major manufacturer of paints and say, 'I want you to make a line of paints that I'll sell under my name,'" Wolfe said. "When someone says he made his own paints, ask him where he got the binders, the resins, and the pigments."

One last point: Success frequently changes people, and it may turn artists who make and sell their own paints into small manufacturers of paints who are no longer practicing artists. Robert Doak noted that he "used to be a painter, but I've been doing so much of this lately . . ." —and the same may be true of a number of other artists who double as art supply makers, including Carl Plansky and Robert Gamblin. Perhaps, the question is not so much whether making art materials is the vocation or avocation of an artist; that the products are "handmade" may be of greatest interest to buyers, and some of these supplies are available in regular art shops. Steve Steinberg, president of New York Central Art Supply, noted that he devotes a section of his store to hand-bound sketchbooks. "You can easily see the difference between hand-bound and machine-bound books," he said. "There's a looseness to the handmade books—you might even say crudity—and they generally use more expensive papers." He added that selling handmade books is "a profitable area of our business."

Custom Art Suppliers

"Part of my responsibility as an artist is to get the materials I feel I need, not just what is readily available," painter Larry Bell said. For that reason, Bell calls on painter Stefan Watson at Watson Paper Company in Albuquerque, New Mexico, for the specialized handmade papers he uses in his works on paper. A small but growing number of artist-led companies work directly with artist-customers to provide the raw materials (such as pigments) or finished products that they seek for their art projects. The prices may be higher than other manufacturers, because of the special orders, or less, since a number of these companies allow artists to purchase materials in bulk. Finding out where one may locate artist-made or handmade (as opposed to mass-produced) artist materials is not always easy, as they are frequently not advertised. "I no longer advertise," Gail Spiegel of Vasari Classic Artists' Oil Colors said. "I can barely make enough for my own store." She does attend certain trade shows, such as the annual Portrait Society of America, as well as Artisan/Santa Fe, and it is at the display areas of trade shows where artists may be able to locate these low-volume, specialty items.

In addition to artists who handcraft art material, certain art stores are also known for stocking materials that include custom brushes, crayons, inks, paints, papers, pastels, pigments, and resins made by artists as well as other top-quality specialty items manufactured in the United States or abroad. See the Resources section of this chapter for a list of producers of handmade artists' supplies and for stores that stock specialty items.

Resources

Mail- and Internet-Order Art Supplies

Aardvark Art Supplies
P.O. Box 434
Belmont, MA 02478
(617) 489–7888
(800) 705–4303
www.aardvarkart.com

Aiko's Art Materials Import
3347 North Clark Street
Chicago, IL 60657
(773) 404–5600
Specializes in Japanese handmade paper and other Oriental art supplies.

American Frame
400 Tomahawk Drive
Maumee, OH 43537
(866) 812–3404
www.americanframe.com
Specializes in frames.

Amsterdam Art
1013 University Avenue
Berkeley, CA 94710
(510) 649–4800
AOE Art Supply
12908 North 56th Street
Tampa, FL 33617
(888) 240–6173
www.aoeartworld.com

Armstrong Products
P.O. Box 979
Guthrie, OK 73044
(405) 282–7584
(800) 278–4279
www.armstrongproducts.com
Specializes in panels used in making booths for art fairs.

Art Xpress
1224 Lincoln Street
Columbia, SC 29201
(800) 535–5908
www.artxpress.com

Art City
(866) 278–2498
www.artcity.com

Art 2 Go
30 King Street
Castle Dougle DG7 1AA
Scotland, Great Britain
(44) 15–56–50–49–36

Art Mart
2081 West Highway 89A
Sedona, AZ 86336
(877) 535–8468
Specializes in Winsor & Newton paints, brushes, and papers.

ArtQuick Corporation
P.O. Box 565
Lincoln, MA 01773

Art Supplies Direct
c/o Starpak
100 Americana Place
Sweet Grass, MT 59484
(866) 273–4278
www.artsuppliesdirect.com

Art Supply Warehouse
360 Main Avenue
Norwalk, CT 06851
(800) 995–6778
www.aswsale.com

Arthur Brown and Bros., Inc.
2 West 46th Street
New York, NY 10036
(212) 575–5555
www.artbrown.com

Artisan/Santa Fe, Inc.
717 Canyon Road
Santa Fe, NM 87501
(800) 331–6375
Dick Blick
P.O. Box 1267
Galesburg, IL 61401
(800) 447–8192 (to place an order)
(800) 933–2542
(product information)
www.dickblick.com

Cartoon Colour Company, Inc.
9024 Lindblade Street
Culver City, CA 90232
(213) 838–8467
(800) 523–3665
www.cartooncolour.com
Specializes in materials for cartoonists.

Cerulean Blue Ltd.
Box 21168
Seattle, WA 98111
(206) 323–8600
Specializes in materials for fiber artists.

Cheap Joe's Art Stuff
347 Industrial Park Drive
Boone, NC 28607
(800) 227–2788
www.cheapjoes.com

Chroma, Inc.
205 Bucky Drive
Lititz, PA 17543
(717) 626–8866
(800) 257–8278
www.chroma-inc.com
Specializes in acrylic paints.

Classic Artist Oils, 1930 Fairway Drive
San Leadro, CA 94577
(800) 872–3262
www.triangle.com

Compleat Sculptor, Inc.
90 Vandam Street
New York, NY 10013
(800) 9–SCULPT
www.sculpt.com
Specializes in sculptors' supplies.

Creatix Pure Pigments
14 Airport Park Road
East Granby, CT 06026
(800) 243–2712
Specializes in pigments, paints, glazes, and inks.

Dakota Art Pastels
P.O. Box 2258
Mount Vernon, WA 98273
(888) 345–0067
www.dakotapastels.com
Specializes in pastels.

Daler-Rowney
Two Corporate Drive
Cranbury, NJ 08512
(609) 655–5252
www.daler-rowney.com

David Davis—Classic Art Materials
D.D. Catalog Corp.
17 Bleecker Street
New York, NY 10012
(212) 260–9544
(800) 965–6554
www.daviddavisnewyorkcity.com

DaVinci Paint Co.
11 Goodyear Street
Irvine, CA 92618
(800) 553–8755
www.davincipaints.com

Designs Plus
P.O. Box 1927
Santa Rosa, CA 95402
(800) 253–7224
www.racksplus.com
Specializes in storage systems for art.

Discount Art Supplies
P.O. Box 1169
Conway, NH 03818
(800) 547–3264
www.discountart.com

Dixie Art Supplies
2612 Jefferson Highway
New Orleans, LA 70121
(800) 783–2612
www.dixieart.com

Easel Connection
P.O. Box 65
Henderson, KY 42420
(800) 916–2278
www.easelconnection.com
Specializes in easels.

Faber-Castell
c/o Arco Services
P.O. Box 813
Akron, OH 44309
www.faber-castellusa.com
Specializes in colored pencils.

Flax Artist Materials
1699 Market Street
San Francisco, CA 94103
(415) 552–2355

Forstall Art Supply
766 Harrison Avenue
New Orleans, LA 70124
(800) 272–9449
www.forstallart.com

Frames by Mail
11440 Schenk Drive
Maryland Heights, MO 63043
(800) 332–2467
www.framesbymail.com
Specializes in frames.

Frame Fit Co.
P.O. Box 12727
Philadelphia, PA 19134
(800) 523–3693
www.framefit.com
Specializes in frames.

General Pencil Co.
PO. Box 5311
Redwood City, CA 94063
(650) 369–4889
www.generalpencil.com
Specializes in drawing implements and erasers.

Genesis Artist Colors
9717 West 16th Street
Department AMAR–501
Indianapolis, IN 46222
(800) 374–1600
www.amaco.com
Specializes in paints.

Graphic Chemical & Ink Co.
728 North Yale Avenue
Box 27, Department AA
Villa Park, IL 60181
(800) 465–7382
www.graphicchemical.com
Specializes in printmaking supplies.

Graphic Media Co.
Dept. A
13916 Cordary Avenue
Hawthorne, CA 90250
Specializes in graphic art supplies.

Gwartzman's
448 Spadina Avenue
Toronto, Ontario M5T 2C8
Canada
(416) 922–5429

The Italian Art Store
Dept. AA–101
40 West Ray Burn
P.O. Box 300
Millington, NJ 07946
(800) 643–6440
www.italianartstore.com

Jerry's Artarama
P.O. Box 58638
Department AM 10
Raleigh, NC 27658
(919) 878–6782
(800) 827–8478
www.jerryssale.com

Kalish Finest Brushes
43 Parkside Drive
East Hanover, NJ 07936
(800) 322–5254
www.kalishbrushes.com
Specializes in Kolinsky and other brushes.

Leo Uhlfelder Co.
420 South Fulton Avenue
Mt. Vernon, NY 10553
Tom Lynch Watercolors, Inc.
P.O. Box 1418
Arlington, IL 60005
www.tomlynch.com
Specializes in watercolor supplies.

H.R. Meininger
499 Broadway
Denver, CO 80203
(303) 698–3838
(800) 950–2787
www.meininger.com

The Mettle Co.
P.O. Box 234
Department Y
Middlesex, NJ 08846
(800) 621–1329
www.mettleco.com
Specializes in metal frames.

MisterArt
913 Willard Street
Houston, TX 77006
(866) 672–7811
www.misterart.com

New York Central Art Supply
Dept. AA–10
62 Third Avenue
New York, NY 10003
(212) 473–7705
(800) 950–6111
www.nycentralart.com

norArt
Harstrup Associates, Inc.
51 Storer Avenue
Pelham, NY 10803
(914) 738–7168
www.mediatekk.com/web/harstrup
Specializes in artists paints.

Nova Color
5894 Blackwelder Street
Culver City, CA 90232
(310) 204–6000
www.novacolorpaint.com
Specializes in artists paints.

Oriental Art Supply
21522 Lurveyor Circle
Huntington Beach, CA 92646
(714) 969–4470
(800) 969–4471
www.ningyeh.com
Specializes in brushes.

Ott's Discount Art Supply
102 Hungate Drive
Greenville, NC 27858
(800) 356–3289
www.otts.com

Paragona Art Products
P.O. Box 3324
Santa Monica, CA 90408
(800) 991–5899

PenCo Artists Supplies Warehouse
718 Washington Avenue North
Minneapolis, MN 55401
(800) 967–7367
www.artsuppliesonline.com

Pearl Paint
308 Canal Street
New York, NY 10013
(212) 431–5420
(800) PEARL–91
(800) 221–6845, ext. 2297
www.pearlpaint.com

Perma Colors Division
226 East Tremont
Charlotte, NC 28203
(704) 333–9201
(800) 365–2656

John Pike Art Products
2926 West Main Street
Caledonia, NY 14423
(800) 882–0417
www.johnpikeartprod.com

Reliable Office Supplies
P.O. Box 1502
Ottawa, IL 61350
Minneapolis, MN 55440
(800) 328–3034
Specializes in graphic arts supplies.

Rex Art
2263 S.W. 37 Avenue
Miami, FL 33145
(305) 445–1413
(800) 739–2782
www.rexart.com

Rochester Art Supply
150 West Main Street
Rochester, NY 14614
(800) 836–8940
www.fineartstore.com

Sax Arts & Crafts
P.O. Box 51710
Department A2
New Berlin, WI 53151
(414) 784–6880
(800) 558–6696
www.artsupplies.com

Selwyn Textile Co., Inc.
134 West 29th Street
New York, NY 10001
(800) 223–3032
Specializes in linen and cotton canvases.

Sinopia
3385 22nd Street
San Francisco, CA 94110
(415) 824–3180
www.sinopia.com

Daniel Smith
4150 First Avenue South
Seattle, WA 98134
(800) 426–6740
www.danielsmith.com

Soto Fine Art
2586 Shadow Mountain Drive
San Ramon, CA 94583
(888) 315–3023
www.sotofineart.com

Stretch-Art
141 East 162 Street
Gardena, CA 90248
(800) 942–8212
www.stretchart.com
Specializes in linen and cotton canvases.

Stu-Art
2045 Grand Avenue
Baldwin, NY 11510
(516) 546–5151
(800) 645–2855
www.stu-artsupplies.com
Specializes in mats, frames, and shrink-wraps.

T-Square Art Supply, Inc.
5140 Plainfield, N.E.
Grand Rapids, MI 49525
(616) 361–0624
www.tsquareart.com

Testrite Instrument Co., Inc.
135 AA Monroe Street
Newark, NJ 07105
Specializes in easels, light boxes, exhibition lights, projectors.

Triangle Art Center
P.O. Box 8079
Princeton, NJ 08543
(609) 883–3600

Tricon Colors
16 Leliarts Lane
Elmwood, NJ 07407
(201) 794–3800

Tubes in Time
P.O. Box 369
New Oxford, PA 17350
(717) 624–8993
Specializes in cardboard mailing tubes.

United Art Education Supply
Box 9219
Ft. Wayne, IN 46899
(800) 322–3247
Specializes in fine art materials and elementary school art supplies.

Utrecht
33 35th Street
Brooklyn, NY 11232
(718) 768–2525
(800) 223–9132
www.utrechtart.com

Wholesale Art Supply Co.
(201) 798–4110
(800) 792–7847
www.wholesaleart.com

Williamsburg Art Materials
1711 Monkey Run Road
East Meredith, NY 13757
(800) 293–9399
www.williamsburgoilpaint.bizland.com
Specializes in artists paints.

Windberg Enterprises, Inc.
8601 Cross Park Drive
Suite 200
Austin, TX 78754
(800) 531–5181
Specializes in art panels.

Yuemei
E.A.C., Inc.
1033 Farmington Avenue
Farmington, CT 06032
(800) 414–9141
Specializes in Chinese papers.

Artists Who Make Supplies for Other Artists

Alchemist Paints & Varnishes
228 Elizabeth Street
New York, NY 10012
(212) 219–2394
(800) 995–5501
www.amberalchemy.com
Sells paints and varnishes made by historic methods.

Robert Doak & Associates
89 Bridge Street
Brooklyn, NY 11201
(718) 237–0146
Makes pastels, watercolor concentrates, oil paints, resins, conservation materials, linen, and cotton duck.

Gamblin Artists Colors
P.O. Box 625
Portland, OR 97207
(503) 228–9763
www.gamblincolors.com
Makes artist-grade and student-grade oil paints and etching inks.

Guerra Paints & Pigments
510 East 13th Street
New York, NY 10009
(212) 529–0628
www.guerrapaint.com
Makes pigment colors, powders and concentrates, resins, additives, thickeners, binders, and oil paints.

Kama Pigments
85 Jean Talon Ouest #4
Montreal, Quebec H2R 2W8
Canada
(514) 272–2173
www.kamapigments.com
Makes pigment colors.

Lapis Arts
1295 South Dahlia Street
Denver, CO 80222
(303) 298–7804
Makes oil paints.

Keith Lebenzon
6200 S.W. Roundhill Way
Portland, OR 97221
(503) 292–4252
Makes brushes.

Carl Plansky
315 Berry Street
Brooklyn, NY 11211
or
266 Elizabeth Street
New York, NY 10012
(212) 219–9535
Makes oil paints.

R&F Encaustics
110 Prince Street
New York, NY 10012
(914) 331–3112
(800) 206–8088
Makes encaustic paints and oil paint sticks.

Vasari Classic Artists' Oil Colors
11 Prince Street
New York, NY 10012
(212) 219–3674
(800) 932–9375
www.shopvasaricolors.com
Makes artists paints.

Watson Paper Company
1719 Fifth Street
Albuquerque, NM 87102
(505) 242–9351

William & Arthur
12–18 Commerce Street
Brooklyn, NY 11031
Makes oil paints.

CHAPTER FIVE

Safety in the Studio

No news to those involved in it, creating art is challenging, rewarding, and fun. The materials used in making art, however, can also be harmful to one's health, affecting all of the major bodily organs, if one's work habits are sloppy or if basic precautions are not taken. The concern with safe art materials dates back to 1940, when members of the Crayon, Water Color and Craft Institute engaged a toxicologist to review product formulas for harmful ingredients. By 1946, a voluntary commercial standard was developed in conjunction with the National Bureau of Standards of the U.S. Department of Commerce, concerning wax and pressed crayons as well as semi-moist and dry watercolors, liquid and powder tempera, several varieties of chalks, pastel crayons, and modeling clays.

Toxic Ingredients in Art Supplies

By 1960, finger paints were added to the list and there was a change in the standard for toxicity. The 1946 standard stated that the included products ". . . shall not contain lead, arsenic or other toxic materials in excess of 0.05 percent," but that was changed in 1960 to read ". . . are certified to contain no known toxic materials in sufficient quantities to be injurious to the human body." Not everyone was convinced by these somewhat loose (and voluntary) standards. In 1981, a study conducted by industrial hygienist Michael McCann, along with Barry A. Miller and Aaron Blair of the National Cancer Institute, found that visual artists had higher rates of bladder, brain, and kidney cancer, as well as leukemia, than the general population. That study was based on reports of the causes of death of 1,598 professional artists. Subsequent studies have only added to the general sense of concern.

Some of the most common toxic materials found in arts and crafts materials are:

Chemical	Art Material	Major Adverse Effects
Ammonia	Found in most acrylic paints	Irritates the skin, eyes and lungs
Antimony	Pigments, patinas, solders, glass, plastics	Anemia, kidney, liver and reproductive damage
Arsenic	Lead enamels and glass	Skin, kidney and nerve damage, cancer
Asbestos	Some talcs and French chalks	Lung scarring and cancer
Barium	Metals, glazes, glass, pigments	Muscle spasms, heart irregularities

Chemical	Art Material	Major Adverse Effects
Cadmium	Pigment, glass and glaze colorant, solders	Kidney, liver and reproductive damage, cancer
Chromium	Pigment, glass and glaze colorant, metals	Skin and respiratory irritation, allergies, cancer
Cobalt	Pigment, glass and glaze colorant, metals	Asthma, skin allergies, heart damage, respiration
Formaldehyde	Most acrylic paints, plywood	Irritates skin, eyes, and lungs, allergies, cancer
Hexane	Rubber cement and some spray products	Nerve damage
Lead	Art paints, enamels, glazes, solders	Nerve, kidney, reproductive damage, birth defects
Manganese	Glass and ceramic colorants, pigments, metals	Nervous system damage, reproductive effects
Mercury	Lustre glazes, pigments, photochemicals	Nervous system damage, reproductive effects
Uranium Oxide	Ceramic, glass and enamel colorant	Kidney damage, radioactive carcinogen

Fortunately, information on which potentially harmful ingredients are contained in art materials, and on how to work with them safely, is increasingly available, but one needs to know where to look. The first place is the product itself. The Labeling of Hazardous Art Materials Act, which went into effect in 1989, requires that art material ingredients that are known chronic hazards be listed on the label with appropriate hazard warnings. Artists should be aware, however, that many pigments and other art material ingredients have never been studied for chronic toxicity. These can still be labeled nontoxic, even when they are related to known toxic chemicals. Caution is still needed when one is working with art materials. This enables buyers to make safer choices and, if artists understand the hazards of particular chemicals, they can use the warning to identify the contents. For example, a yellow material labeled with warnings about cancer and kidney damage is likely to contain a cadmium pigment. A material labeled with warnings about reproductive damage, birth defects, nerve, brain, or kidney damage may contain lead. (Unlike ordinary consumer paints, artists' paints are still permitted to contain lead.)

Manufacturers of products containing toxic elements are also bound by state and federal "right to know" laws to fill out Material Safety Data Sheets, which are provided to those in employer-employee relationships. Artists may write to manufacturers for these data sheets, although in many states the manufacturers and distributors are not required to provide them to individual consumers. Most responsible manufacturers, however, will supply this information. A second source of information on what is in art materials and how they should be properly used are several private and public agencies concerned with these and other related issues, and one can receive written material and advice over the telephone. Among the agencies are:

Occupational Safety and Health
Administration
U.S. Department of Labor
200 Constitution Avenue N.W.
Room N3101
Washington, D.C. 20210
(202) 523–8151 (information)
(202) 523–0055 (publications)
www.osha.gov

Centers for Disease Control
1600 Clifton Road, N.E.
Atlanta, GA 30333
(404) 639–3311
(800) 311–3435
www.cdc.gov

Arts, Crafts and Theater Safety
181 Thompson Street, No. 23
New York, NY 10012
(212) 777–0062
www.caseweb.com/acts

Arts and Creative Materials Institute
100 Boylston Street
Boston, MA 02116
(617) 426–6400
www.creative-industries.com

In general, the largest problem for artists, both hobbyists and professionals, is that the majority of them pursue their art in their homes rather than in a studio located elsewhere. Dusts from clays and pastels, solvents in turpentine and aerosol spray paints, lead found in stained glass and ceramic glazes, and a variety of other toxic substances may become a permanent part of their home environment, affecting everyone who lives there. Airborne contaminants may enter the lungs, while other harmful elements are able to penetrate the pores of the skin or be ingested orally when on one's hands (which touch the mouth) as well as when toxic materials settle on food. In a separate studio, the health risks are confined to the individual who is involved in the art project for the few hours a day that the room is used, whereas in one's house—especially in a kitchen or living room—there may be people around all the time.

The danger is greatest for young children, as they have a higher metabolic rate than adults and will absorb toxic substances more quickly into their bodies. In addition, since children's lungs and body defenses have not yet completely formed, they are more susceptible to disease that may damage them permanently. Often, when a child is born, the room previously designated as the studio will be converted to a nursery, and the parents begin working on their arts-and-crafts projects in more heavily trafficked rooms, such as the kitchen or living room. There is then a greater probability of contamination through the air or skin, as well as the chance for a serious accident, such as a child drinking from a former milk container that the parent is now using to store turpentine, pottery glaze, or other hazardous substance. The potential risks are great.

Safety Tips for Paints and Pigments

Some art materials are inherently more dangerous than others to artists and their families, such as those that leave a dust that may be inhaled (the largest problem), absorbed through the skin (a rarer occurrence), or cause a skin irritation. Artists may breathe in raw, powdered pigments, as well as the dust from chalks, pastels, paint that is sanded; in addition, the preservatives regularly used in paints—including bleach, formaldehyde, fungicides, and pesticides—may evaporate into the air and be inhaled. Unfortunately, paint manufacturers rarely identify the additives used in their products.

How dangerous common paints are depends on a number of factors, including the individual artist's predisposed sensitivity to certain chemicals, the amount of exposure, how the art materials are used, and the degree to which basic precautions are taken in advance to neutralize the potential toxicity. There are, according to Monona Rossol, a number of methods to limit the harmful effects of art supplies. (For in-depth information about all of these supplies and how to work with them safely, see Ms. Rossol's book *The Artist's Complete Health and Safety Guide*, Allworth Press, 2001.)

- As dry pastels and powdered pigments are the most likely to be inhaled, artists should stick with premixed paints and oil pastels.
- Whenever possible, water-based products are preferable to those containing solvents (acetates, acetone, methyl alcohol, mineral spirits, paint thinner, petroleum distillates, toluene, turpentine, among others), since these have the potential of damaging the eyes, skin, nervous system, and certain internal organs.
- Regular brushwork of wet paint on a substrate is preferable to spray painting, which makes potentially toxic particles airborne. Similarly, the sanding of dried paint or sprinkling of dry pigments on wet paint increases the potential for contaminants to be inhaled.
- Have all containers of art materials closed while not in use. To further protect themselves, artists should wear gloves and full-length smocks and otherwise attempt to avoid skin contact with paints and pigments. Studio apparel should remain in the studio and not be brought into the rest of the house, because that would spread contaminants more widely. Clothing worn in the studio also should be laundered separately from other articles.
- Unless one is using products that pose no health risks, such as pencils and watercolors, the home studio should be isolated from the rest of the house, sealed off by tightly fitting doors. Parents are generally advised to segregate their art activities in rooms that have a special outside entrance and that are locked to prevent small children from entering, such as a garage or outbuilding. The studio needs ventilation, such as one or more windows, or some exhaust system if particularly hazardous materials will be used. The surfaces in the studio, such as floors, shelves, and tables, must be cleanable (floors, for instance, should be sealed), and they should regularly be cleaned.
- Make sure that the air inside the studio is fit to breathe. A simple ventilation system for many individual studios requires windows at opposite ends of the room. The window at one end is filled with an exhaust fan, and at the other, it is opened to provide air to replace that which is exhausted by the fan. This system should not be used in studios where dusts are created, although it is acceptable for painting and other arts activities that produce small amounts of solvent vapors.

Printmaking Hazards

All of the same potential hazards in painting (pigments, preservatives, and solvents for clean-up) exist in printmaking; however, depending upon the type of print process (engraving or etching, lithography, screenprint, woodcuts, or linoleum cuts), other toxic materials may be used, such as carbolic, citric, hydrochloric, and nitric acids. These acids irritate the eyes and skin; they may damage the respiratory system and, if they come into contact with certain solvents or other materials, acids have the potential to ignite. Among the recommended precautions for using printmaking supplies are:

- Keep acids stored separately from other products and, possibly, from each other in specially designed acid storage cabinets.
- Using water-based inks will lessen the need for strong solvents. Similarly, disposable screens are preferable to screens that must be cleaned with solvents.
- When designing a printmaking studio, a safety consultant should be brought in. They can be found through the American Industrial Hygiene Association (*www.iaha.org*), which will provide a list of its members, or at a local university where there are departments of health and safety. Industrial hygienists "may not know much about art, but they will know something about the chemicals you are using," Rossol said. "They have to put all sorts of protections in the science rooms." At a minimum, ventilation systems should be installed, such as exhaust fans and fume hoods, where solvents and acid baths are in use. Respirators, gloves, and goggles also need to be worn.
- As with painting studios, a printmaking studio should be isolated from the rest of the house. Food should not be prepared or eaten there; protective clothing should be worn, and all apparel used in the studio should stay in the studio. Also, all surfaces should be cleanable and cleaned regularly with wet mops and sponges rather than brooms, which often make dust airborne. Similarly, ordinary household and shop vacuums ought not to be used, since their filters will pass the small toxic dust particles back into the air.
- Install a sink and, perhaps, a shower to wash off acids, inks, and solvents with which one's eyes and skin may come into contact. First-aid supplies should also be on hand for chemical burns.
- The safety consultant should explain how all inks, solvents, and other chemicals are to be disposed of, in accordance with environmental protection statutes. In addition, one may learn about the requirements for toxic waste disposal by calling the local sanitation, environmental protection, or public works department. Laws vary widely, depending on the type of waste treatment in one's community. Pouring solvents down the drain is against environmental laws everywhere, as well as a danger to the artist and his or her family. Solvents in drains and sewers tend to evaporate, producing flammable vapors that may cause explosions. Many communities have a toxic chemical disposal service that will accept waste solvents and other toxic waste created by households and hobbyists. Professional artists may be required to hire hazardous waste disposal companies to pick up their toxic refuse. Usually, ordinary waste from consumer art paints and materials can be double-bagged and placed in the regular trash.

Lead metal scraps, on the other hand, can be recycled. Again, one should call local authorities for advice on disposal of art materials, as the fines for violating the laws can be quite high.

Health Tips for Sculptors

Sculpture is, in general terms, the process of building up (with clays, waxes, papier-mache, pastel, or metals) or carving down (stone or wood), and both techniques create significant amounts of dust, especially when electric tools are in use, and flying chips that may damage the eyes. Additionally, heavy lifting may be involved, causing muscle strains and other injuries, and power tools often create significant amounts of noise (damaging one's hearing) or slip from one's hands. Stone dust varies with the type used, and some are more hazardous than others: Limestone, for example, may contain silica, which is associated with lung disease and impairment, while dust from alabaster is only a minor irritant to the unprotected eyes and lungs. Many of the products used in cleaning metal, such as ammonia, cyanide, hydrochloric acid, nitric acid, sulphuric acid, as well as a variety of solvents and other materials used to color or patinize sculpture, contain chemicals that can be quite toxic. In addition to the other recommended studio practices, there are the following:

- Obtain a chemical or mineral analysis of the stones that may be used, and look for stones with the lowest levels of toxicity.
- Wear safety or impact-resistant goggles (rather than ordinary spectacles without side shields) to protect against dust and flying chips; there are also industrial-type welding goggles (preferably with plastic or mesh face shields) and helmets for those involved in heavy grinding and welding. Additionally, artists should wear steel-tipped shoes, in order to protect their feet, and some type of hearing protection (fire-resistant ear plugs or muffs, for instance). Hair, of course, should be tied back.
- The ventilation should be tailored to fit the type of work done in the studio. For example, all kilns need to be vented, and there are several commercial systems that can be purchased for them. More complex equipment may require an engineer to design a proper system.
- Along with a ventilation system, there might be dust masks or respirators. Some respirators supply air, although few artists are likely to face a lack of oxygen. More practical are respirators that purify existing air through filters—the filters also should be matched to the type of dust that will be created.
- Follow directions for the safe use of machinery and products. For those with limited experience in welding, two organizations—American Welding Society, 550 N.W. LeJeune Road, Miami, FL 33126, (800) 443–9353, and the Hobart Institute, 400 Trade Square East, Troy, OH 45373, (800) 332–9448—regularly offer courses in proper technique throughout the United States and Canada.
- When heavy machinery and materials are to be used, make sure that the floor can support the weight. Those artists planning to weld or forge metal may also want to install fireproof materials in the floors and walls.

- Good housekeeping—cleaning up and putting items away properly—is always recommended. However, the accidents resulting from tripping over something in a room with large, heavy materials and operating machinery are likely to be more severe than in a painter's studio. Items should not be left around the floor casually.
- For sculptors working in wood, lumber that has been treated with chemical preservatives, such as arsenic or creosote should be avoided. The studio should also be equipped with a sprinkler system or fire extinguishers, and smoking should never be permitted.

Darkroom Precautions

Darkrooms often have a certain smell emitted by the photochemical baths, a reason that they need to be amply ventilated. It is often the case that artists create their darkrooms in converted bathrooms, kitchens, and basements, where light may be minimized, without ventilating these facilities. Prolonged exposure to darkroom chemicals—such as acetic acid, formaldehyde, hydrogen sulfide, sulfur dioxide, and various solvents—has been associated with respiratory disease (asthma, bronchitis, pneumonia) and other ailments. Among the recommended studio precautions are:

- Kodak suggests that proper ventilation include at least ten air exchanges per hour; obviously, an adequate supply for replacement air should be available. There also should be localized exhaust systems for toners and solvents.
- Acid and other baths should be covered when not in use, in order to keep gases and fumes from spreading.
- Check with water treatment facility officials to find out which (if any) chemicals may be put down the drain; arrange for a commercial toxic waste disposal service to regularly remove those chemicals that cannot be put in the drain.
- Chemical absorbents should be used for breakage and spills, and barriers for chemical containment should be built into the darkroom floor.
- If chemicals splash onto clothing or skin, wash immediately with an ample supply of water. Wearing gloves, goggles, and an acid-proof apron will also help.

Additional, general advice for artists includes obtaining and reading the Material Safety Data Sheets from the manufacturers for all products in order to identify the toxic, active ingredients, as well as keeping children out of the studio when hazardous chemicals are being used.

The concern over potentially hazardous ingredients found in many art supplies has led to new laws (as noted above), as well as to efforts by manufacturers to reformulate their products in order to exclude the most toxic elements. There are also a growing number of alternatives and substitutes for the more dangerous materials, such as talc-free, premixed clay (in place of clay in dry form), water-based inks and paints (instead of solvent-based inks and aerosol sprays), vegetable dyes (rather than fiber-reactive or commercial dyes) and wax crayons or oil pastels (in place of dusty pastels and chalks). Artists, especially those with children, should contact the various private and public agencies about safe materials to use. Few artists have any desire to work with gloves, goggles, and respirators unless absolutely necessary, and they will have less need to do so if they use safer materials.

Studio Insurance

A lot of things may happen to artists in a lifetime—big-time commissions, rave reviews, a museum retrospective. They may also become incapacitated, see their work damaged or lost through fire and theft, or get sued for millions of dollars by someone who tripped over the scaffolding in their studio. One cannot ensure great success in a career, but artists—from the least well-known to the most established—may insure against some of the worst hazards.

Various insurance companies have what they call "studio insurance" or "artist floaters" that offer levels of protection of the physical premises of the studio as well as the tools, materials, furniture, and artwork (commissioned or not, completed or unfinished) therein. In addition, artists may purchase transit insurance (when objects are being shipped to a gallery or art fair, for example), general liability coverage (for someone hurt moving the artwork, for instance, or a visitor injured in the studio), workmen's compensation (for the artist's employees), and disability insurance (if the artist becomes unable to work).

Not every artist requires every type of insurance coverage. Conceptual artist Sol Lewitt, whose works have an international market, spends "tens of thousands of dollars a year" on various types of insurance, according to his business manager, Susanna Singer. Sculptor Glenna Goodacre pays $8,000 in yearly insurance premiums, which doesn't include workmen's compensation. However, policies exist for those in need, regardless of their stature in the art world, and at far more affordable prices.

"All artists have something to lose if there is a fire in their studio, even if they've hardly ever sold any works," said Tony Newman, vice president of American Phoenix Corporation, which provides studio and other related types of insurance policies for members of the Chicago Artists' Coalition, American Crafts Council, and several other crafts organizations, with annual premiums starting at $250.

Regular homeowner policies would likely cover damage to a studio in one's house if the artist is a hobbyist (although the existence of a studio and its contents should be noted on the policy), but artists who are able to earn any money from selling their work might want to consider special studio insurance. "As soon as you've sold a work, you have a market," Robert Salmon, vice president of Allen Insurance Associates, stated, and that market gives value to unsold pieces sitting in a studio. Artists who have reason to view themselves as more than hobbyists (whose artwork is solely intended for personal enjoyment) will find that homeowner policies regularly exclude commercial activity, such as an art studio, from their coverage.

There is no rule of thumb for determining how much in premiums buys how much insurance protection. Different carriers require certain minimum premiums

(Flather & Perkins's is $250, Huntington Block's is $500, Chubb's is $1,000, Allen Insurance Associates' is $2,500), and costs are determined based on where one lives, the amount of the coverage and of the deductible (usually between $500 and $5,000), the existence of a twenty-four-hour central-station alarm system, location of the studio (in the artist's house, in the woods, near a fire hydrant, in the downtown section of a city) and its construction (wood, metal, brick), fragility of the art (glass and ceramics are high-risk items, bronze sculpture far less so), and what kinds of insurance protection are required. Except with studio insurance offered to groups, coverage is usually tailored to the circumstances of the individual artist.

It is not uncommon for artists to buy a certain maximum amount of insurance coverage, which is less than the full value of their art and studio, as a way to keep the premium lower, with the hope that no fire, for instance, would result in a total loss. Bill Christenberry, a Washington, D.C., painter, photographer, and sculptor, has a $75,000 policy for his studio and the artwork in it, even though there is several hundred thousand dollars worth of art there and the studio itself would cost $100,000 or so to replace. He pays $1,200 in premiums for this coverage from the Fireman's Fund "because that's all we can afford," his wife, Sandra, said. "We have three children, and two of them are of college age. We just have to hope that no damage or theft occurs that's more than $75,000 worth." Other artists, such as Corpus Christi, Texas, sculptor Kent Ullberg and Northampton, Massachusetts, painter Scott Pryor, have coverage for their studios but not for the work in them because "it's rare that I have more than one work in the studio at any one time. When a work is finished, I frame it up and send it out to one of my galleries," Pryor stated.

The studios of both Bill Christenberry and Kent Ullberg have been burglarized, which included the theft of artwork. At the time, Christenberry had no studio insurance at all, suffering a total loss. Ullberg later installed a central-station alarm system for his studio, which resulted in a small savings on the overall insurance premium. However, damage, especially for works in transit, is a far greater problem than theft. Because of the higher probability of loss, a policy solely for transit insurance is often the most difficult to obtain unless coverage for the artwork itself already exists.

Some insurance carriers require central-station alarm systems, while others may lower the premium up to 15 percent for artists who install them. These alarm systems, however, may cost as much as $1,500 to put in and another $30 or $40 per month to monitor. Some artists choose to forego the alarm system, as the expense may outweigh the discounted premium.

At times, artists may be required to purchase insurance—for example, by a contract that a corporation or public art sponsor may use when making a sculpture commission, and this coverage usually is for general liability. Such coverage would include, for instance, a workman hurt moving or installing the piece as well as someone injured because of faulty construction or a material weakness. Most other types of insurance are optional. One kind of general liability protection that is available for commissioned work covers disputes between artist and buyer over what the piece should be or look like.

Insurance carriers are most willing to provide studio coverage for commissioned works, because the stated price of the work in the contract alleviates the need to hire appraisers and determine market values. These companies will also frequently accept claims for commissioned works that were not completed, paying the percentage of the insured value proportionate to the degree that the work was finished. Valuations and completed and unfinished artworks that have not been commissioned can become an area of contention between artists and the insurance companies. "We're very reluctant to underwrite studio policies for artists because of the difficulty of valuing the things," said Dr. Dietrich Von Frank, senior vice president of Nordstern Insurance Company, which insures art dealers, museums, and "one or two artists only. . . . The artists have to prove that their work has value and, if it hasn't sold or they haven't sold all that many works in their careers, that may be difficult."

The burden of proving that something of value was lost, and how much that loss is, falls on the artist. Insurance companies may write a policy for an artist for a certain level of coverage, take a premium based on what the artist says his or her art is worth, but not pay what the artist claims he or she has lost. Artists can help themselves in proving the value of their work by keeping good records of what they have sold, to whom, and for how much, as well as a list of all the pieces they have in their home or studio and the individual values they place on them. These records and lists, of course, should be placed somewhere else or in a fireproof safe.

If determining the value of completed works is complicated, unfinished pieces are more trouble still. "We don't do incomplete works," Robert Salmon said. "Was the work half-done, two-thirds? Is it all in your head but just not down on paper? What are we dealing with? With completed works, you insure more cleanly." Still, some of the larger insurers of artwork, such as Chubb and Huntington Block, will underwrite policies for unfinished works, determining the stage of completion through discussion between the agent and the artist and valuing the artwork on a pro-rated share. The Washington, D.C.–based National Artists Equity Association's fine arts insurance program with Northbrook Property and Casualty values "works in progress" at "cost of materials and labor but not to exceed $5,000 for any one work."

The valuations made by insurance carriers are usually "net values," that is, the market price of the work less the standard commission that the artist's dealer would have charged. Insurers will agree to pay the entire market value to those artists who commonly sell out of their studios without middlemen. There is a range of coverage areas for artists, but insurance carriers also include in their contracts a number of exclusions, some of which may be modified by purchasing additional coverage. Standard among these exclusions are inherent vices, dishonesty by the artist or his or her employees, wear and tear, gradual deterioration, rust, corrosion, dampness of atmosphere, wet or dry rot, mold, change in temperature, freezing, insects or vermin, water that backs up through a sewer or drain, loss of market (the artist's work becoming less sought-after), damage due to restoration by the artist, mysterious disappearances or inventory shortage, theft from unattended vehicles, earth movements (earthquakes, volcanic eruptions, landslides), floods, war, and nuclear disaster. Insurers may also set limits to the amount of liability they will accept for works damaged in transit or for any one item.

PART THREE

Exhibiting and Selling Artwork

CHAPTER SIX

Exhibiting One's Work

Making art offers a variety of personal rewards for the artist, from solving technical and formal problems in the work to discovering areas of thought and wonder in oneself and expressing them in a coherent manner. However, art is a form of communication with the outside world, not simply an internal monologue, and this communication best takes place when the work is exhibited publicly. Eventually, all artists want to show their artwork for reaction and comment.

Where to Exhibit

Artists show their work because they want to share their vision and point of view and receive feedback. Of course, most artists hope that the public exposure of their work will lead to its sale. Selling artwork is one of the most difficult acts for artists, many of whom dream of collectors who will "discover" them or dealers who will take over the responsibility of marketing their work. At least in the beginning, however, artists cannot escape the responsibility of creating their own markets.

The first step in the process is showing one's artwork to the public. Fortunately, there is a wide variety of sites suitable for an exhibition in almost every town, of which a commercial art gallery is but one possibility. Banks, restaurants and cafés, churches, art supply shops, libraries, town halls, community centers, schools (secondary schools and colleges), and office buildings are often hosts of art displays as the art does not cost them anything and may bring more people in. For the artist, especially one who has not had much experience in exhibiting artwork in the past, this kind of show creates the opportunity for comments, praise, suggestions, meeting other artists, and perhaps even a sale.

Exhibition is about exposure. Certainly, some sites are more favorable to a serious appreciation of one's artwork than others. For instance, while a great many people visit a café or restaurant, sitting perhaps within inches of an artist's painting, the non-art setting of this exhibit may lower its esteem as art. People may run their fingers over the surface of the work; coffee may be splashed on the painting; if smoking is permitted, the canvas itself may pick up the smell of tobacco; the bulb in the lamp on the table may burn an area on the canvas. I was once in a restaurant where the walls all held large abstract paintings by a particular artist. At one point, I went to the washroom, where another large abstract painting was hung over the toilet—this work was a composition largely of yellows and browns: How the artist benefitted from this display is a mystery.

As much as many artists over the past century have claimed to want to break down the barriers between art and daily life, a certain formality needs to be maintained in the presentation of art in order that it be taken seriously. One of the reasons for mats and frames around artworks is to physically separate artwork from everything around it, to make art an object of contemplation rather than part of the scenery. Equally, every type but public art needs a setting that removes the distractions and encourages thoughtfulness.

Nonprofit or alternative art spaces are also venues for lesser-known artists (or those whose art is outside of the mainstream) to display their work. A growing number of fine art museums have created exhibition series that spotlight the work of younger and regional artists. Charity auctions offer yet another way to put one's work before the public, this time in a setting that affords the artist a pat on the back. Artists attending a class or school are usually permitted to enter work for student shows, and those who are members of societies or clubs exhibit with these groups at their annual shows (see chapter 12).

Juried competitions and sidewalk shows (some juried, some not) are yet other possibilities for exhibiting one's work. There are reportedly 10,000–15,000 arts and crafts shows held somewhere around the United States each year, usually during the summer months in the North and during the winter in the Southern states. Many of the larger shows are listed in publications for artists.

A Short Course in Marketing Artwork

Before trying to sell anything, one needs to find the appropriate audience. This is the central concept of marketing, and it is as true for artwork as it is for toothpaste and automobiles. Not everyone is going to want to buy a work of art, and not everyone who collects art is likely to purchase a particular artist's work. Finding the right niche—the specific galleries or juried art shows featuring a certain type of artwork, for example—is the most important first step to developing sales.

There is often a lot of trial and error in marketing, as artists winnow down the potential avenues for sales to those that show the best results. "I used the spaghetti method of marketing," said James Wall, a painter in Charlottesville, Virginia. "You throw spaghetti at the wall and what sticks you stay with." He tried sending out brochures of his work to art consultants ("haven't done a great deal for me"), art dealers ("not a lot of interest"), licensing agents ("nothing has happened"), and print publishers ("nothing"). He offered to paint a mural on the wall of a restaurant for the modest price of $2,000, believing that "a lot of people will see my work that way," and that has resulted in some sales to diners.

Most successful for him has been entering local art exhibitions, where giclée reproductions of his botanical-motif paintings have sold to both Charlottesville natives and tourists, usually while he is present. For all the effort Wall has put into his paintings and brochures, it is his personality that assures potential buyers that his artwork is the product of someone in whom they can feel confidence. "I used to worry about what to say to people when they looked at my work," he said. "Often, I didn't say anything, or not much. Then, I relaxed about the whole thing and just started talking naturally to people, about their children, about the weather, about anything. If they asked me questions about my work or my technique, I would answer them, but I never put pressure on anyone to buy something." Based on his experience, Wall now makes a point of being at shows of his work as often as possible, "because my presence really has an effect."

New York City abstract expressionist painter and printmaker Mike Filan also struck out in a variety of directions when he first began to seek his market, investing $8,000 one year for a booth at the annual Art Expo in Manhattan ("I sat there for a week, and people just walked by") and $300 for a booth at the annual conference of the American Society of Interior Designers ("it didn't pan out for me"). Yet another $300 was spent on bottles of wine ("good wine seemed like the capper") for a three-day, open-studio sales event that a friend who was looking to become a corporate art consultant organized on his behalf, but that also didn't result in any sales. In contrast to James Wall, the benefit of his presence and personality did not create any converts; however, Filan did have more luck than Wall with brochures.

He spent $2,000 to print four thousand foldout brochures that featured a number of color images of his work with a small bio on the back, and another $2,000 for mailing, but Filan was fortunate that the design of the brochure by another friend only cost him one of his prints in barter. Several hundred dollars were also spent on purchasing mailing lists of art dealers and consultants. Between 5 and 7 percent of those people to whom he sent a brochure responded to his mailer and, "out of that, 3 percent have actually sold work," he said. "All you need is one, two, or three corporate consultants, to sell your work regularly." Most of the sales have been prints—a dealer in Florida sold five, while a dealer in Texas sold ten, and there were sales of five others to Colgate-Palmolive, ten to Pfizer, and twenty to a group of teachers. All in all, Filan has earned $30,000 from that one mailer.

Joan Gold, a painter in Eureka, California, has also had success marketing artwork to consultants who, in turn, act as agents for her work to private—usually corporate—clients, taking a percentage of the sales price (from 30 to 50 percent) as a commission. "Eureka is at the end of the world," she said. "There aren't many galleries close by." She added that her few experiences going from one gallery to the next were "just plain bad."

Gold purchased her list of consultants from artists' career advisor Caroll Michels and sent each person on the list a brochure of her work. The result was responses from dozens of consultants to whom she began sending out her original paintings, rolling her canvases and placing them into hard cardboard tubes that are sent through Federal Express. "The benefits of consigning work to consultants is that you get a commission without additional expenses," she said. "The consultant pays for framing." Gold works with thirty consultants, of which twenty are actively promoting her paintings at any given time, and "I keep in touch with all of them by cards, mailers, phone calls—they need to be reminded of who you are and what you do." One or two paintings (with an average price of $3,000–$6,000 before commission) sell somewhere each month, although Boston Corporate Art in Massachusetts has been the most active in selling her work and has sold between thirty and forty paintings over the years.

There are probably as many successful approaches to marketing art as there artists who have sold their work; some artists have sold work through a Web site, while others earn a following at selected juried art competitions. Yet other artists maneuver to know the right people. However, every success has involved finding the proper audience. Exhibitions are often valuable in determining who a particular artist's audience might be. Shows, which tend to be short-lived and quickly disappear from public memory, need to be thought of primarily as marketing tools rather than the end product of marketing. It is wise for artists, and perhaps an observant friend, relative, or spouse, to be in attendance at shows in order to see who responds positively to their work—men, women, homeowners, renters, under forty, over forty, politically conservative or liberal, Caucasian, people of color—since this will help narrow the search for the most likely audience. Ultimately, artists want to show where their most likely buyers are going.

It was more than serendipity that enabled Denise Shaw, a yoga instructor and painter of abstract imagery on Japanese rice paper using oriental brush techniques, to sell all of the works from a show hung at the Yoga Connection in downtown Manhattan. A suitable mix of Eastern-oriented art and an audience of people involved in an Eastern exercise and meditation was the key. The Yoga Connection did not have a gallery space, but Shaw identified an opportunity and seized it. She also received several commissions for new work from people who practice yoga there and saw her art. "My work appeals to a certain kind of person who practices yoga who is into my use of psychological concepts and poetry," Shaw said. Noting that her work is regularly displayed at the Yoga Connection, she called the studio "a pretty good venue for me," far superior to the commercial, nonprofit, and co-op galleries where her work has been exhibited in the past without resulting in sales.

While some marketing efforts are hit-or-miss, others are the result of painstaking planning and research. Long Island, New York–based painter and printmaker Anne Raymond scours art and general interest magazines (*Art in America, ARTnews, The New Republic,* among others) for the type of artwork that is appreciated and bought in certain cities around the United States ("the prices for my paintings are just too low for New York City, under $10,000"). She hones in on the galleries that feature realist painting in these cities, looking for the type of artists represented there and the price range, as well as noting how long they have been in business, and their location. Many galleries also have their own Web sites, from which other or corroborating information may be obtained. Finally, Raymond travels to the city—she averages two of these business trips per year (to Santa Fe, Scottsdale, Boston, Philadelphia, Chicago)—to look at the galleries in person and show her work.

The level of courtesy that she finds at the gallery is very important to her—"if anyone is snobby or rude to me, that's a turn-off right away from an artist's point of view or a customer's"—and Raymond also checks that the information she read or heard about a gallery is borne out.

"I go into a gallery and tell them, 'I'm Anne Raymond. I live in New York, and I'm going to be in town only two days. I'd really like you to look at my work.' It's important that I mention only being in town for two days, otherwise they might never get back to you." When she visited the Peter Bartlow Gallery in Chicago, she brought a sheet of slides, and the gallery director asked to see originals, of which there were some in her hotel room. "Since I was only going to be there for two days, the director agreed to see my work that afternoon." At first, the Bartlow gallery took on her monotypes, but later began handling her paintings and has since sold a number of both. There are now three other galleries around the United States that also show and sell her art.

Open-Studio Events

"There are a lot of open-studio events in the spring and fall around here," said Nancy Fulton, a painter and organizer of Somerville Open Studios in the city of Somerville, on the outskirts of Boston. Somerville's May event takes place the same weekend as that of neighboring Brookline, and, even if the date were changed, conflicts would undoubtedly occur with open-studio days in Boston and other cities around Boston. There lies the success and the challenge of open studios as a means of providing exposure and generating sales for artists and their work.

Artists know about open-studio events, seeing them as an opportunity, and the public enjoys the opportunity to tour spaces to which they otherwise might have no access, possibly picking up a piece of art at a very discounted price in the process. For artists, the goal must be to insure that the experience has positive, tangible results: Everyone seems to be doing it, but is anyone doing it right?

The term "open studios" has itself become all-purpose, referring to a variety of activities. Artists' Web sites now frequently go by that term, and the Benton Foundation in Washington, D.C., has established a program called "Open Studio: The Arts Online," which provides financial support for artists and arts organizations to use the Internet. Two municipally owned artist studio space facilities in Virginia, the Torpedo Factory in Alexandria and Columbia Pike Artist Studios in Arlington, both have "open studios," but these are open to visitors year round. In essence, they are tourist attractions where artists may also work.

For most artists, open studios are a once- or twice-a-year event, in which the public is invited into the creative workplace to meet the artist, look at artwork that is completed or in progress, and perhaps buy something. Many artists simply pick a day to allow visitors into their studios. In a growing number of instances, groups of artists band together to open their studios on the same day during the same hours, encouraging the public to visit some or all of the others.

"For a lot of the artists, the only place that people can see their work is at the Crawl," said Craig Thiesen, coordinator of and participant in the St. Paul Art Crawl, which has taken place over two days (Friday evening, 6:00–10:00 P.M., and Saturday afternoon, 1:00–6:00 P.M.) in the spring and fall since 1991. The Crawl encompasses over 180 artists in thirteen downtown buildings, and the 7,000 estimated visitors may get to one-third or less of the studios. There is no jurying of artists who wish to participate, and their principal obligation to the event is the payment of a $20 fee. Few of the artists earn a living solely from their artwork; Thiesen, himself a Web designer who also paints landscapes, said that "I generally don't sell anything at the Crawl. I do make some good contacts, and occasionally that results in a sale sometime later."

Nancy Fulton's own experience in Somerville has been similar. She is an architectural consultant who also paints and does not pursue the marketing of her work much beyond the open-studio event. "I've sold a few small pieces," she said. "Nothing much. However, someone bought my work in the fall who had first seen it at the open studio in the spring."

Tallying up how many sales artists chalked up, and how much money they earned, during these open-studio events is never easy. Thiesen noted he sent out a questionnaire one year and only a handful of artists sent them back. Both the St. Paul Art Crawl and the Somerville Open Studios receive grants from the state arts agencies and their city governments to pay for advertisements, maps, brochures, and other promotional materials, because these events are seen principally as increasing tourism—shopping and eating in restaurants—in less utilized areas of town. The Art Crawl takes place in the Lower Town section of St. Paul, an abandoned railroad district that artists began to use as loft space for studios and living quarters beginning in the 1970s. However, it still is "a pretty sleepy area that twice a year is transformed when thousands of people come for the Art Crawl," said Jeff Nelson, director for cultural development for the City of St. Paul. "That's very good for shops and restaurants in the area."

The City of Decorah, Iowa, also has its eye on the tourist dollar, scheduling the Northeast Iowa Artists' Open Studios to "double up with the annual foliage tours" of the area in October, according to Margaret Davis, business manager for the Decorah Regional Arts Council. Grants from local agencies, as well as from the Iowa State Department of Cultural Affairs, enable the Decorah Regional Arts Council to place advertisements in newspapers in Minneapolis–St. Paul; Madison, Wisconsin ("we try not to conflict with the Wisconsin studio tour," Davis said); throughout Iowa and into Illinois. Entertainment—musical events, mostly, but occasionally theater and even stand-up comedy—is coordinated to coincide with the three-day open studio weekend, and even the local churches get involved by preparing and selling soups and sandwiches.

Unlike the open-studio tours in St. Paul and Somerville, there are fewer participating artists in Decorah (thirty or so), and they don't all work within walking distance of each other. Visitors will have to drive, in some cases, as much as five or ten miles from one artist to the next (the entire span of this showing is forty-five miles). To encourage visitors to travel these distances, those who go to eight different studios are eligible for a contest in which three winners will receive donated artwork by a few of the participating artists.

With such a heterogeneous group of people visiting open studios around the country, actual sales may or may not take place but they cannot be predicted. Some people just want to poke their heads in a studio to see what's happening. "Friday is the social night of the Art Crawl, and a lot of people are here on a date," Thiesen said. Jeff Nelson noted that many visitors came to Lower Town "to see the really cool loft spaces and maybe get a sense of a different lifestyle." That kind of voyeurism may vex some artists, who are primarily looking for serious collectors and sales, Thiesen said: "A lot of people just want to see what your place looks like. You can blockade the bedroom, and still you see people trying to get around the barricades. I personally don't put out any chairs or food or drink—I don't want people to settle in and take things. It's not a wine crawl." The Somerville Open Studios committee attempted to solve this problem by allowing artists who live in residential studio spaces to display their work in community spaces in public buildings, although this seems to contradict the concept of the open studio.

The ability of artists in group-open-studio events to generate sales and potential buyers depends on a number of factors:

- Artists should notify their friends, family members, collectors, and acquaintances about the open studio, rather than relying on an organization to spread the word effectively. As noted above, municipalities and many open-studio organizers view these events as generating tourist dollars, not art dollars. Margaret Davis noted that a number of the participating artists take brochures about the open-studio weekend to the art shows and fairs they attend in the Midwest. She also encourages these artists to link their Web pages to the Decorah Regional Arts Council's Web site in order to allow visitors "to preview the artist's work. I know of at least one visitor who bought a $500 work after previewing it on the Web."
- Talk about the artwork. There may be throngs of people in the studio at any one time, and many have little or no experience talking about art. "I tell people to ask me questions," said C. J. Lori, a painter and one of the organizers of the Brookline Artists' Open Studios in Brookline, Massachusetts. "There are no such things as stupid questions. I don't want people to go away with questions." She added that artists should not take offense at non-art comments ("Why did you make that so big?") but help visitors find a way to discuss the work—that's the artist's part of this public-service event. Artists should also try to discern members of the crowds who seem most serious. Visitors who spend longer looking at works might be approached with general comments about how the pieces were made, about sources of inspiration, or about influence or the subject of them. Conversations that ensue may be followed by giving the visitors a brochure, postcard, business card, or other information about the artist, and the artist should also take down the visitors' names, addresses, and telephone numbers.
- The studio should be visitor-friendly. An artist needs reasonably good interpersonal skills to make a go of an open studio, and biographical material about the artist, perhaps a portfolio, statement, and price list, should be easily accessible. "I've been to open studios, where I don't know the artist—there's no name on the wall or any information about the artist when you walk in," Lori said. "You might see a bowl of cheese doodles out. The artist is sitting with his friends, with his back to you. Unless I absolutely love the art, I'm just going to walk away."
- The event should have a range of media and styles. A gallery generally has a certain unity, in terms of style, medium, and pricing, but visitors expect to be surprised when they move from one studio to the next. Since there rarely is jurying in open studios, it is difficult to control who will take part, but the organizers should be sensitive to the need of keeping the offerings diverse.
- If a group open-studio is not primarily about sales, what can be gained from it? Sales can and do take place, but they generally occur in the souvenir price

category of $25–$50. Artists whose work sells for considerably more than that might frequently offer sketches, studies, and prints at bargain prices as a means of starting a relationship with a collector. That may not work for everyone. C. J. Lori noted that "I have few things under several hundred dollars. I could make some reproductions of the paintings and paint a less expensive work, but that would take a lot of time and I'm not sure they would sell anyway." (In fact, Nancy Fulton made some prints especially for the open-studio event, and they did not sell.) However, open studios are more about meeting new people, some of whom may eventually become buyers, helping the uninitiated learn to appreciate art, and absorbing the comments of visitors. "Sure, I have to filter the feedback," said Matt Carrano, a painter and participant in Somerville Open Studios. "You can't take everything people say to heart, but art is about communication. Artists have something they want to say, and they want other people to understand them. I want to know what's working with the stuff people respond to, and I want to know what's not working with the stuff people don't respond to."

Art Career Help

No one is born with the knowledge of how to market and sell artwork, and information is frequently difficult to come by. A book such as this is clearly intended to provide basic information, ideas, and resources for artists looking to put their work out into the world (the bibliography also lists other books that similarly offer assistance to artists at various phases of their development). Still, some artists may have very specific questions or require one-on-one counseling, which is available. Certainly, artists should learn about career development workshops offered at professional art schools where such topics as how to approach galleries and art and the law are discussed—the costs of these events are often quite reasonable or even free. There are also artists' advisors, who work with both professional artists and serious amateurs to help them create and publicize exhibitions, as well as to sell works. These advisors charge either (or both) by the hour or by the project for a range of services.

Artists' advisors is a relatively new profession; they can be distinguished from artists' representatives (whose aim is to sell work) and public relations firms (whose aim is to publicize) by the fact that they look to set their clients on the right road that makes selling and publicizing artwork possible. Most, although not all, of their clients are in the "emerging" category, with either little or poor experience exhibiting or selling their work. "I get retired people, people switching from commercial to fine arts, art teachers who want to pursue their work more seriously and sell it, graduates from art schools who have been out of school for three or four years and find that the world isn't the way their teachers described it, people who have never been to art school at all and are self-taught," Sue Viders, an advisor in Denver, Colorado, said.

Viders, as many others in her field, has found that the number of artists seeking career help has grown enormously. "A lot of them had felt, and some still do, that if they create the perfect picture the world will come to them," she stated. Even those who do look for assistance may set certain unspoken limits on how much they will change their attitudes or artwork. "My biggest challenge is fighting an unwritten artist etiquette book," Caroll Michels, a Long Island, New York–based advisor, said. "Artists often think that if they don't have an extensive résume, they shouldn't ask very much for their work—that they should price their work according to their résume. I tell them, 'Be ballsy and demand what you want. If the work is good enough and collectors want it enough, they'll pay it.' Artists think that they shouldn't demand a written contract with their dealers, because it might turn off their dealers, and so they accept terrible treatment from these dealers. I tell them, 'Get out of the Dinosaur Age, and demand your rights.'"

With all of these people, most of the actual consultations occur over the telephone, and artists will be asked to send in portfolio material (slides or photographs of their work, résumes, press releases) for the advisor to view. "I have a cauliflower ear, and I never get hoarse," Los Angeles advisor Calvin Goodman said, although Sue Viders purchased a telephone headset "because, otherwise, by the end of the day my ears hurt from the telephone receiver."

Advisors are primarily selling their knowledge of the art world and art market, a knowledge that is presumably large enough to encompass the different media and styles of work that their artist clients may bring in. "I always worry that my personal opinion may become a part of the problem of helping an artist market his work," Calvin Goodman said. "I try to put my subjective feelings aside—realizing that I'm not buying it, it's not for my collection—but attempt to see what work the artist is best at, which has the greatest market potential. There is a market for just about everything, but some markets are better than others, and I want to steer the artist in the most marketable direction possible."

Still, advisors have their preferences and dislikes, and artists should ask questions in order to be certain that they will be well served for the money. In general, artists should ask various questions, including: How long have you been in this business? How many other artists have you worked with over this period (get names and addresses of some, and contact them about their experience with the advisor)? Will you provide a general marketing strategy for my artwork, or specific contacts at galleries, or both? Are there certain media (oil painting, ceramics, collage, sculpture, for example) or styles of art (abstract, realist, portraiture, surrealist, for instance) that you have found to be more or less difficult to market?

Once, Goodman did tell a client that he was wasting his time and money because the would-be artist did not have sufficient talent—other advisors also told of recommending to their clients that they take more art classes—but the general aim of advisors is to determine their artists' capabilities and accentuate them.

Some advisors also candidly acknowledge that they cannot do much with certain styles of artmaking. Sue Viders, for instance, noted that "95 percent of my people are into realism, and I understand that market better. If someone is really abstract, I tend to send them to other people." Another advisor, Laura Stamp, explained, "I have a problem with surrealism, because those paintings are not very saleable. They repulse people." It is wise for artists to determine in advance whether or not a prospective advisor will be able to help them market their particular kind of artwork.

Most advisors are not full-time, practicing artists themselves. That may suggest to potential artist-clients that advisors are relatively neutral on aesthetic questions, or that they are less knowledgeable about what it takes to succeed in the art world because they've never done what they are recommending (if they're so smart, why aren't they rich?). Successful—that is, self-supporting—artists, however, generally don't counsel those who are younger or lesser known on how to get ahead in their careers. In some instances, they do not wish to recall their own trial-and-error efforts at receiving recognition; it is also possible that they know little more than their own experience, which may not be applicable to many others. On the other hand, Beth Ames Swartz, an artists' advisor in New York City, noted that "It's important to me that I'm a bona fide artist, someone substantial and successful who has been through it."

Some artists' advisors advertise themselves in magazines, while most receive clients either through word-of-mouth or a seminar on marketing strategies that they have given. Listening to a potential advisor at a seminar discuss his or her approach to marketing an artist's work is an excellent way to gauge that person's competence or suitability. Art dealers, print publishers, and business art advisors may also recommend artists' advisors with whom they have worked and in whom they have confidence.

Many artists' advisors have published books in their field. Often, those books may obviate the need for hiring the advisor who might otherwise do little more than read his or her book to the artist-client. Calvin Goodman, who has advised artists since 1958, is the author of the continually updated *The Art Marketing Handbook*, while Laura Stamp has self-published *How to Become a Financially Successful Professional Artist by Selling Your Own Fine Artwork*. Sally Davis is the author of *The Fine Artist's Guide to Showing and Selling Your Work*; Sue Viders wrote *The Marketing Plan for Artists* as well as *Producing and Marketing Prints*; Constance Smith is author of *Art Marketing Handbook for the Fine Artist* and *ArtNetwork Yellow Pages*, and Caroll Michels is represented by *How to Survive and Prosper as an Artist*. Other advisors have their own books, or have written articles for art magazines. Alan Bamberger has written periodically for a number of publications, including *American Artist Magazine*, *The Artist's Magazine*, and *Art Calendar*, and his own Web site contains the text for a number of those articles. Some advisors, among them Katharine T. Carter, may not have published articles or books but regularly give talks on career subjects for artists, and it may be worthwhile to attend an upcoming lecture. Sylvia White has a ninety-minute videotape of tips and instructions for neophyte artists, and Jennifer Gilbert, who is otherwise a Boston art dealer and not an artists' advisor, sells two videos on marketing artwork. Articles, books, speeches, and videos should be examined critically for their quality and depth of information and advice before artists consider hiring an artists' advisor. See the Resources section of this chapter for a listing of advisor contacts.

As a growing number of artists look to the Internet to see, show, and, perhaps, sell artwork, they may also find a burgeoning supply of career advice directed at them. One of the newest Web sites in this area is Artist Help Network (*www.artisthelpnetwork.com*), which was created by artist career coach Caroll Michels. The information on the site is not so much specific advice as resources of interest to artists, divided into seven categories: Legal; Money; Career; Exhibitions, Commissions & Sales; Presentation Tools; Creature Comforts; and Other Resources. Under each heading are numerous regional, national, and international organizations (identified by name, address, telephone number, and a brief description), many of whose own Web sites may be accessed by a click. The information on this site is actually the appendix of her book, *How to Survive and Prosper as an Artist* (Henry Holt & Company), now in its fifth edition. However, as opposed to a book, the information on the Web site will be continually updated and amended. "I want to keep people current," Michels said. "The problem with a book is that you write it and then every address and phone number changes."

Michels also has a separate Web site that focuses exclusively on her consulting work for artists (*www.carollmichels.com*). Other artists' career advisors, however, combine information on their services with free information and advice for artists, such as Alan Bamberger (*www.artbusiness.com*), Geoffrey Gorman (*www.gormanart.com*), Susan Schear (*www.artisin.com*), Constance Smith (*www.artmarketing.com*), Sue Viders (*www.sueviders.com*) and Sylvia White (*www.artadvice.com*). The advice and help come in different forms—Bamberger writes medium-length essays on a number of topics, Gorman sends out a free e-zine every month with brief tips and news reports to interested artists, while Viders takes and answers questions online in an "Ask Sue" column—but, put together, artists may obtain a free education in the business of art.

There's yet more: The Toronto-based Arts Business (*www.artsbusiness.com*) is an e-zine of resources, opportunities (commissions, calls for art, job openings, etc.), and art business news covering Canada, Great Britain, and the United States. Another free e-zine, *Selling Art on the Internet*, published by Benecia, California, artist Marques Vickers (*www.marquesv.com/ezine.htm*), looks at Web-based marketing and sales approaches, while Chris Maher's "Selling Your Art Online" Web site (*http://1x.com/advisor*) also offers a variety of articles and resources for artists in this new and daunting field. Perhaps the most all-encompassing career development site for artists on the World Wide Web is the Philadelphia-based Art Biz (*www.theartbiz.com*), which charges a membership fee—$125 per year, $45 per year for students—for access to opportunity databases (updated daily), an electronic newsletter, a professional exchange page that includes information on approximately 30,000 artists and potential art buyers (art dealers, interior designers, corporate art consultants, corporate art buyers, among others) and a downloadable artist career development tutorial. The Art Biz also features an online bank, operated by BankCorp.com, that offers no-fee, no-minimum checking, and savings accounts for artists, and one need not be a member of Art Biz to open an account. According to Dana Sunshine, president of The Art Biz, incentives for opening an account with the bank include a gift certificate for art supplies.

Marketing Work During the Periods Between Shows

In the lives and careers of visual artists, exhibitions tend to be the highlights. These events focus attention on the artists and their work, creating opportunities for sales, praise, reviews, and even controversy. Their psychological value to artists is immense; it allows them to communicate with and be recognized by the world outside of their studios. Small wonder that the categories of one-person and group shows dominate most artists' résumes.

Shows, however, are short-term, and there may be months or a year or more between one exhibit and the next. Few artists will earn a year's livelihood from one annual show, and they can only hope that visitors to this year's exhibition will remember them next year. Artists must learn to see exhibits as but one element of their overall marketing efforts, which must carry forward during the long stretches of time in which there are no shows.

Exhibitions offer the chance not only to sell but to collect the names, addresses, and telephone numbers of those people who express interest in an artist's work. That list is the difference between the short-term and the ongoing, as artists may keep in contact with those potential buyers through personal correspondence ("I enjoyed meeting you, and hope that you would visit me at my studio . . .") or general mailers. A month or two "before Christmas is a particularly good time to send out note cards," Barbara Ernst Prey, a painter in Oyster Bay, New York, said. "A lot of people are looking for a gift idea for a spouse."

Some artists send out postcards—picture of artwork on one side, written information on the other—that describe some work (series of prints, major commission, new subject matter) that recently has been completed. Other artists mail "newsgrams" to their collector list, noting upcoming shows or describing highlights of the preceding year. Perhaps, an opportunity to see or buy the work is mentioned, such as a studio sale or a private showing for past buyers.

A collector list needs to be more than a series of names and addresses, according to Sue Viders. "The biggest problem of people who exhibit their work is that they don't know who their audience is," she said. "Shows give you a chance to meet and collect information on the people who have some interest in your work." She added that a gallery sign-in book is valuable to learn the names and addresses of visitors, "but it is always better for the artist to be at the exhibition, to talk to visitors about their likes and dislikes. If someone buys a work, the artist should personally deliver it to the collector's home. You can see the type of home they have, the type of furniture they buy, the color scheme they use, whatever other art they own. Artists should keep as extensive a file as possible about anyone who has bought their work, and call or write these people if your work fits them or their house."

When they are meeting the public or potential buyers, many artists are accompanied by assistants (perhaps spouses or relatives), who do the actual collecting of names and addresses and handle the exchange of money and other important but mundane tasks, freeing the artists to be charming and conversational. Inviting past or potential collectors to the intimate setting of an artist's studio allows the work to sell itself, and the artist need only answer questions or otherwise be polite in the face of non-artistic comments. Studio invitations also should be extended to art dealers, art consultants (who buy for corporations), art critics, other artists, museum officials, and independent curators, as any one of them may become buyers or recommend the work to others.

Exhibitions place artists in the public eye, but the period between shows provides opportunities in which artists and their work may receive public notice. Teaching an art workshop or an adult education course, offering work at a charity auction, staging a demonstration of one's technique, or painting a mural all may generate attention, perhaps some extra income and the chance to make some sales. Even non-art-related activities, such as volunteering for a United Way Fund Drive, is a way to meet company executives and other people with money who could be added to a mailing list and who may eventually turn into buyers of one's artwork.

If there are long periods between exhibitions, it might seem obvious for an artist to have more shows. Art dealers, however, cannot always squeeze another show into their schedules, and they may be reluctant to "arrange an out-of-town show, because the dealer has to split the commission with someone else," said painter Nancy Hagin. Exhibitions are usually thought of as affairs that are arranged by others, but artists may also create their own events. Hagin, along with fellow artists Janet Fish, Sondra Freckleton, and Harriet Shorr, decided each to paint the same group of objects but in their own separate styles. At the end of this exercise, they decided to exhibit all their paintings in a combined show, which they arranged with an alternative art space in New York City. "If a dealer won't generate some attention for your work," Hagin said, "you try to generate things on your own."

In a variation on the same theme, sculptor Elyn Zimmerman, who participates in two or three group shows per year and has one solo exhibit every other year, noted that "I try to put my work somewhere on loan—at colleges, museums, or sculpture parks." She contacts these institutions herself, finding that many of them are interested in short- and long-term loans. Her reason for doing this is that "maybe two or three works sell from a show and the rest take more time to sell. Meanwhile, I've got all these big sculptures to store while I'm making others. If I can put my work on display where people can see it, it's better than my paying to store it. They have guards and insurance, so I don't have to pay for that, either. An added benefit is that I can bring people out there to look at it—that may result in a sale."

Alerting the Media to One's Artwork

Politicians call it "living off the land"—generating attention through newspaper or magazine articles rather than buying short radio or television spots for expensive commercials. They schedule press conferences or press walks, issue policy statements and appear on talk shows, all of which keeps their costs down and their visibility high. Artists also need to know how to get a free ride in the media, offering a public demonstration, scheduling an art exhibit opening, teaching a class, opening one's studio to the public, or anything else that qualifies as news. Journalists rarely just write about an artist unless there is an event that calls for coverage. News and feature articles, interviews, and reviews all keep an artist's name before the public even when sales of artwork are slow or nonexistent, and the media attention itself may result in sales later on as more people become aware of the artist.

The getting of that attention, therefore, becomes a major concern for artists, especially the creation of a press release. Two critical points are: to whom the release should be sent, and how to write the release. One does not just send off a release to a local newspaper and wait for a reporter to call. Relationships with critics and journalists should be ongoing whenever possible, creating an investment in one's career on the part of the particular media. This relationship may involve telephone calls or a meeting at a gallery as well as in one's studio.

Relationships with critics and reporters must also be flexible, as journalism is a nomadic profession where reporters move from one publication or station to another with some regularity. Journalists also migrate from job to job within their companies, moving from the features to the business pages, for instance, based on the serendipity of new editors or some new management concept. Mailing lists must be kept up-to-date, verified by telephone calls. Artists also must be prepared to like the next writer as much as the last one. "The New York artists I represent, who have become friendly with freelance art critics, are generally the most successful," said Jane Wesman, who heads a New York City–based public relations firm of the same name, which specializes in artists and writers. "You need to cultivate the people who can be helpful in your career."

There are various ways to determine who is eligible for a release or press package (more about creating a press release and package below). One of the more expensive ways is by purchasing printed lists (or preprinted labels) of specific editors (such as arts-and-entertainment editors or features editors) at newspapers and magazines nationwide. These can be obtained from Burrelles—Media Labels Department, 75 East Northfield Road, Livingston, NJ 07039, (201) 992–6600—and cost between $150 and $200 for a thousand names. The same information and more is available in Burrelles's multi-volume *Media Directory*, which includes newspapers (two volumes: $180), magazines (one volume: $180), and broadcast (one volume: $225)—the entire four volumes (Media Directories Department) sell for $450, although these books may be available at certain libraries, college, public, and university.

A less expensive way is to read, on a regular basis, the publications in one's own region in order to determine who covers openings, who writes about art, who writes about women, who reports on education issues, and who does personality profiles. In most newspapers and magazines, the pages devoted to the visual arts are very limited, and artists should look for other areas in the newspaper or magazine for coverage. Those other sections may have considerably more space and the same readership as the arts section. Wesman noted that artists should not confine themselves to art magazines in their press marketing efforts, perhaps sending press material to an airline or fashion magazine. "You want to broaden your audience to people who don't necessarily read art magazines, because those people may have money and interest, too."

Through telephone inquiry to a newspaper, one may learn who is the calendar editor (listings of upcoming events), as well as the arts-and-entertainment editor, features editor, lifestyles editor, home editor, magazine editor, Sunday editor, education editor—they assign the reporters. One should probably send press releases to different journalists and their editors even at the same newspaper, as it is unlikely that a single press release is passed on from one person to another. Usually, if the press release isn't absolutely pertinent to what the editor or reporter is doing, it is tossed out. Journalists also are inundated with press releases, which requires that the information they are sent be eye-catching, concise, and followed up with additional releases and telephone calls. A somewhat cynical rule of thumb in marketing events to journalists is, the second you hang up the telephone, they have forgotten the entire conversation. Second mailings should note that there had been a conversation with the journalist, with a clear and concise summary of what the artist wants the journalist to do.

Magazines have a longer "lead" time than newspapers, and artists should prepare press releases and packages for them as much as six months in advance. With newspapers, six weeks is usually sufficient, unless there is a holiday tie-in, which may involve a special section and more time.

Creating the Press Package

A press package includes a release, illustrations (slides, photographs, or high-quality color copies), biography or résume of the artist, artist statement (if relevant), and clippings of past articles about the artist's work or career (those with photographs of the artist and/or his or her work are most likely to catch the eye of a journalist, who may not choose to read the entire article).

In most cases, a press release should mimic a news article in a newspaper, with a headline in bold letters that quickly tells journalists something about the event and keeps them reading. "You could write, 'Jane Wesman to Talk about Art World at Conference,' which is all right if everyone knows who Jane Wesman is," she said. "Probably better is, 'World's Greatest Publicist Presents Inside Look at the Art World.'"

The press release should be in a newspaper's inverted pyramid style, with the most important news featured at the beginning and the less vital information at the end. Many smaller publications place news releases directly into the newspaper, and, if there are any cuts to be made (usually for reasons of space), the editing is done from the bottom up. The most important information is what is happening (exhibition, demonstration, class) when (time and dates) and where (street address, floor number), noting the significance or uniqueness of the event (for instance, printed by photogravure, first time these works have been shown publicly, honoring a recently deceased parent or public figure). Depending upon the nature of the event, this initial lead could be followed up by more information about the artistic process, the cost of attending the class or demonstration, or a quote by the artist or a third party (a critic or gallery director, perhaps) about the nature of the artwork.

The artist's previous experience (where exhibited or taught before) and educational background may have greater value to the local media if that show or class or schooling took place locally, and it might be placed higher in the press release; otherwise, this information should appear further down.

If the artwork is key to the story, as in an exhibition or demonstration, there should be an accompanying image, or more than one. Bombarded by a myriad of press releases, journalists need their information presented in the most time-efficient manner, and a good-quality image—no snapshots—says more than a thousand words. Color copies (usually costing between 90 cents and a dollar per copy) are one way to provide visual information to a journalist, but they usually are not a satisfactory illustration for a review or story, which may take place if the newspaper or magazine simply scans in the image from the copy by computer. For that reason, actual photographs or slides (costing, on the average, between 75 cents and $1.25 per slide) should accompany the copies. The number of visuals that are sent out, as well as the number of repeat mailings, is often dependent on the artist's budget, as press packages may be sent out to a number of journalists and editors.

RESOURCES

Artists' Advisors

California

Alan Bamberger
2510 Bush Street
San Francisco, CA 94115
(415) 931–7875
E-mail: *alanb@artbusiness.com*
www.artbusiness.com

Todd Bingham
1016 Eucalyptus Avenue
Vista, CA 92048
(800) 697–8935
www.tbfa.com

Michelle Carter
4790 Irvine Boulevard
Suite 105
Irvine, CA 92720
(714) 730–6128

Contemporary Artists' Services
Sylvia White
2022-B Broadway
Santa Monica, CA 90404
(310) 828–6200
www.artadvice.com

Constance Smith
P.O. Box 1268
Penn Valley, CA 95946
(916) 432–7630

Calvin Goodman
c/o GeePeeBee
11901 Sunset Boulevard
Unit 102
Los Angeles, CA 90049
(310) 476–2622

Colorado

Hilary DePolo
Denver, CO
(303) 722–8676
E-mail: *hdelwthin@aol.com*

Sue Viders
9739 Tall Grass Circle
Littleton, CO 80124
(800) 999–7013
(303) 799–1220
E-mail: *viders@worldnet.att.net*

Florida

Katharine T. Carter
P.O. Box 2449
St. Leo, FL 33574
(352) 523–1948
E-mail: *ktcassoc@icanect.net*
www.ktcassoc.com

Maine

Susan Joy Sager
ArtBiz
P.O. Box 222
South Berwick, ME 03908
(207) 384–2759
www.artbiz.info

Massachusetts

Jennifer Gilbert
DeHavilland Fine Arts
39 Newbury Street
Boston, MA 02116
(617) 859–3880

Michigan

Chris Maher
P.O. Box 5
Lambertville, MI 48144
(734) 856–8882
E-mail: *chris@1x.com*

New Mexico
Sally Davis
7209 Oralee Street, N.E.
Albuquerque, NM 87109
(505) 822–9118

Geoffrey Gorman + Associates
2013 Kiva Road
Santa Fe, NM 87505
(505) 989–4186
E-mail: *ggaarts@aol.com*

New Jersey
Susan Schear
879 Amaryllis Avenue
Oradell, NJ 07649
(201) 599–9180
www.artisin.com

New York
Art Information Center
55 Mercer Street
New York, NY 10013
(212) 966–3443

Artists' Advisors:
The Art Planning Group
12 White Street
Dept. I, New York, NY 10013
(212) 388–7298

Katherine T. Carter
24 Fifth Avenue
New York, NY 10011
(212) 533–9530
E-mail: *ktcassoc@icanect.net*
www.ktcassoc.com

Contemporary Artists' Services
Sylvia White
560 Broadway
Room 206,
New York, NY 10012
(800) 239–6450
E-mail: *artadvice@aol.com*
www.sylviawhite.com

Caroll Michels
19 Springwood Lane
East Hampton, NY 11937
(631) 329–9105
E-mail: *carollmich@aol.com*
www.carollmichels.com

Renee Phillips
200 East 72nd Street
Apartment 26L
New York, NY 10021
(212) 472–1660
www.manhattanarts.com

South Carolina
Laura Stamp
The Quarters
1211 Metze Road
Unit B–5
Columbia, SC 29210
(803) 798–8903

Texas
Marie Bahr
1701 South Mays
Round Rock, TX 78664
(512) 246–7519
E-mail: *artcareer@aol.com*
www.tintartgallery.com

Virginia
Lj Bury's Art Business Advisory
21310 Windrush Court
Suite 34
Sterling, VA 20165
(703) 430–8167
(800) 343–3444

Washington
Dan Fear
Art Support
300 Queen Anne Avenue North
Seattle, WA 98109
E-mail: *artsupport@att.net*
www.gonesouth.com/artsupport/index.html

Wisconsin
Deka
Kathy Heep
P.O. Box 322
Delavan, WI 53115
(262) 728–1216
E-mail: *kheep@pensys.com*

CHAPTER SEVEN

Presenting Your Work Professionally to Dealers, Competitions, and Buyers

Increasingly, artists have taken upon themselves the job of selling their own artwork, bringing their work to arts-and-crafts fairs, entering pieces in juried competitions, opening their studios to visitors, mailing full-color brochures to prospective buyers, even developing their own home pages on the Internet. Still, most artists tend to measure their career achievements in terms of gallery representation. (The ability to claim that one's work is shown in a New York gallery—almost any gallery there—often outweighs the fact, in many artists' minds, that sales are rare and few or no one-person exhibits take place.) When you present your art—whether it be to a dealer, a gallery owner, or a potential buyer—you want to make sure that it is shown to its best advantage.

The Value of a Gallery Connection

The value of a gallery connection, even to artists who sell very little, is more than boasting rights. The existence of a third party—the art gallery owner or dealer—to speak on behalf of someone's artwork is a powerful psychological boost for both the artist and potential collector, as it suggests that the work has at least met with one expert's approval. A dealer's mailing list is likely to be larger than the artist's, which will bring in more (and different) people to view the work than if the artist created the show him- or herself. Art critics are also more apt to attend and write about an exhibit at a gallery than visit an artist's studio; as journalists, art writers describe news events (the show) that are available to their readership (in a public space, such as a gallery).

Art dealers may well be interested in representing one's work, exhibiting it in group or one-person shows. The kind of dealer who will promote an artist's work, increasing the volume of sales, bringing in higher prices for individual pieces and placing the art in prestigious private or public collections, will generally want that artist to already have an established market which can be built upon. While dealers rarely turn a nobody into a somebody, those with significant contacts may turn a somebody into a somebody bigger. In order to interest that kind of dealer, an artist needs to develop a history of exhibiting his or her work with an equal history of sales. Dealers also rely on endorsements of artists' work from people they trust, such as other artists they represent, other dealers, certain critics, museum curators, or academics. This requires artists to become a part of the art world, displaying their work widely and taking time to meet people who may not be buyers themselves but are in a position to influence dealers and collectors.

In addition, artists should only approach those dealers who represent artwork similar to their own—an art gallery of realist painting is an unlikely bet to represent an abstract sculptor. Artists should research galleries and dealers either by visiting them to determine the type of art that would be eligible for display there, or by looking through the *Sourcebook to the U.S. Art World*, published every summer by *Art in America*, which lists many galleries around the country and the artists represented in them.

Introducing Your Artwork to Galleries

Traditionally, galleries require slides of work they might consider showing; however, that does not rule out albums of high-quality color photographs. In fact, a growing number of art dealers and gallery owners welcome photographs, in albums or in some other format. "It is difficult to tell from little slides what the work actually looks like," Kathy Jackson, director of the Linda McAdoo Galleries in Santa Fe, New Mexico, said. "We tell artists, 'Bring in photographs, or we'll be happy to look at slides.' Most artists don't ask, but some do. About 15 to 20 percent of the artists who come in bring photographs of their work."

Chris Skidmore, director of Gremillion & Co. Fine Art in Houston, Texas, noted that it is no more trouble for him to look at slides than through albums of photographs, since the gallery owns both a Viewfinder and a light table. However, "if the artist is bringing images of their work to the gallery in person, it's easier to look through photographs because you don't have to set up the Viewfinder."

There are some obvious advantages of good-quality color photographs—generally four-by-five-inch prints, although they can be smaller—over slides, such as the fact that not all dealers and galleries have light tables or slide projectors (or screens) to view the work adequately. Frequently, dealers just hold the slide up to an overhead light source for a second or two, and move on quickly—obviously, craning one's neck and looking into a light fixture are not conducive to careful, long-term examination. Photographs, especially those in an album, are more apt to be looked at longer, and the album may be left open on the gallery owner's desk, enabling that person to take a second look.

Slides are also usually far more expensive to produce than photographs, so artists may find themselves paying more for something that is likely to be viewed less. This is not to say that slides are out-of-date or inadvisable and photograph albums are problem-free. Juried art competitions, for example, almost always demand slides. Show sponsors equip jurors with slide carousels for the purpose, and a photo album would prove cumbersome for them.

Slides fit easily into plastic slide sheets, which are relatively lightweight when preparing a self-addressed stamped envelope. One may look at a sheet of slides and gather a lot of information about an artist's work, in a relatively short period of time. Photograph albums, on the other hand, are much heavier, adding to the cost of the return postage—that may negate the savings on photographs as opposed to slides. These albums also take considerably longer for someone to plow through, which may not be to that person's liking. Whether slides or photographs, each image should note the name and address of the artist as well as the title, medium, and size of the work. Unidentified photographs or slides, especially if a slide falls out of the sheet, or photograph out of the album, will only work to the disadvantage of the artist.

The question of whether to send photograph albums or slides may be determined by what the recipient requests. Artists should call or write the dealer (or gallery, or corporation, or art school, or juried competition, or magazine) to find out what is wanted and when. Some dealers only look at slides once a year—in the summer, for instance. Artists who send a packet of slides or an album of photographs to such a dealer in January and ask that they be returned within a month or two will miss the viewing opportunity.

In general, fifteen to twenty slides or photographs are the upper limit for dealers, corporations, or schools, unless they specifically request more—juried art competitions specify how many slides they will look at. Dealers and corporations prefer to see an artist's current body of work and subject matter, with an emphasis on consistency, rather than a retrospective of one's entire career. However, art schools hiring faculty are more likely to be interested in a more retrospective approach, as that indicates an artist's versatility and capability of teaching a wide mix of students.

Artists should prepare a package of information for the recipient that includes the slides or photographs, résume (or list of exhibitions and critical notices), a "cover letter" that introduces the artist and mentions what one is looking for (gallery representation, a job, a commission), and a self-addressed stamped envelope. The return-postage envelope is very important, as galleries are unwilling to spend money to return something that was generally unsolicited to begin with, and they also resent the artist's failure to include it. Unless a dealer agrees to hold the material for the artist, it is best not to drop off the packet and say, "I'll be by Wednesday to pick it up." That creates a storage problem for the dealer and increases the possibility of the packet being lost.

The more contained this packet is the better, as a cumbersome package of loose clippings and other bits of information that are difficult to contain or to put into the return-postage envelope make a poor first impression. Many art dealers receive between ten and thirty of these packages a day; by necessity, they approach them hurriedly, and a messy presentation engenders an irritation with the artist, which is a poor way to begin a relationship.

As the world becomes more and more oriented toward the use of computers, there may be opportunities to put images of one's work (plus information about oneself as well as an artist's statement) on a CD-ROM, as some artists' advisors have suggested. If you have digital versions of your artwork, and a CD burner, this could actually be an inexpensive way to display your images. Artists with Internet home pages might also inform dealers where their work may be found on the Web; yet placing slides or photographic images in front of someone may still be more efficient that hoping that the dealer proactively turns on a computer.

Besides slides and albums of color photographs, there are other ways of presenting one's work that may be considered. Color xerographic copies of photographs are often less expensive than making additional copies from the photographic negatives, and the quality may be good enough for the purpose—once again, find out what the recipient wants. Caroll Michels, an artists' advisor on Long Island, New York, recommends creating a brochure, with pictures of one's work and information about the artist, that may be sent along with a "cover letter that says, 'If you're interested, I will be happy to send slides.' You have to look at the initial outlay. The cost for each packet of slides and postage on the self-addressed stamped envelope is likely to be $15–$25, while a brochure may cost 85 cents a copy. With a brochure, you save money on those who aren't interested in your work."

To Frame or Not to Frame?

"Artists shouldn't be in the framing business," one contemporary art dealer said, "and they aren't always the best judges of what kinds of frames to use." Still, most dealers and gallery owners require artists to bring in paintings and works on paper that are ready for presentation, and that usually means fully framed (with works on paper framed, matted, and glass-enclosed). On occasion, a dealer will arrange for the framing but deduct that cost from whatever the artist is owed after a sale takes place.

Considering the fact that many collectors discard the frames anyway, purchasing ones that better match the decor in their homes, who should pay for the original frames? As one might expect, artists and dealers are of different minds on this question. Dealers usually believe that framing makes a work of art complete and is therefore the artist's responsibility, while some artists see framing as part of the domain of making a sale, which is why the dealer earns a commission. Dealers contend that an aesthetically appropriate custom-made frame dramatically influences a potential buyer's decision about purchasing a work of art, while many artists view expensive frames as superficial trappings. Buyers should only purchase works based on their pictorial merits, they feel.

"Emerging artists especially don't understand that presentation is everything. Some artists are so cheap that they won't pay for a real frame," Sue Viders, an artists' advisor in Denver, Colorado, stated, but the cost of framing can be prohibitively expensive, particularly for emerging artists whose market may be too limited to recoup these (and other) expenses. Marcia Lloyd, a Boston painter who is able to support herself from sales of her work, spent $4,000 to frame the paintings and works on paper in her most recent exhibit. "I had to put out the $4,000 up front," she said. "A lot of people who collect just assume that the gallery picks up the framing charge."

Lloyd used to make her own lattice wood (strip) frames but, since 1983, has paid professionals to create more polished-looking framing. It seems to be worth the expense. "The more professional a work looks, the more likely that you can sell it for more money," she said, adding that her frames are neutral in color in order to appeal to a wide range of tastes and decor. "I have no way of knowing for sure, though, that using a professional framer has increased either my sales or my prices. It's just a matter that the quality of the framing has increased with the prices." To cover the expense of framing, Lloyd stated that she has had to raise her prices, and her dealer—Boston's Portia Harcus of the Harcus Gallery—deducts that amount from the gross receipts before taking her commission.

Raising prices will not work for every artist, because that might drive prospective buyers away. Michael Ingbar, a New York City dealer of contemporary art in the "emerging" category, said that a number of his artists "scour flea markets for frames." He doesn't recommend that they spend hundreds of dollars on new custom frames because, "if the framing is very expensive, it might put the work out of my clients' price range." As with Portia Harcus, the framing costs are not part of his commission.

For Memphis, Tennessee, painter Burton Callicott, the expense of framing—and he strongly believes that all works should be framed—is more one-sided, falling entirely on him. Callicott builds his own frames using architectural molding, the same material placed on doors and walls. He applies three coats of flat black oil-based paint, then rubs it with steel wool, and gilds the top rim of the frame. The molding extends beyond the surface of the canvas in order to protect the picture's surface, "because I have done jurying for art shows in the past, and I know what happens behind the scenes. Paintings are stacked one against another, and the surface sometimes gets scratched and damaged." All of this care and know-how in the framing is Callicott's expense, without reimbursement from a dealer. What's more, he stated, "when a dealer thought that another kind of frame would be more suitable for a client, the dealer put a new frame on it and charged me" by taking that expense out of his earnings. "Galleries don't give you anything, and I think that's unfair."

The issue boils down to what a dealer owes (or believes he or she owes) an artist. Stephen Rosenberg pointed out that "dealers don't get their commissions from getting works framed and running errands. Dealers get their commissions from making sales and getting the artist's work known." His best offer is to split the cost of framing with the artist, which is still better than what the majority of artists receive.

In the past, dealers were more prone to assume the financial burden of framing, but the high costs of gallery rent, advertising, travel, salaries, and other expenses associated with dealing in art have led to higher commissions and fewer free services for artists. Like juried competitions, most dealers now expect artists to bring them works ready for elegant presentation, the cost of which is not their concern.

However, a more old-fashioned approach can be found here and there. Louis Newman said, "I take my commissions for selling works, which involves marketing and presentation, and that includes framing. I pay the rent for the walls the paintings are hung on, and I pay for framing."

Crating and Shipping Artwork

Sending off slides of one's art for juried competitions or to art dealers is an important step, but it is only the first step in placing work before the public. The actual art objects must eventually be transported to the shows or galleries where they have been accepted, and this takes care on the part of the artist. Works of art are frequently a casualty of moving, especially when the hired movers don't have specific expertise in transporting art. "We've had people come to us who have used general movers in the past," said Bob McCracken, president of Richard Wright, Ltd., an art moving firm in Massachusetts. "They tell us stories: someone's foot went through their painting; things were dropped. General movers hire from pools, people who say they have moved things before."

Works of art require special handling, as even a light bump can cause paint to fall off a canvas or permanently unbalance a sculpture. The glass covering a print or watercolor may shatter and tear the artwork underneath, or a frame may break and create a pull on the canvas. Transporting art even short distances can prove troublesome. "You can strap a painting into the back seat of your car and hope you don't hit any potholes along the way," said John Buchanan, registrar at the Metropolitan Museum of Art in New York City, "but there are a lot safer ways to do it." Those ways can also be considerably more expensive, and the Metropolitan Museum spends over half a million dollars a year moving objects from one place to another. The cost is high because of the risks.

Federal Express, for instance, discourages people from using the company to ship artwork, because of the high probability of some sort of damage. "Things with a high intrinsic value have a high breakage rate," a company spokesman said. There are, however, a number of sensible precautions one can take, some of which are quite inexpensive. One of the more painless things to do is remove the hanging devices from behind a painting—the screws and wires—and take the picture out of the frame. Both the canvas and frame may expand and contract under certain climatic conditions, brushing against each other, and that may knock off some paint. Museum conservators often recommend putting some felt or foam between the frame and canvas, then wrapping it all up in brown paper. This provides protection against dirt and dust, as well as a cushion against a small bump. Disassembling a work for shipping, of course, is not always an option, as art shows frequently require artists to send in their pictures ready for hanging out of the crate. Frank Marcotti, national operations manager for U.S. Art Co., said that it is "common sense to pack and ship a painting upright, the way it is hung on the wall. If it is tipped on its side, the artwork may move, the canvas may be stretched, and paint could pop off."

Movers typically wrap a painting in a buffered, acid-free glassine paper, then wrap it again with bubble wrap, and finally, place the piece in a cardboard box that is at least three inches larger on all sides than the wrapped picture. Within that three-inch space, McCracken noted, one might put Styrofoam "plastic peanuts" or even cooked popcorn. "You can feed the popcorn to the birds afterwards," he said. "It's environmentally friendly." The cost of the packing, for a single thirty-by-forty-inch painting ranges from $35 to $45, Marcotti stated. Some art movers are also willing to simply pack artworks, which can later be trucked by more general home movers.

If the picture is covered by a sheet of glass, one might also choose to place a couple of strips of tape across it, securing the glass in one piece if it breaks rather than allowing it to shatter all over the work. To remove the tape, pull it back slowly along its own length so that it is almost doubled over itself—pulling it back at a right angle may cause the glass to break from the stress. The tape may leave a residue on the glass when it is later taken off, which can be tricky to remove, especially if it is ultraviolet Plexiglas whose glazing material may be damaged by the potent chemicals in some household cleansers, such as Fantastic and Formula 409. Those chemicals, by the way, also give off vapors that may damage the art. The tape residue should be removed with hexane or mineral spirits, dabbed on a cotton swab; nail polish remover is also usable, although not on ultraviolet Plexiglas. Razor blades may also be used to scrape off residue. A number of museums now cover the glass with clear contact paper, which quickly allows one to see what the work is and also lessens the problem of tape residue.

Works may also be cushioned in bubble wrap, which is available at many hardware stores, although the entire package should be wrapped again in brown paper, because bubble wrap is difficult to tape down securely. An unfortunate problem with bubble wrap is that it tends to retain heat and moisture that may harm the art. Wood, for instance, may warp inside bubble wrap; paint may flake off, or a metal sculpture may develop rust. One way to avoid this problem is not to pack or move on a rainy day, and it is possible to stipulate to movers that they should not come if the relative humidity is above 65 or below 40 percent, or when it is raining.

An alternative is to demand in writing that movers not store works left overnight on a loading dock where heat and humidity levels, not to mention dirt, are likely to be unregulated and the possibility of theft is quite real. It is possible to demand that the moving van itself have temperature and humidity controls (a practice of many larger art museums), although this is rather costly. In addition, one should resolve in advance with the mover the amount of insurance as well as instructions on how the art objects should be handled, and this should be in writing. Shipping one's creations can be traumatic, but decisions should not be avoided by letting whatever happens happen.

It is not uncommon that paintings and delicate works on paper are shipped in wooden crates. For almost any sculpture, this is mandatory, and crates can be constructed at a cost of between $100 and $1,500, depending on how careful one wishes to be. A crate is relatively easy to build. It is a simple pine box, reinforced with three-quarter-inch plywood and lined with waterproof paper and a layer of polyurethane foam. One must make sure that objects do not bang against the sides but are fitted snugly inside. Screws, rather than nails, should be used to attach the lid of the crate, as hammering may prove quite jarring to the works inside that one is trying to protect. Many conservators also suggest coating the outside with oil paint as it adds an extra sealant to protect against rain. It is also advisable to place skids on the bottom of the crate, so that the prongs of a forklift are able to slide underneath easily, and some ornament on top, so that the crate could not be shipped upside down.

The heavier the crate, the more expensive the shipping charge. A 250-pound sculpture, for instance, may require 1,200 pounds of crating material just to ship it safely. Certain other factors also determine the cost, such as where the shipment is going, the time of year, the amount of insurance one places on the objects, and the ways in which they will be cared for along the way. Many artists and collectors ship valuable objects by air, as the storage cabins of most planes are pressurized and environmentally controlled to degrees that are not destructive to most works of art.

John Buchanan stated that "outside of the major urban areas, there are very few commercial movers who know anything about how to pack or move works of art. You really take your chances with some of them." He recommended calling museums to ask who has moved objects for them. There are a number of companies regularly used by most museums, and they are equipped to provide a certain level of insurance coverage for valuable pieces, although most collectors and museums get additional insurance elsewhere. The classified sections of a number of art magazines, such as

ARTnews and *Art in America,* are also good places to look for companies that are equipped to handle art objects.

The more one ships works of art, the greater the likelihood of some damage taking place, but it can be minimized by providing certain kinds of care. Understanding the needs of one's art objects is the first requirement, and it may be the most important one for reducing the worry over whether or not these pieces arrive safe and sound at an art show or gallery.

Should an Artist Be Told What to Do?

A common area of frustration for artists is when collectors or dealers want to alter some aspect of the artist's work, for instance, to get the same image but in different colors. Sculptors may be told, "Why not do smaller things that people can and will buy more easily?" Who makes these decisions—the artists or their dealers?

Art world opinion divides evenly on this question, and for obvious reasons. Artists believe that they have the final word, while dealers claim that collectors run the show. In large measure, both sides are right: No one can (or should) tell an artist what to do or how to do it, and collectors are free to buy or not to buy whatever they choose. However, having staked out these positions, both artists and collectors look for basic areas of common interest. Artists who are creating art to satisfy their own internal needs should determine whether or not they also wish to satisfy a market, which to artists' advisor Sue Viders translates into making "ego art or consumer art. You have to ask yourself, 'Who are you creating the art for, and why are you creating the art in the first place?' If it is to sell, then you have to accommodate the market."

It is not always the case that an art dealer will bluntly tell an artist to make smaller works because that's what collectors want. Frequently, a dealer will mention which pieces are selling, and, if those happen to be all smaller works, the artist is apt to catch the subtle hint to work smaller. Arthur B. Davies, the noted American painter, is reputed to have advised his students back in 1915 not to paint pictures that were longer than their arms, as they probably would be carrying their works around with them from gallery to gallery in search of someone to represent them. Station wagons, vans, and other types of modern transportation, however, may have solved part of that problem.

Collectors may not be the only reason that a dealer suggests the artist create smaller pieces. "We can't show paintings that are bigger than six-by-nine-feet," Penelope Schmidt, co-owner of New York City's Schmidt-Bingham Gallery, stated. "Larger than that, the painting won't fit through our front door or in the elevator. With sculpture, too, there is a storage problem, especially for very large works." However, trying to tailor one's art to a particular market or the physical constraints of an individual gallery owner doesn't necessarily make for good art. The scale of the art may be very important to the art or the artist, and finding the market for this work can be difficult. Artists should, therefore, look carefully for the right dealer, art consultant, or corporate buyer who can place large-scale public artwork in the proper venue.

CHAPTER EIGHT

Selling Work Independently

Marketing your own artwork takes a lot of courage, and it also calls for qualities that might, in other circumstances, be called bad manners. You have to talk about yourself, and do a lot of it—what you do, what you have done, why you are doing it, why what you are doing has some value. It is so much easier when someone else does that talking for you, such as an art dealer, but most artists cannot rely on some third party to make the case for them.

For one thing, most artists are not represented by a dealer or gallery, and dealers aren't likely to take on an artist before that person has demonstrated that he or she has a following. (Does that sound like a vicious circle?) Second, most art dealers do very little on behalf of the artists whose work they show in their galleries, and very few gallery artists actually sell enough of their work to support themselves. Some artists have found a variety of creative ways to be aggressively proactive, by taking independent and leadership roles in the art business, setting up a booth at arts-and-crafts fairs, running their own sales soirees, and setting up galleries of their own.

The Private Studio Open House

Perhaps, group open-studio events (see chapter 6) are more suitable for artists at the outset of their careers or for those who are not pursuing the marketing of their artwork steadily. The sometimes circus atmosphere and the uneven quality and content of the work in these open studios may begin to work to the disadvantage of artists whose work has reached a higher level of appreciation. For them, selling $25 knickknacks would be a humiliating step down. These artists may continue to hold open studio events, but just for their own studio and by invitation only. Their focus primarily will be on sales, commissions, and establishing relationships with serious collectors.

"I sell so much at my open studio," said Lynn Peterfreund, a watercolor painter in Amherst, Massachusetts, who opens her studio to collectors, friends, and colleagues twice a year. "I make thousands." She noted that big group open-studio events have "an exhibitionary value to artists, but my aim is to sell."

Practice has made (almost) perfect for Richard Iams and Buck McCain, two painters living in Tucson, Arizona, who have been holding a joint annual open studio—actually, open house—every March since 1993. Organized and run by their wives, Donna Iams and Melody McCain, the event drew 30 walk-ins the first year and grew to the point where it is an invitation-only affair for 350 collectors. (The final number may be higher, since many invitees bring guests who they believe might also be interested in the artwork.)

From this experience, Donna Iams has learned what does and what does not work:

- "Start planning the open-studio six or seven months in advance," she said. That planning includes checking that no other major events are taking place that day at neighboring colleges or in the NCAA Final Four basketball tournament ("someone once asked us if we had a television"), scheduling the printing of brochures, flyers, and postcards; hiring caterers, florists, and parking attendants.
- Notify people months in advance. "When we first started, we tried telling people a month in advance, but so many people had already made other plans," she said. "They told us, 'We wish you had let us know earlier, so we could have put in on our calendar.'" Richard Iams's holiday cards (Hanukkah for Jews, Christmas for Christians) each contain a brief handwritten note about the show, followed up in late January by a postcard with information about the open-studio event and an image of a painting that will be on display. One month before the event, a newsletter is mailed out, containing between four and six images, the times and date of the showing, a map and a request for an R.S.V.P. ("The first time we had more than three hundred people, we ran out of food.")
- Make it one day. "The first few years, we did shows over two days, on Saturday and Sunday, from 2:00–5:00 P.M., but that was very exhausting," she said. "You have to set up twice and take everything down twice. We switched to a one-day show, from 10:00 A.M. to 7:00 P.M., and that's worked out a lot better." A problem with the second day, she noted, is that collectors believe that "if they didn't come the first day, everything will be gone, so they didn't come the next day." Over the course of that nine-hour day, she found that the flow of visitors was relatively constant.
- Have a range of artworks to show. Each artist puts out approximately twenty artworks, consisting of five paintings and the remainder sketches and small studies for larger pieces. It is the less expensive sketches that are most likely to sell, especially to visitors who are just starting to collect. "For the first three years," Donna Iams said, "we tried to make the display look like an art gallery," but they switched to a far less intimidating and formal approach, putting unfinished and unframed pieces on the floor, perhaps in a corner. (Their house looked like a house again.) "People like to root through things. When they find something out of the way, they feel as though they've made a discovery."
- Provide food and drink. As the open studio becomes an all-day event, the foods need to change for different times of the day ("no one wants to eat a sandwich in the morning"). Before noon, the serving is similar to a continental breakfast, with cinnamon rolls and fruit, changing to carrots and celery sticks, chips and salsa, chimichangas and fajita sticks (kept in warming hot plates) by the afternoon and evening. "Sandwiches don't work," she said. "They dry out." Guests are limited to two free drinks, including beer, wine, and juices. "We try to use top-end wines, costing generally $15–$20 a bottle. We don't

want to invite people in and then give them cheap things to eat and drink. I've heard at gallery openings people say, 'Gee, this gallery must not be doing well if this is what they serve,' or, 'I think this wine has been watered down.' We want to project an image that we can provide nice things."

- Make yourself available. For the first three years, Donna and Melody prepared and served all the food and beverages themselves, "and we never had time to talk to people." That talking has proved quite valuable, discussing the business side with collectors (prices, commissions, how and when to make deliveries), making sure that visitors sign the guestbook, and stepping in to continue conversations with visitors when their husbands are being monopolized by individual guests for too long. They hired a caterer and a bartender, both of whom were allowed to put out their business cards. As a result, the caterer drummed up a considerable amount of business, too, and gave Donna and Melody a sizable discount (10 percent the first year, 50 percent most recently).
- "Name tags don't work," she said. "People hate them." Visitors prefer to remain anonymous to one another but are usually willing to put their name, address, telephone number, and e-mail address in the guest book, although they may need to be shepherded over to it.
- Flower arrangements add to visitors' pleasure, while parking attendants alleviate concerns about where to park and about the safety of the cars. For her own peace of mind, Donna Iams removes prescription medications from the bathrooms, breakable pottery that may be bumped by people walking through the house, and pocket-size valuables (small sculpture, for instance) that might be stolen. She also purchased additional liability coverage for her homeowner's insurance policy (approximately $50) for that one day. The entire cost of staging the open studio is $1,500, including $575 for catering, $300 for wines, beers, and hard liquor, $150 for parking attendants, and the remainder for printing and mailing.
- Every visitor takes away a packet of images—postcards and brochures, mostly, and biographical information about the artists. Donna and Melody have also set up a print stand where visitors may purchase reproductions of their husbands' paintings.
- After the event, every visitor will be sent a handwritten thank-you note for coming. At the open studio, Donna and Melody hire a photographer to take pictures of visitors, posing actual buyers with the artist and the work purchased. These photographs will accompany the thank-you notes.

Artist-Owned Galleries

Art galleries are the glamour end of the art world, where artworks are displayed in a way that focuses visitors' attention just on them, where dealers stand ready to laud the artist and handle the exchange of money. There is something about those white walls, having a dealer, not seeing one's art competing with a bowl of soup (when it is exhibited in a restaurant), and the knowledge that potential collectors may look at and buy it, that gives artists a sense of getting a fair hearing. For many artists, gallery representation is the ideal arrangement, but not for printmaker Charles Harden. "I can't afford to sell my work at a gallery somewhere," he said. "Galleries take a 50 percent commission and, when you take out the costs of matting and framing, there's almost nothing left. I could raise my prices, but I'm not sure anyone will buy them. I don't want to price myself out of existence."

Harden solved the problem by opening his own gallery in Barnstable, Massachusetts: Harden Studios, which also shows the work of four or five other artists. It's a solution that a number of Massachusetts artists (as well as artists elsewhere) have tried, ensuring that their work is always on view, displayed in its best possible light, and without middlemen to take half the money and or the need to curry favor of dealers or others in the art world.

There are generally not enough art galleries in the country for all the artists who want to be represented in them, and relatively few of those live up to the hopes and expectations of the artists who have found a place in them: the dealer doesn't advertise and promote exhibitions or the artist; the art is displayed randomly; the overall quality of the art in the gallery is uneven; commissions are too high; and the artist isn't paid promptly when a sale does take place. These are standard complaints, and one frequently finds that, when artists get together, they are more apt to discuss what their gallery or dealer isn't doing for them than what they are currently working on.

A clear benefit for artists of having their own galleries is simply being present for those who stop in. "It matters to collectors to meet the artist," said Jan Collins Selman, painter and gallery owner in East Falmouth. "They hope to have personal contact with an artist at work. I make sure to work at the gallery once a week and let people see the magic of an image taking shape before their eyes." Meeting collectors has also been useful to Geoffrey Smith, owner of Aries East Gallery in Brewster, as some of the summer tourists who have bought his work in the gallery have given him commissions to paint specific scenes. One of those summer visitors was Stephen Brown, chief executive officer of John Hancock Insurance Co. in Boston, who asked Smith to create a suite of paintings in Boston neighborhoods for the lobby of the building. "I meet a lot of people by being in the gallery, and the rapport I develop can go a long way," Smith said.

A personal rapport may be extremely important in a tourist environment, where visitors come for a weekend, a week (perhaps two), and may not come back next year. Two-thirds of the buyers at painter Debbie Hearle's gallery in Chatham are first-time collectors for her; unlike many other artists, who send out postcards and announcements to past buyers in order to describe upcoming shows, Hearle hasn't developed a mailing list because she doesn't expect collectors to buy her work another time unless they happen to be visiting Cape Cod (and Chatham) again. "Everything I sell is right here," she noted. "People don't buy my work from other parts of the country." The personal touch helps her sales in that she also does portraits, which some tourists will want "while they're here on the Cape."

Other artists who are gallery owners report similar percentages of first-time collectors—Selman estimated 60 percent and Smith 70 percent. "You want a lot of new customers every year," Smith said, "because people don't vacation on the Cape every year. There's no predicting who will be a repeat customer." Paul Calvo, a painter who closed his Chatham gallery in February 1998 after the rent was increased substantially, noted that 90 percent of his collectors were "walk-ins," tourists with no previous connection to Calvo or the gallery. The artists also describe a significant number of sales, but usually for lower-priced pieces, perhaps bought as souvenirs. Selman sold 260 pieces in 1997, earning $54,000; Smith sold approximately $50,000 in art, while both Calvo and Harden had receipts in the $20,000–$25,000 range.

A history of selling to one-time buyers rarely adds up to star power in the art world. Most viable galleries rely on a base of collectors who regularly purchase most of the pieces sold there; the artists' standing in the art world depends on the reputation of the gallery and of the collectors. "My career isn't developing as fast as it would if I showed elsewhere," Harden said.

Owning a gallery solved the problem of where and how to exhibit one's art for painter Barbara Halliday Montgomery, whose decision to open the short-lived West End Market Gallery in North Adams, Massachusetts, in 1988, for instance, "evolved from my needing a place to display my own work." Art generally needs a certain artistic context in order for it to be viewed as art—that is what separates graffiti from graffiti art—and a gallery can help an artist feel more like a professional. "The gallery atmosphere has a certain formality," Richard A. Heyer, owner of the Beaver Pond Gallery in Williamstown, Massachusetts, said. "You walk in and really feel you are looking at serious art." A watercolorist of landscapes, Heyer added that, since starting up the gallery in 1978, he is "not just pursuing art without a goal. The gallery creates goals for you, such as finishing enough paintings and having them all in frames and looking presentable."

There are some notable examples of galleries owned and run by individual artists in major cities—Alfred Stieglitz's "291" gallery in New York City back in the 1910s featured his own photography in addition to photographs, paintings, and sculpture of fellow modern artists, and a number of the loosely structured East Village galleries in Manhattan in the 1980s were established by avant-garde artists—but these types of galleries are most commonly associated with small towns and rural regions. Today's artist-owned galleries grew out of the idea of artist cooperatives, which are art spaces that a group of artists pay for and jointly run in order to show their own work and gain control over their careers. Frequently, galleries owned and run by an individual artist are located on the first floor of that artist's house, which is both convenient and allows substantial business write-offs.

For watercolorist Lou Lehrman, owner of The Gallery at Mill River in Mill River, Massachusetts, an entire gallery "gives me a showcase for my painting, and people can see my work in depth. I am represented by other galleries—a couple in Scottsdale [Arizona], one in Sedona [Arizona], and another in West Hartford [Connecticut]—but they may only show two of my paintings. They may have another two paintings, but they're probably somewhere in the back, maybe in a bin. You have no control in other people's galleries, but, in my own, I can show more of my pieces as I like. I also get to keep 100 percent of the sale, since there is no commission."

On the positive side, of course, although the dollar amounts are limited, the artists needn't share their proceeds with another dealer. However, these artists don't receive the benefits of having a dealer promote their work. As dealers, these artists are not particularly active in advancing the interests of the artists whose work they represent. "It's hard to sell other artists' work," said William Davis, a painter who closed his Dennis, Massachusetts, gallery in December 1997, after six years. "Of course, I'm primarily going to try to sell my own work but, if I notice people aren't interested in my work, I might point them in the direction of other artists." For her part, Selman noted that gross sales of work by the other twelve artists in her gallery were $23,000, less than a third of the total. "I'm the draw. My name is first on the list in ads," she said. "Patrons who have enough of my work may become interested in other artists' work." The reason for establishing a gallery rather than just opening up her studio to the public is that it gives "a context for my work, and it's also refreshing to see other artists' work. It challenges me to do better." Over the years that he ran his gallery, Alfred Stieglitz quarreled, and ultimately broke, with most of the photographers whose work he represented over matters of aesthetics. Artists who are considering consigning their work to a gallery owned by an artist, created largely to showcase that artist's work, should be confident that the gallery will represent their work and ideas fairly.

One of the largest entrepreneurs in the artist-as-gallery-owner arena is the painting couple of Robert and Michele Kennedy, who live part of the year in Key West, Florida, and the other part in Cotuit, on Cape Cod. They own sixteen galleries (called either Kennedy Gallery or Kennedy Studio, depending upon whether one-of-a-kind or prints are primarily sold there), located on Cape Cod, Key West, and several other tourist destinations, all of which are operated by employees of the Kennedys. At these galleries, close to 80 percent of the sales are for the work created by the Kennedys, according to Robert Kennedy, who added that "my wife selects the other artists in these galleries. They are artists who are local to the area where the gallery is, and she picks artists whose paintings complement the work we do."

As well as creating the opportunity for commissionless sales, gallery ownership offers considerable potential drawbacks, including the cost of renting a gallery space (which can be quite high in tourist areas, where every shop owner wants to be on the beaten path) and interruptions of one's work. Both Calvo and Smith noted that they paint during the winter months in order to build up an inventory for the summer, but Davis found that his gallery took too much time away from his painting, "and my career was starting to suffer. I was not doing any major paintings"—twenty-four-by-thirty inches in size—"but just smaller eight-by-twelve-inch pieces for other galleries that show my work, just to keep them satisfied. Mystic Gallery called me up once to say that someone had come in looking for a big work of mine and they had nothing to show him." He added that his inability to create larger paintings (which usually take longer to produce) meant that he was "not getting into big shows. I was slipping into obscurity." As a result, he closed the gallery in order to concentrate on the larger world of high commissions and the chance of renown.

Nina Pratt, a business consultant to art galleries, stated that having one's own gallery is "not the easiest or the best way to show or sell your art. It's much more practical to just have shows out of your studio once or twice a year or even to use your studio as a gallery. You might see three or four people a day; you wipe your hands off and shake hands with the people who come in. That way, you don't have the huge overhead of a gallery and use up time that might otherwise be spent on your art in maintaining the gallery."

Operating a gallery, even in one's home, can become a major expense. Clements Kalischer, a commercial and fine art photographer and owner of Image Gallery in Stockbridge, Massachusetts, which he started in 1965, doubts that "the gallery has ever broken even, not when you figure the overhead, the taxes, the heat, the electricity."

It cost approximately $59,000 to buy and another $20,000 to convert a family-owned meat market into the West End Market Gallery, taking down and putting up walls, replacing flooring and adding lights, putting in parking spaces, landscaping the back and installing a second bathroom with handicap access. Meanwhile, electricity cost a monthly $200, the telephone another $100, printing and mailing amounting to $75, and wintertime heating (oil) averaging $200–$300 per month. The expenses quickly proved too much and, despite the money Barbara Montgomery earned as a singer (in her now ex-husband's folk band) and the fact that she "received some help from my family to open the gallery," the gallery closed.

Any business expense may be written off, whether the gallery is located in one's home or elsewhere, but if there has been no profit in three out of five years, the Internal Revenue Service will disallow the deductions, viewing the gallery as a hobby rather than as a serious commercial enterprise. Artists contemplating creating a gallery of their own work need to know what regular art dealers know—how to sell art and make money from it. In the smaller towns where these kinds of galleries are more likely to be found, there does not tend to be an active market for art, certainly with prices for individual works that can support an individual or gallery.

Most artists already have some pay-the-bills job, often a full-time job, and creating art itself requires a lot of time. There is very little time left to run a gallery, and the art is usually the first thing to go. "To do it right," Kalischer noted, "you have to do it more than just on a part-time basis, but, if you have to live on it, you can't possibly do it full-time."

Co-op Galleries

The battle required simply to enter the art world, and the difficulties and expenses involved in operating a private, commercial gallery, have led many people to band together and join cooperative art galleries, which are run (and paid for) by their artist members. Co-ops solve the where-can-I-show-my-work problem for artists, although they are less likely to lead to substantial sales. The cost of joining a co-op and paying monthly dues may prove a drain on some artists' bank accounts, and a stigma is occasionally attached to co-op artists for apparently not being good enough to get a "real" art dealer to represent them. For some artists, however, co-ops are places where careers may begin, although advancement frequently means that the artist moves on to a commercial gallery.

The AIR (Artist-in-Residence) Gallery in New York City, which was founded in 1972 as a feminist cooperative, has launched a number of noted and successful artists. For some, the co-op was a clear starting point in their success, attracting the attention of collectors and commercial art dealers, while others found success coming despite their association with AIR. Nancy Spero, one of AIR's founding members, who left the co-op in 1983, stated that her work "didn't really sell much there, but it was seen by a lot of people, including dealers who later asked me to show at their galleries." For her, among the benefits of being in a co-op were "learning how the art world worked and understanding how to pursue my own interests, not being pushed around," as well as creating art without having to keep an eye on the market. "The work I did at AIR was crucial to my artistic development," said Spero, who is currently represented by New York's Josh Baer Gallery. "I wasn't worrying about sales. I was supporting myself in other ways. Being able to create and exhibit noncommercial art, and get feedback from people on it, gave me a lot of confidence when I finally went to a commercial gallery."

That freedom is not without cost, as AIR requires a one-time $500 acceptance fee from new members as well as monthly payments of $90 to cover the costs of heat, light, power, rent, and incidentals. At other co-ops, there may also be a commission—smaller, certainly, than those charged at commercial galleries—for all pieces sold, with that money used to pay salaries or other expenses. One cannot be assured of recouping that money through sales of artwork, as co-ops are not the main stops for serious collectors, and newspaper or magazine reviews of exhibits at these spaces are rare.

For Dotty Attie and Barbara Zucker, who were members of AIR from 1972 to 1987 and 1972 to 1974, respectively, the opportunity to have their art exhibited, especially in the context of a politically oriented artistic cooperative, was vital to their careers. "AIR gave me the opportunity to show my work," Zucker, a sculptor, stated. "Once you've shown, that's a rite of passage. You have a different view of yourself once you've had a one-person exhibition, and what I also learned was how to show my work." As with Spero, dealers came to Zucker, either having seen her work at shows at the co-op or through hearing about her from those who had been to her exhibitions. Dealers also told Attie that they admired her work at the co-op ("I always remembered those dealers and had a warm feeling for their galleries," she said), which proved encouraging when she decided to move to a commercial gallery. "Through years of being at AIR, I was able to build up a reputation," she noted.

Attie began inviting dealers to her studio in September of 1987. By December, the New York City gallery PPOW asked her to join, giving her a one-person exhibition the following September that completely sold out in one month. "At AIR, I wasn't able to support myself by selling my work," she said. "After the first show at PPOW, I was able to, and I've been able to ever since." The ability to reach a larger, more serious audience of collectors is a major reason these women left AIR and others leave their co-ops; it is the difference between starting out and making a career move. Attie stated that no museums showed her work during her almost sixteen years at

AIR, but, within a short period of time after moving to a commercial gallery, the Brooklyn Museum and the Museum of Modern Art in New York City both exhibited her pieces.

Elaine Reichek, a past AIR member who currently exhibits at the Michael Klein Gallery in New York, said that it is "hard to sell collectors work from a co-op. They look to dealers to guide them in what to buy." While attributing her growth as an artist to the freedom of exhibition without the pressure to sell artwork at AIR, her move from co-op to commercial gallery had less to do with the prestige she earned at AIR than with her efforts to make contacts with people during those years. She was introduced to dealer Michael Klein, for instance, through friends of friends rather than at an AIR exhibition. "Everyone at AIR functioned as her own marketer," Reichek stated. "AIR did give me a place to show my work, but it certainly didn't advance my career."

There are scores of cooperative, artist-run galleries around the country, and they each are as individual as their current roster of member artists. All of them exist because artists need somewhere to exhibit their art, although only some of them are viewed by their members as places to start careers. That is because becoming a self-supporting artist isn't a primary goal for many members. "Back when we started, in 1966, there was hardly anywhere in Reno to show your work," Marge Means, president of the Nevada-based Artists CO-Operative Gallery, said. "Now, there are a lot of galleries where you can show your work in Reno, but a lot of people just like being part of a co-op."

At both Artworks Gallery in Hartford, Connecticut, and the Artists' Cooperative Gallery in Omaha, Nebraska, members are more likely to leave the co-ops because they have moved elsewhere or stopped doing their art than as a result of stepping up to a commercial gallery. "We have a number of activities that people want to be part of," Judith Green, director of Artworks Gallery, noted. "We bring in guest lecturers; we hold juried exhibitions. A lot of the members like to spend time with the other members."

Co-op galleries certainly do entail maintaining a personal, as well as financial, commitment to a group, and they permit a greater diversity in styles and subject matter than is found at many (if not most) commercial art galleries. Cooperatives, however, may not be for everyone. The commitment of time and energy can be enormous. "You have to be on committees; you have to sit at the gallery," Dotty Attie said. "You have to do all the work, and you just get burned out after a while."

Co-op membership also changes over time, and older members may feel less affinity with some of the newer ones, resulting in a withdrawal of that initial commitment. Ultimately, co-ops are statements about the art world, a claim by certain artists that they have been shut out of the process, due to the kind of artwork they create, the exigencies of commercial art dealers, the race and gender of the artists, or some other cause. In this regard, they are as much political as aesthetic groups, and political ideas change with new faces and the passage of time. There may be a certain time limit after which career-minded artists will move on from a co-op.

Although over the past two hundred years there have been instances of artists cooperatively taking control over the display of their work—all of the French

Impressionists' exhibits of the 1870s and 1880s, or the Ashcan School's shows in the United States in the first decade of the twentieth century, for example, were organized without benefit of commercial dealers—the co-op as alternative art venue took hold widely in the pluralistic 1970s. Many co-ops and alternative art spaces came into existence at this time and some, such as AIR, drew critics, dealers, and collectors.

The 1980s signaled a retreat from alternatives, with both new and established commercial art galleries as well as a number of major and smaller museums reclaiming the enthusiasm for discovering new artists. That decade's association of artistic novelty and excitement with monetary worth meant a turning away from the noncommercial emphasis of co-ops. Whether the art world shifts back to an interest in alternative spaces and co-ops during the 1990s and beyond is yet to be seen.

Another potential drawback of co-ops as starting points in an artist's career is an unstated stigma attached to these kinds of galleries, perhaps because of their perceived association with political rather than purely aesthetic concerns. With AIR, "a lot of people complained that an all-women's co-op ghettoized women artists," Nancy Spero said. "I think belonging to AIR may have set me back," artist Mary Beth Edelson stated. "Co-op artists are generally stigmatized in the art world and, through my association with AIR, commercial galleries assumed that I had made a commitment to exhibit my work in a certain way." After her 1992 departure from AIR, where she had been a member for almost ten years, Edelson claimed that she needed "to reinvent myself" in terms of how the art world perceived her, becoming involved with the artists and galleries gaining popularity in Manhattan's East Village during the early and mid–1980s. Art dealers began to give her work a second look at this time.

Winning an audience, a dealer, and recognition in the art world is a battle, however one goes about it. Co-op galleries are but one line of attack for artists, some of whom will draw the attention of collectors and dealers, while others gain the experience of exhibiting their work and running a gallery, free from the pressures of earning a living in this way. "Many commercial gallery owners have a very fixed idea of what they want to show," said Sarah Savidge, director of AIR Gallery. "You may not fit into that fixed idea, and many artists have found co-ops to be an answer to that problem."

Geoffrey Homan, president of the board of directors of the one-time Association of Artist-Run Galleries, noted that there is often a "conspiracy of silence" among the critical establishment about co-ops, a result of economics: "Dealers are fearful of losing market share, and art publications, which rely on advertising from dealers, don't want to offend the dealers by reviewing an artist-run space." However, he stated, the benefits of belonging to a co-op outweigh the disadvantages, since there are no expectations about the sale of one's work and "you can control your own destiny as an artist. At a lot of commercial galleries, the plan is to have all of an artist's work sold before the show even opens. If the work doesn't sell very well, or doesn't sell at all, the dealer may just kick you out of the gallery. Now, that's got to interfere with the creative process. You avoid all that at artist-run galleries."

CHAPTER NINE

The High Cost of (Non)Success

Me? Invited to be in an art exhibit in Paris? That's what the advertisement seemed to say. Paris! Ooh-la-la! Actually, anyone can be in it just by sending five paintings and a check for $800 to Paris's Centre Internationale d'Art Contemporain. Oh, well, it sounded good for a moment. What about an "Artist's-Dream-Come-True show in famous SoHo NY Gallery"? That one asks me to send slides of my work, plus a $25 "processing fee," to Palace Pyramid Promotions, which isn't listed in the telephone directory and only has a box number address in Beverly Hills, California. Hmm. Maybe I should think twice about it.

Or I could be listed in a directory, such as *Artists of New England*, published by Mountain Productions, Inc., of Albuquerque, New Mexico, or the *Encyclopedia of Living Artists*, published by ArtNetwork in Renaissance, California. Then, people will have heard of me. Well, maybe not. I would have to buy space in either book for a reproduction of my work and a brief biographical summary, just like an advertisement, costing $900 for a half page and $1,500 for a full page for *Artists of New England*, $398 for a half page and $598 for a full page in the *Encyclopedia of Living Artists*. Besides, there is hardly a library in the country that stocks these vanity publications.

Not Every Chance to Show One's Work May Be Worth It

A tour through the classified sections of major art magazines leads to a growing number of services offered to artists, generally involving exhibition opportunities and art directories. Once, art was the expensive thing; now, it appears that promoting one's work may cost a small fortune. Just like anything else they might pay for, artists need to approach gallery shows, juried competitions, and other career aids as consumers, asking hard questions and making informed choices.

One advertisement, for instance, announces: "Have a show in SoHo. We take no commission, so any sales you make, you keep." A show in SoHo, however, doesn't mean in a known gallery or art space, as Manhattan Fine Art Storage has merely set aside two rooms off its storage areas for exhibits. A show in SoHo also doesn't mean for free, as those two rooms are for rent, costing either $56 or $75 a day, depending upon whether or not an artist has work stored at this facility. Artists who simply need somewhere to display their work in order for potential buyers to see it in quantity, for instance, may consider this a reasonable amount to pay, but others who hope to have their art reviewed by newspaper or magazine critics or looked at by walk-in traffic are more likely to be disappointed.

The opportunity to claim that one's work has been exhibited in SoHo is very tempting, just as artists may be anxious to have their art shown in Paris, but vanity shows are not accorded any prestige in the art world. In fact, they tend to be looked down upon, indicating, not that a gallery believes in the artist's art, but that the artist had enough money to get his or her work displayed somewhere. Those who want to build up their credibility as artists by loading up a résume with various shows of this sort may find that this is a very expensive and not particularly effective way to establish themselves or their work as good or marketable.

Another magazine advertisement reads: "Artists wanted to exhibit in our Georgetown, Washington, D.C., gallery, our dynamite Public Spaces program, and our New York show." The Michael Stone Collection doesn't provide these services for free, however, charging $95 per month (twelve-month minimum) or $110 per month for those who only want to try it for six months in addition to a 30 percent commission on all sales. The Public Spaces program currently consists of exhibiting works in various offices (such as the national headquarters of the American Society of Interior Designers) in the Washington, D.C., area for up to six months. This certainly gives an artist's work considerable exposure, which may lead to sales. Many commercial art galleries also place work in corporate offices as well as in private homes for a period of time, but they usually charge the company a rental or leasing fee, and most of that money goes to the artist—artists generally don't pay to decorate corporate office walls.

Yet a third advertisement, this placed by the Chim Gregg Art Gallery in La Puente, California, calls for artists whose work is abstract and two-dimensional to apply for representation, submitting four slides of their work. However, interested artists are told to submit a check for $5 as a "jurying fee," which is unheard-of in the gallery world. Art dealers and gallery owners look at slides for free; it is their job to seek out new talent, not a favor they are performing for artists. In a separate letter to interested artists, the Chim Gregg Gallery's director, Bobby-Lou Hargis, also states that "The Gallery owners only insure the works that belong to the gallery," and there is "a fee for services rendered, as the artists do not have to be here to help with Gallery sitting." Again, it is customary for galleries to provide insurance for all works, owned or consigned, on their premises, but highly unusual for artists to be required to pay a fee for gallery "sitting"—isn't being present in the gallery one of the main jobs of a dealer? This letter also notes, "The ARTISTS that we represent can advertise, using the Gallery name and address in their ads." For many artists, the ability to refer potential collectors to their gallery itself is worth various extra expenses; clearly, this is a service that the Chim Gregg Art Gallery believes is worth paying for.

Many of these advertised "opportunities," especially those offering a show in a SoHo gallery, appear to be aimed at artists who don't live in (and hardly, if ever, visit) New York City but see an exhibit there as a measure of achievement. Vanity art shows, like vanity publishing, however, carry no prestige. They may lead to sales, if the artists themselves find buyers and get them to come to the exhibit, but these kinds of shows are not stepping stones to better things.

Fighting Back

National Artists Equity Association recommends that artists ask a series of questions of potential gallery owners before paying them any money. Among these are: Who are the owners of the gallery and what qualifications do they have to exhibit or sell art? Do they have contacts with collectors and critics as well as museum curatorial experience? When was the gallery started? Does it have a reputation in the local arts scene? Have exhibits there received critical attention in local or national media? Are the owners members of any dealers' association? How is the gallery organized to make money—charging fees of artists or actually selling artwork on which it makes commissions—and does it have a reputation for selling? Artists Equity also recommends asking the gallery owners for names of other artists as references and obtaining detailed information on how the money paid to the gallery will be used, such as by examining a sample exhibition budget.

A great many advertisements for juried art competitions demand an up-front payment. Jurying or entry fees have long proven troublesome for artists. A variety of visual artists membership organizations, such as the Boston Visual Artists Union, the Chicago Artists Coalition, and Artists Equity, have advised their members not to participate in shows that require artists to send in money along with slides. Their view is that, just as writers don't pay editors to read their manuscripts and dancers and actors don't pay theater companies in order to audition, visual artists shouldn't have to pay someone to view slides of their work. This view has been endorsed by the New York State Council on the Arts, the Oregon Arts Commission, and the Washington, D.C., Commission on the Arts and Humanities, which have adopted rules prohibiting these agencies from giving money to groups that charge artists entry fees. Peer review panels at the National Endowment for the Arts also turn away applications from groups that call for fees, although there is no official policy on this by the federal arts agency.

The organizations that charge these fees defend the practice, claiming that art shows are expensive to mount. However, a show sponsor's expenses should not be transferred to artists, a group that includes those who paid for someone to look at their slides and then were rejected. Artists already have enough expenses in creating, framing, photographing, crating, shipping, and insuring their artwork without being told that they must pay for someone to look at their art. There are also other ways for show sponsors to recoup their costs (such as charging a commission on sales, charging admission to visitors, or publishing a catalogue of the show, which can be sold), which are fairer to participating artists. In the past, the even-yeared open exhibitions at the Manhattan-based National Academy of Design were paid for in large measure through the $20 entry fees that artists were required to submit with their slides. Since an average of two thousand artists vied to be among the three hundred artists regularly admitted to the show, the fees raised $40,000. More aggressive fundraising on the part of the Academy has allowed the institution to drop the entry fees, much to the relief of many within the institution. "I happen to be against entry fees," Gregory Amenoff, a painter and president of the Academy, said. "It says 'amateur.' You end up with two thousand people sending in money and one slide, with a 15 percent chance of actually getting into the show, which means that the show is financed by people who didn't get into the show. We wanted to professionalize the show by getting rid of the entry fee and, again, treat artists in the same way they are treated at other New York institutions." Many top-flight artists had not entered the Academy's open exhibition in the past, nor would they dream of doing so now, he noted, if the fee were reinstated. Improving the quality of the show, as well as its standing among artists, meant eliminating the entry fee.

Whether or not artists refuse to take part in competitive juried shows that require entry fees, they should at least make their unhappiness with these fees known to the show sponsors. If enough artists complain, perhaps a change may eventually result.

Other show sponsors, such as those holding art fairs, sometimes require artists to submit a check for a "booth fee" with their slides and applications, and the amount may range from $40 to hundreds of dollars or more, depending upon the booth rental charge. This fee is given back if the artist is not accepted, but it may be months between the time when the application was sent in and the time the money is returned. The check the artist receives is often that of the show sponsor rather than his or her own, which means that the sponsor has been able to draw interest on this money instead of the artist. Once again, artists may wish to protest a situation in which they find themselves subsidizing people who claim to be aiding the arts.

Before You Sign . . .

Whenever there is a jurying system, artists should be informed who the judge(s) or juror(s) will be in advance of applying, as it is the prestige of those persons that gives importance and validity to the event. If one also knows something about the juror—he is a dealer of mostly avant-garde art, she paints watercolor landscapes—that may help potential applicants assess the chances of having their work selected. It doesn't tell potential applicants much when Art Enterprises of Lompoc, California, announces that its First Annual Art Competition will be "juried by professional artists." Similarly, the "International Biennale" (sic), organized in Miami, Florida, for the Musée d'Art Moderne in Bordeaux, France, will have art chosen "by international selection committee appointed by museum director." For some artists, the possibility of having their work displayed abroad may outweigh not knowing who the jurors are, the existence of an entry fee ($20 for three slides, $5 for each additional slide submitted), and the unwillingness of the French museum to take responsibility "for loss or damage of any kind for any work." It is a difficult decision to make, but artists should at least know what they are facing.

The sponsors of many competitive exhibitions will develop a prospectus, outlining what the show is, where and when it will take place, how many artists are to be selected, the type of art (subject matter and media) that will be featured, the names of the jurors, the liability of the sponsor (in the event of damage, fire, loss, or theft), how art is to be shipped, whether or not there will be prizes offered (and in which categories) and commissions on sale of artwork as well as any other charges. Artists should send for this information before submitting slides and any money to be in the exhibits. Similarly, artists should see in writing what kinds of arrangements galleries or other exhibition spaces that advertise for artists have in mind in advance of sending slides and, certainly, before shipping original work.

Buying One's Way into an Art Magazine

Traditionally, fine artists have been thought of popularly as scruffy types without much money. Not anymore, obviously, as a growing number of art magazines have created opportunities for artists to pay to get their artwork displayed within their pages. Both *Art New England* and *ARTnews*, for instance, have created "Artist Directory" sections, in which artists may display their work in exchange for a fee ($279 and $400, respectively). In a similar vein, *The Crafts Report* has a regular "Showcase" section, which costs $400 for a quarter-page advertisement (one image plus fifteen words of descriptive copy and artist contact information).

A survey of artists who have placed advertisements in *ARTnews* reveals that none of the respondents could report, as a result, any sales of artwork or commissions to create a piece; none were asked to exhibit in a gallery or hired to teach, lecture, or give a demonstration of their techniques. Curtis Salonick, a photographer in Wilkes-Barre, Pennsylvania, had a typical artist's experience, reporting that "what has transpired since the ad are very few inquiries; nothing concrete." Ana Maria Sarlat, a painter in Miami, Florida, noted that she was "contacted by a gallery in Puerto Rico that was interested in my work, but they dealt with realism so it wasn't a good fit. Someone else called about my work, but it sort of fizzled out." Kathleen McKenna, a painter in Shaker Heights, Ohio, stated that she had been contacted by a couple of galleries, "and we'll see if anything comes of that." Los Angeles painter Ione Citrin claimed that she has received "about a dozen responses to which I immediately replied and followed through." However, "they were totally zero insofar as anything concrete." Ginger Bowen of Lahaine, Hawaii, Mary Farmer of Atlanta, Georgia, and Olive Reich of Brooklyn, New York, all claimed to have received inquiries but no immediate buyers. Barbara Starr, a painter in St. Louis, Missouri, reported no buyers and no contacts. "It's not likely that I'd place another ad in *ARTnews*," she said.

Blurring the distinction between a contest and an advertisement are *Art Calendar*, *Manhattan Arts*, *American Artist*, and *The Artist's Magazine*, all of which hold competitions for artists to have their work displayed in the respective publications. *Art Calendar* has a centerfold contest four times per year (in which the work of 20 artists out of 400–500 applicants is displayed), as well as a separate annual magazine cover competition, and the entry fee for submitting three slides is $25 for each. *Manhattan Arts*' annual cover contest requests a $25 entry fee for submitting three slides, and *American Artist* also asks $5 per slide for its annual competition. For its part, *The Artist's Magazine* holds an annual contest (in which the work of 30 artists out of an average of 13,400 applicants is exhibited in the December issue), with each applicant paying an entry fee of $10 per slide.

The respective magazines do not keep track of how well these artists have done in terms of sales of work, commissions, opportunities to teach, or contacts from dealers, collectors, and museum curators resulting from the advertisements or exposure. Perhaps, the magazines themselves are the biggest winners. According to Sandy Luppert, manager of ancillary products and marketing for F&W Publications and the coordinator of *The Artist's Magazine's* art competition, the average applicant submits three slides. At $10 per slide, multiplied by the 13,400 applicants, the magazine takes in over $400,000 in entry fees, well in excess of the $16,500 in contest prizes awarded, payments to jurors, and other administrative costs related to the competition.

Not Every Honor Bestowed Upon an Artist Is Worth It

When does an honor become an insult to an artist? Perhaps when the honor represents a sizable loss of income or a diminution of the artist's reputation. It may be an honor, for instance, when an artist's work is selected out of a juried show for a purchase award, as this offers recognition and hard cash for the artist. However, many show purchase awards are in the hundreds of dollars—sometimes as low as just $100—whereas the artists may price their work much higher. Artists may find themselves in the awkward position of drastically discounting their work or trying to push the award sponsor to kick in more money or simply declining the award, which may alienate a prospective buyer in the process.

It may be an honor when an artist is asked to donate a work to a charity auction, which again increases artistic exposure and enhances his or her reputation as a good citizen. However, current tax law only permits artists to deduct on their tax returns the cost of materials for artwork they donate to charitable institutions, as opposed to the full market value of the art, which a collector may declare. Artists also may feel resentment over how little their work sells for at charity auctions—free dinners at restaurants tend to be more coveted, especially at mixed auctions, and that is often the price range for bidders at these affairs—and that they have somehow damaged their own market.

Artists must balance the interests of good publicity against a financial loss, and their decisions may change from one event to another. Joseph LaPierre of Palm Beach, Florida, turned down a $300 purchase award for a $700 painting at a show in Alabama, because "that award was sponsored by a major corporation, and they could have afforded the full price." However, he accepted another $300 purchase award at a show sponsored by the Art Guild of Ponce Inlet, Florida, "because that award was sponsored by a mom-and-pop business that put up the $300 as a way to help the cultural life of the community. With that kind of sponsor, I won't object to taking less."

In many smaller arts-and-crafts shows, purchase award sponsors are individuals or local businesses, who make their own selections rather than await the decision of a judge, and they usually look for artworks within the price range of their award. Local merchants pledge amounts ranging from $100 to $500 for purchase awards at the Roswell Fine Arts League National Show in Roswell, New Mexico, according to show chairman Richard Cibak, and these businessmen also pick the works for these awards. "It is often the case that the award may be considerably less than the market value of the work," he said, "and it is up to the sponsor of the award and the artist to negotiate a final price." It is likely that the chosen artists feel some pressure under the circumstances to cut their prices.

Purchase awards sponsored by museums are likely to be for larger dollar values, and there is also a résume value in being able to claim that one's work is in the collection of some major institution. In 1981, Howard Terpning of Tucson, Arizona, won the Prix de West purchase award from the Cowboy Hall of Fame in Oklahoma, receiving an amount that was "several thousand dollars less than what I thought the painting was worth, but it was a significant honor to win, and I didn't mind taking a little less." Subsequent events more than compensated for the loss of income, as Terpning won the 1990 Hubbard Art Award for Excellence, a purchase award worth $250,000 for the artist's entry ("Transferring the Medicine Shield") that was otherwise priced at $185,000.

Worse than accepting less than a piece is worth is being asked to give one's work away. Some smaller arts-and-crafts shows also have door-prize raffles, at which the winners receive a work by the exhibiting artists. Grumbling results from the pressure on exhibitors to donate their work for these raffles, which cuts into potential sales and may give the entire event a carnival-like quality. Charity auctions equally may raise troubling concerns for artists, who want to be supportive of a good cause but may not have the ready cash to donate. "Very often, I'll do a painting for some worthy cause, which my dealer could sell for a good amount of money, but the worthy cause turns out not to be a very good marketer of artwork," said Robert Bateman, a painter in British Columbia, Canada. "I may help out some conservation group, but you find that environmentalists don't have any money and my work sells for very little. This becomes a blot on my escutcheon. If I put someone up the flagpole and I don't get much of a salute, it can be a little bit embarrassing and diminish my reputation."

The problem, many artists find, is that once they make a donation of artwork to one charity, they are inundated by requests from others. "I can nickel-and-dime my career away with all these good causes," Bateman noted. Similarly, sculptor Glenna Goodacre found that "you give to one group and you get fifteen more requests the next week. People don't believe it when I tell them I don't have anything to give them." She and others pointed out that charity events are not sensitive to the tax disincentives for artists to give their work but see artists as having an inexhaustible supply of available merchandise. Also, charities return to the same artists again and again.

"The number of requests for donations of your work jumps up geometrically after you give once," photographer Nicholas Nixon said. "You find yourself on everyone's list. They sometimes treat you as though they're entitled to your work and, once you start to say no, they are not particularly sympathetic. Sometimes they sneer." Other artists have found the same to be true. "I get annoyed at the way you get asked again and again to give something," printmaker and sculptor Leonard Baskin noted, adding that "artists don't get a lot of feedback from the donation of works."

Artists handle this problem in different ways. Some donate a reproduction of their work or create a line of low-cost items. Sculptor Kent Ullberg, for instance, has a line of more affordably priced bronzes from which he may select a work for a charity auction, and Goodacre said that she does "a series of terra cotta plaques every year around Christmas, and those I give away. They're inexpensive to produce, and I don't mind the loss of income. I certainly don't give away my big, expensive pieces."

At some charity auctions, artists are allowed to establish minimum bids. This would ensure that the art is not sold unless the bidding reaches a certain amount, ensuring that the sale price does not have a deleterious effect on the artist's market and reputation. The National Museum of Wildlife Art in Jackson Hole, Wyoming, holds an annual "Western Visions" show of two- and three-dimensional miniatures, and all of the works (usually a hundred) are put up for sale at a silent auction at the conclusion of the exhibition. The artists set a minimum price for their work and receive between 60 and 80 percent of the auction proceeds, with the remainder going to the museum for collection conservation. This style of charity auction prevents works from selling below market value and, if the pieces do not sell at all, from becoming a public embarrassment to the artist.

Also at some charity auctions, artists are permitted to offer works for sale, donating the money earned (or a certain portion of that money) to the charitable cause, which they may deduct in full on their tax returns. George Koch, president of National Artists Equity, noted that "charity auctions should not pressure artists to offer their pieces but, instead, approach collectors rather than artists to donate works. Collectors can receive the full fair market value of the work as a charitable deduction on their taxes." Otherwise, he added, artists should try to gauge what their feelings will be if they see their work selling for relatively little money. "If the prospect of that is too painful, they probably should not donate their work."

A Pop Quiz

Who or what is an artist, and what makes an artist a professional? Neither question generates an easy answer but, perhaps, there are ways to approach them.

The United States government has answers for both questions; however, the answers contradict each other because different agencies are looking for specific kinds of information. The Census Bureau (whose data on artists is extrapolated by the National Endowment for the Arts), for instance, claims that there are something over 100,000 visual artists in the country. The decennial census asks at what job an individual worked on April 1, or what career activity occupied the largest portion of that day, and, for statistical purposes, the answer to this determines one's employment area. Someone who painted most of that day is a painter unless the respondent indicates otherwise.

The Internal Revenue Service, on the other hand, does not consider someone a professional artist—able to deduct art-related expenses from gross income on tax forms—unless that person made a profit on the sale of his or her work in three out of five years. The government, therefore, may deem someone an artist on one hand but a rank amateur on the other hand.

The art market may or may not provide answers to these questions. Certainly, there are many people who exhibit their artwork in galleries and in other art spaces; a portion of these people sell their work regularly, while others sell occasionally, or just enough to cover expenses, or sell rarely if ever. Anyone can sell something once, if only to a parent. Somewhere on this continuum one may want to place the idea of being a professional, or even being an artist at all, if it is decided that collectors define what art is through their purchases.

In addition, if sales define an artist or his or her professional standing, where does one place Vincent van Gogh, who only sold one or two paintings during his lifetime but was lionized as a towering figure posthumously? Was van Gogh an amateur in life and a professional in death?

Perhaps, an artist is someone who attains an art degree (a Bachelor or Master of Fine Arts, for example) from an art school or even teaches art privately or at a school. Many artists also belong to professional associations, such as a watercolor society or an artists union, which exist to help members' careers in some fashion. However, the lack of a market for their work may undercut the claims artists may make for themselves, regardless of where they studied, or where they teach, and to what groups they belong. Most faculty at art schools would have no other money coming in if they gave up their teaching.

Within that 100,000-plus group that the National Endowment for the Arts has defined, there is a wide spectrum of talents and marketability. Categorizing people in too fine a manner often results in numerous exceptions and contradictions. The twentieth-century view, first articulated by Marcel Duchamp, is that artists define themselves, with no other external forms of validation required. One might add to this that artists who behave professionally are professionals.

Part of being a professional is understanding, first, the variety of ways to exhibit and sell one's artwork, second, the value of joining an artist membership organization or society, third, what art schools look for in prospective faculty members, and, fourth, what the federal government requires for artists claiming art-related deductions. In fact, a number of profitless artists have successfully defended their deductions to the IRS on the basis of having made efforts to exhibit and sell their work, belonging to an artists' organization, earning an art degree or otherwise taking art classes, as well as teaching at an art school. Saving receipts and maintaining good records, these artists have been able to document the extent to which art is their vocation, and this process establishes them as professionals.

PART FOUR

Seeking Inspiration, Alone and in Groups

CHAPTER TEN

Finding Inspiration, Overcoming Frustration

The mythical view of artists has placed them in their studios or garrets, waiting for the Muse to inspire some great new idea or image. Were that the case, the wait could be a long one, leaving artists with little to do between brainstorms. In fact, most artists rely on good work habits to solve technical, aesthetic, or intellectual problems. These include maintaining a regimen of drawing or painting for a certain amount of time every day as well as pursuing certain ideas to their completion in the hope that they might lead to other, new and interesting concepts. In the mostly hands-on profession of art, inspiration comes from doing.

In Search of the Muse

No artist is free from dry periods or mental blocks, when the old ideas seem to lead nowhere and new ones are hard to find. There are really two aspects to this problem: The first is the feeling of having run out of ideas, which tends to be a very temporary condition; the second is a general lack of enthusiasm about creating art itself and losing a sense of what makes art exciting, which can be far more troubling. For artists who have established a market for their work, fear of negative criticism or turning off past collectors may also enter their thinking. "When I'm at an impasse," photographer Sandy Skoglund said, "I try to do whatever feels good. The internal satisfaction has to be the focus." That may be more easily said than done, as some methods work, others don't. Jackson Pollock, who was stung by criticism of his later work, largely gave up painting in the last few years of his life. Italian comic opera composer Gioacchino Antonio Rossini's mental block lasted for the better part of three decades, as he wrote almost nothing of any length or importance for the last half of his life.

Different artists have approached the problem in various ways. Pablo Picasso, for instance, periodically looked for rejuvenation in various media (ceramics, printmaking, sculpture, stage design) and subject matter (copying Old Masters, ancient Greek mythology). Painter Janet Fish "started doing watercolors as a way of loosening up my use of color. I had begun to find that subject matter had come to dominate my painting." Ben Shahn, who by 1950 felt trapped in the socially conscious work he had done in the 1930s and 1940s, took a teaching position at Black Mountain College in North Carolina, which proved stimulating to him. "Black Mountain was a very argumentative place. A lot of the abstract expressionists were there," said Shahn's widow, Bernarda Bryson Shahn. "It helped clarify his ideas, and his work also went in a variety of directions after that. He moved from just continuing on with the same subjects that had come out of the Depression—the poor, hungry, and homeless people—to more universal themes."

The search for a way out of a dry period may also lead to new ideas for artwork as well as energy for the task. Edward Hopper, who is best known for his paintings of urban life, lived most of the year in New York City but he frequently became restless there, unable to paint. His restlessness led him to travel around the country and to Mexico, subsequently yielding a sizable body of paintings devoted to people on trains and highways, at gas stations and hotels.

Painter Will Barnet, whose career is known for having undergone numerous stylistic changes, has also been prone to dry periods. Born in 1911, Barnet was a realist who focused primarily on social problems in the 1930s. His imagery became increasingly abstract by the early 1940s, and he again returned to realism by the late 1950s. "The dry periods came more during the early years," he stated. "There have been fewer since then. In the early years, they also lasted longer, sometimes up to a year. The problem always was that I wasn't quite sure how to handle my forms. I was searching for something elusive, and it took a while to find the key."

One of the things that helped him find that key was printmaking, first woodblock and later color lithography. It was a natural choice for Barnet, who had worked in the 1930s as a printer and taught graphic art for forty-five years at the Art Students League in New York City. "The flatness of the print, the solid blocks of color that you use, especially with the woodcuts, helped me get away from all the gradations of color, helped me get away from the realistic figure, to something more abstract." Barnet's interest in abstraction led to his participation in what was called in the 1940s and 1950s the "Indian Space" school of painting, which adopted imagery from the designs of the Mayans, Peruvians, and Native American tribes of the Northwest. "It was abstraction that wasn't so dependent on self-expression," he said. "You didn't only deal with yourself but with other, larger cultures."

By the late 1950s, Barnet had again reached a crossroads and was looking for a new key to painting, this time using more realistic, people-oriented subject matter. Like Ben Shahn, Barnet was also searching for a realism that went beyond social problems but he was unsure which themes held enough interest for him. Again, color lithography allowed him to experiment with ideas and techniques that he could take back to the canvas. "With prints, you are still drawing, still composing, still using color, just as in a painting," Barnet said, "but you can change the drawing or composition or colors in the print in a way that you can't with a canvas. The canvas is right there in front of your nose." He has continued to make prints from time to time, to sketch regularly and, until recently, to teach, all of which have provided him with a high degree of artistic stimulation.

Another source of inspiration, or an antidote to a dry period, has come from his fellow artists, seeing what they are doing, listening to the ideas they are pursuing, and talking with them about other artists and their work. "I'm not the kind of person who likes to live in the country all by myself," he said. "I'm a people person. I like to paint people, and I like to be with people. I like living in New York City for that reason."

A student of art history, Barnet also gained inspiration for new ideas from visits to museums, especially the Metropolitan Museum of Art and the Frick Museum in New York. Honoré Daumier and Juan Gris were early sources of inspiration for him—Daumier for his portrayal of the social condition of the poor and oppressed, Gris for his use of color and sense of cubist form—but, later, Barnet gained a new appreciation of the work of Jan Vermeer. "Vermeer could make a universe out of the corner of a room," he said. "I had been thinking about moving inside, from making paintings of people in the street—the old social condition stuff—to paintings of families, my family. A family is an interesting, organic thing. You can watch it start, as it grows and develops, and mark all the important changes that take place along the way. When I saw how well Vermeer could manage interior scenes, I gained the courage to try out what I had been thinking about."

While Barnet has remained interested in the art of the recent and distant past, which he calls "connecting up with art history," as a source of ideas, many other artists feel a bit more detached, or want to get away from the art of the past altogether. Photographer Mary Frey noted that she gets "solace and sustenance from looking at the work of artists of the past but, after all, I'm a contemporary artist and I need to find the work of contemporary artists. I think that my work has become part of a dialogue with contemporary art, and so it is more important to me to see what similar or not-so-similar things other artists are doing currently." Noting that a mental block indicates "something that you are trying to avoid," Janet Fish said that a dry period "can lead you to stop working entirely. As they say, when you fall off a horse, you have to get right back on the horse because, the longer you wait, the harder it becomes to get back on the horse. You just have to keep painting. Going to museums can easily become another way to avoid working. It certainly is that way for me."

For many artists, the act of creating a work of art is analogous to following a train of thought, developing and reworking ideas that may or may not come together to form a successful piece. A dry period may arise when artists have not pushed their ideas far enough or when a particular problem has already been solved—leaving artists only to repeat themselves. Janet Fish has found that her response to a problem in her work is to open herself to new ideas and experiences, and to keep working. "Sometimes, I work small when I'm not sure about what I'm doing," she said. "Better a little bad painting than a big bad painting." Fish noted that it is important to distinguish between a dry period, when problems in one's work need to be confronted, and just having a bad day, when nothing seems to go quite right. A particularly rough dry period can lead an artist to "do anything to avoid dealing with the painting." To her mind, the worst thing to do is "indulge in a dry period and let yourself quit working altogether. That way, you lock yourself into a mental block. If you get too polemical, or overly embroiled in a certain narrow idea, you can't go anywhere."

Finding New Inspiration, Creating New Art

Exactly how new styles and concepts in art are born may be the secret of creativity, a power of mind that doesn't become clearer to anyone through knowing that it stems from the right or left side of the brain. Innovation comes through trial and error, experimenting with ideas until something that is both distinct and personal is developed. Artists often develop some sort of moat that effectively distances them from the outside world, and most agree that they must in some way blind themselves to the real world to envision the unseen.

Painter Philip Guston consciously sought to avoid both contemporary and historical art as he prepared himself to start a new work. First, according to his New York art dealer David McKee, Guston would go out to some double feature, picking the trashiest movie he could find so that, by the time he got back to his studio, all the art history he knew and the knowledge of what other artists were doing would be obliterated. Then, he began painting something that he hoped wasn't imitative.

There are a lot of ways artists prepare themselves to begin a new piece, but they all know the fear Guston had. No one wants to express him- or herself in a work of art only to realize that Matisse did the same thing seventy years earlier. It is increasingly difficult for many artists to get around this problem—a large number of them work in universities and find themselves teaching to students the very stuff they are trying to forget when it's time to create. Since the early 1980s, the postmodern art-about-culture, as well as "appropriationism" (quoting of other art in one's own work) by some contemporary artists, reflects a wholly different attitude to this issue. To this newer generation of artists, creating in the Information Age does not always mean creating something original. Rather, creating art becomes defined as taking in data, processing or manipulating it, and feeding it back to the world. This reflects a greater faith in the external than the internal world, and it raises questions concerning how artists can create something that is new. The idea of "the new" itself is a modernist concept that many postmodernists reject.

Still, most artists believe that their personal viewpoint is of value, and that they can offer more than commentary on past images. Far more than reveling in their sources, artists over the past hundred years have frequently sought to distance themselves from, as well as reject, art that has influenced them. "History . . . is a nightmare from which I am trying to awake," James Joyce wrote, and the Italian Futurist F. T. Marinetti proclaimed in a manifesto, "Come on! Set fire to the library shelves! Turn aside the canals to flood the museums! Oh, the joy of seeing the glorious old canvases bobbing adrift on those waters, discolored and shredded!"

Attending trashy double features is one way to block out the rest of the world, but there are many others. "I generally clean the house a few times, or go shopping," noted painter/sculptor Lucas Samaras, "all sorts of stuff to wipe my consciousness clean of what everyone else is doing." "The further I get into my own books, the less capable I become of reading other people's works," author Judith Rossner said. "I read magazines, watch TV. Any stupidity is all right." Painter Larry Rivers also claimed: "I guess that I am guilty of setting up egotistical defenses against intrusions from the outside world from time to time. Every artist has to make himself a little stupid, a little blind, a little insensitive and a little arrogant—everything we don't want to be." For her part, painter Lois Dodd stated that her recipe is to "get myself some time and space to think, just clear my head of other stuff. Of course, I paint landscapes, and I can generate excitement from just going out into a landscape and looking around. I think it's harder to get excited when you are standing around in your studio."

Within a self-imposed solitude, most artists claim that the first construction, even before the work itself, is their identity that will create the art. The persona or vision is really what the art is about and, within this identity, the artists put their stamp on experiences. This personal voice gives the past a freshness and vitality that moves tradition into innovation.

New art opens one's eyes to the world in a new way—although the line between what is new and what is old is somewhat blurred, because newness is something measured in small degrees. Major breakthroughs are few, and they largely derive from already-existing genres, as Picasso's cubism is partially indebted to Cezanne and African art, and Kandinsky's abstract paintings owe much to the Fauvists. Artists make a small turn of the dial from what they know, and this moves the new work into its own arena—divorced from, yet carrying on, tradition. Tradition is not a forward-looking entity, and historians only discern it by looking backwards, for instance, identifying how photorealism derived from Pop Art, which itself grew out of the principles of dada, many of whose practitioners were greatly influenced by cubism. The approved artists of the nineteenth-century French academies, who denounced the Impressionists, thought of tradition as something to follow but, for most of them, it led nowhere other than obscurity. Artists of the past are silent unless those of the present give them validity through borrowing ideas and expanding on them.

Historians will show how something that looks new is actually part of a long line of development, but that ignores the fact that the art of our time still looks new to us. What an artist brings to a tradition is the present—a set of ideas, assumptions, and circumstances that gives every time period its distinct character—and this finally does wake us up, as James Joyce hoped, from what has gone on before. Contemporary art wakes us up to ourselves. "This history of art is all part of the baggage you take along as an artist," painter Chuck Close said. "I try to purge my work of other people, but there is no sense in reinventing the typewriter when you want to compose a novel. You are an artist because you turn what you have seen, and know, into something else."

Dealing with Criticism and Rejection

In the life of every artist, from the newest kid on the block to the most revered, there is far more rejection than acceptance and success. Juried competitions may not want one's work, private or public arts-funding agencies may not provide a grant to help create it, commercial art dealers may not be interested in displaying or representing it, critics or reviewers may ignore or pan it, and collectors may pass it by with only a glance (if that). Every artist must learn not to take rejection personally.

Making peace with the opinions of other people is a key element in the maturation process of an artist. Onlookers may make comments or ask questions that seem insulting: "What is that?" "Is that a horse?" "Can you do that in green?" "That might work over my sofa if you made it larger and more horizontal." Count to twenty before responding, whatever helps keep one's cool. Some artists are simply not temperamentally suited to selling their work directly, but that is the artist's problem rather than the collector's. Those with gruff personalities will have to put their careers entirely in the hands of dealers and other middlemen who can respond cordially to possibly tactless questions.

Feeling hurt or disappointed by the reaction of others is natural. Artists have to remain focused, however, both on their art and their career, and remember that the enjoyment of creating artwork—rather than proving something to someone else—is the reason they started in the first place. There may also be a degree to which the opinions and reactions of others may allow artists to look at their work from a different vantage point; perhaps, some changes are worth considering.

Beyond this, opinions are not static and judgments vary from one person to the next. Art competitions usually have different jurors from one show to the next, so there is always the likelihood that the subjective opinions of someone who rejected certain artists one year will not hold sway the next. Art dealers may decide against showing the work of a particular artist, not as a result of something's being wrong with the artwork but because (1) they already have too many artists in their stable; (2) the artist's work doesn't fit into the specific style (realist or abstract, for instance), media (photographs, watercolors, prints, drawings, and mixed media are often difficult to place and, as with works on paper, don't bring as much money), or theme (landscape, portraiture, regional artists, for example) of the gallery; (3) the artist is not of the stature of the other artists in the gallery; or (4) the artist does not have a sufficiently established market.

Artists are less likely to feel personally wounded when rejected by collectors and dealers (who represent the commercial side of the art world) than that of art show jurors, art critics, and museum curators (who theoretically inhabit a realm of pure aesthetics). Artists must keep in mind that these individuals aren't the final word on one's art—there is no final word—and that vindication often takes time. Alfred Barr, who for many years was the guiding intellectual force at the Museum of Modern Art in New York City, once stated that he felt vindicated if one contemporary work of art out of every ten that he acquired on the museum's behalf turned out to be validated by history as a good choice.

Art critics may seem to be more of an obstacle, as their tenure is generally longer. Few issues get artists as incensed as the subject of critics, and many artists have tended to build up the assumed power of critics to mythic proportions: Critics determine the market for art; art gallery goers decide what to.look at based on what was favorably reviewed; a negative review can ruin an artist's career; currying favor with a critic, perhaps even giving him or her an artwork, will get you on the critic's good side.

In reality, some critics do wield some power, while others do not. Theater critics, especially those in larger cities, are thought to have the most power—that is, the ability to make or break a show. The reason for this is not because their ideas about what constitutes good theater or good acting necessarily influence anyone reading them; rather, the cost of putting on a production may be so great that, if the backers fear that not enough theatergoers will fill the seats, they will close down a show early in order to cut their potential losses. Movie critics, on the other hand, have very little sway with the reading public. Consider the fact that certain actors—say, Sylvester Stallone—rarely if ever have received favorable reviews, yet so many of their action films rake in hundreds of millions of dollars. Probably, no critics have less influence than pop and rock music critics; radio and MTV airplay has far more to do with recording artists achieving popularity and brisk sales.

Art critics may have a bit more influence on their readers than film or pop music critics but not nearly as much as those reviewing theater. Beyond this, there are no documented instances of a critic irreparably damaging an artist's market or career. One recalls that many French art critics condemned the work of the Impressionists but Impressionism clearly triumphed and the words of its detractors have been long forgotten.

An art critic's role, as far as the interested public is concerned, is to indicate what is happening where, which is more in the line of straight journalism than opinion-making. For this reason, artists should make sure that they notify the newspaper or magazine well in advance about any upcoming exhibitions, and they should provide high-quality photographs of their work—black-and-white or color, depending upon the needs of the publication—for illustration. Getting one's name in the paper and, better yet, a picture of one's work, is what readers look for, because they are not nearly as likely to remember what the critic said as the fact that there is a current or upcoming exhibition they might like to take a look at.

This view contradicts what artists too often believe—that a critic's words are examined at length and revered by readers as gospel—and it also denies what critics themselves like to believe. Anyone who labors over words wants to believe that others will spend an equal amount of time thinking about those words. Deconstructivist critics have gone further, announcing that art itself is simply "text," which needs to be deciphered by a critic in order to be rendered intelligible to the public. It doesn't bode well for the artist, for instance, when critic Donald Kuspit writes that "it is inevitable that one acknowledge, however reluctantly—for both critic and artist—that 'the critic is artist,' in the fullest sense that the eroding idea of 'artist' retains. All the weight of meaning in the formula of their relationship is now on the critic rather than the artist." It serves the ego and the self-interest of certain critics to believe this, but only other critics of this bent and some impressionable (or insecure) artists will concur.

Counteracting the views of nonartists, a number of artists themselves have written art reviews, usually during the early stages of their careers. This exercise provides, perhaps, the fine artist's perspective on art and, in the process, makes the artist/critic known to the editors of publications that may someday publish articles about them. Sculptor Donald Judd and painters Peter Halley, Peter Plaegens, and Fairfield Porter all have written reviews of artists' exhibitions. Whether or not their criticism is superior, inferior, or no different than that of nonartist reviewers is open to debate. They certainly did not write about their own shows and, as soon as they have disparaged some other artist's work, they opened themselves up to the same sort of complaints all other critics hear.

Artists do expose themselves to public scrutiny and comment when they exhibit their work, and it certainly seems unfair to put themselves in that position only to have some critic render a negative judgment. However, critics also expose themselves publicly when they discuss and offer their opinions on an artist's work. Readers are perfectly able to determine whether or not a critic has exercised sound reasoning and shown sufficient knowledge or understanding. Critics don't simply say, "I like it," or, "I don't like it"; it is the explanations for their comments on which they are judged.

It is true that critics (and the public in general) may not understand what the artist is attempting to say in his or her artwork. Once a work of art is exhibited publicly, it is open to the ideas and interpretations of anyone who sees it; in effect, it no longer belongs to the artist in the sense that the artist is the final source of meaning but, rather, it becomes the property of the world. However they may want to, artists cannot control how their work is perceived. Critics are the most visible target of an artist's sense of, and frustration with, losing control. Artists certainly do not lose any of their power, because that power exists within the work itself, and someone else's opinions do not really affect what the artwork is.

It is best for artists to understand that, in all but the rarest instances, negative criticism isn't personal. Critics may write unfavorably about exhibits or artists because they prefer a different style or type of art—no single newspaper or magazine reviewer can be so knowledgeable and objective about all the art, past and present, which he is required to write about that he can comfortably judge it equally. As Lawrence Alloway, the critic who coined the term "Pop Art," has pointed out, most art writers are only interested in artists of their own generation, as "the critic's entrance into the art world also becomes a cut-off point."

Foundations, corporations, and governmental agencies that provide grants or commission art each have their own idiosyncratic way of deciding who gets what. It is best to keep in mind that more people, including artists and critics, have been historically unhappy with the selections so-called experts and judges have made than pleased with them. The "Salon des Refuses" in 1863, for instance, best known for introducing the world to Edouard Manet's painting "Le dejeuner sur l'herbe," was created by decree of the French government after the official salon (the Royal Academy of Painting and Sculpture) rejected a record 4,000-plus paintings. The Nazi regime in Germany, on the other hand, wanted to control public judgment on contemporary art, creating a hostile "Degenerate Art" exhibit of European modernist painting for people to scoff at while lauding other official art exhibitions, now-forgotten pictures of hardworking Aryan laborers and patriots.

Errors in judgment, of course, are not limited to Europeans. The federal government of the United States thought so little of the artwork created under the Federal Artists Project of the Works Progress Administration that it baled thousands of canvases (by such artists as Adolph Gottlieb, Jackson Pollock, and Mark Rothko), storing them in a mildewed state at a warehouse in the Flushing section of Queens, New York, and later selling them at an auction for four cents a pound to a junkman in 1944—the junkman and the antique dealers who bought canvases from him at $3 or $4 apiece all did much better than the government.

CHAPTER ELEVEN

Kindred Spirits

By the nature of their profession, artists tend to be loners who use solitude as a way of collecting their thoughts and finding the right visual means to express them. However, working in isolation for too long can prove personally wearisome and even become a detriment to one's art, as art is a form of communication with others and not solely a conversation with oneself. For this reason, artists over the centuries have frequently banded together in some way, meeting in particular cafés or studios to create or talk about their art or just commiserate together.

Increasingly, the tendency of artists groups is less to define a specific style of art than to provide encouragement, instruction, information, camaraderie, career assistance, or opportunities for exhibition and sale of their work. Throughout the country, there are hundreds of artist clubs, local, regional, and national societies for painters and sculptors, artist-run art spaces and cooperative galleries, as well as membership organizations that offer services to artists. They each have somewhat different reasons for being, and artists may select the groups that best meet their particular needs.

Support Groups for Artists

Artists have a variety of very tangible needs—among them, art materials, time to work, a studio in which to work, and a place to exhibit their work—and some less tangible ones, too. Inspiration (or one can just say ideas) and confidence in their own creativity are no less essential but are more difficult to discuss in a general way because these come from within. Where Jackson Pollock got the idea to wave a stick full of paint at a canvas on the floor, and how he allowed himself to exhibit these drip paintings are among the great questions of twentieth-century art.

The desire to create a supportive environment for creators has become more widespread since the early 1990s, as hundreds of artist support groups around the country have sprouted. In addition, a growing number of psychotherapists have begun to specialize in arts-related issues, leading groups or working with individuals. Although it cannot be guaranteed that one emerges a Jackson Pollock, artists may feel more understood, more like part of a community, and grow more confident in the pursuit of their art.

When she first moved to New York City from Alexandria, Virginia, in 1997, Barbara Ratchko was "lonely and wanted to be part of a group of other artists, to talk about what's going on with our work." In the classified section of the magazine *Art Calendar*, she found an advertisement from a woman in Manhattan who wanted to form that very type of group—"she also felt the lack of people to talk to," Ratchko said. "You feel very isolated in New York, too." Within a matter of weeks, Ratchko became part of a group of fellow women artists, talking about their work and their experience as artists.

Support groups for artists like this one pop up in various forms all over the country. They differ from "crit" groups in that the individuals are not specifically looking for critiques of their artwork from other members; they differ from associations in that they are not necessarily pursuing common economic interests; and they differ from societies in that they are not formed around the idea of staging an exhibition. Support groups focus on the emotional aspect of being an artist.

"There are a lot of feelings of isolation, of not being connected to a community, and we talk about what that's like and how we deal with it," said Rivkah Lapidus, a Somerville, Massachusetts, therapist who "facilitates discussions" of groups of artists and writers. Among the commonly brought up issues in groups are mental blocks to starting, or completing, an artwork, anxiety about exhibition, making time to make art, and seeing themselves as artists in a positive light. "With so many artists, their minds are hung up on suffering," said Linda Shanti McCabe, who leads support groups for artists in San Francisco. "We think that artists are starving, or addicted, or mentally ill, or it doesn't count."

Sometimes, artists' minds are "hung up" on some notion of perfection that, almost by definition, they are unable to attain. Their work must not be just good but important, significant, a breakthrough, and failure to reach these dizzying heights leads them to quitting trying. The writer Henry James, who himself worried that his own creations were mere escapism rather than a "gem of bright quick vivid form," identified such a character in his short story "The Madonna of the Future." The genius painter, Mr. Theobald, whose canvases were all blank, announces proudly, "'I may say with some satisfaction that I've not added a grain of rubbish to the world. As proof of my conscientiousness'—and he stopped short, eyeing me with extraordinary candor, as if the proof were to be overwhelming—'I've never sold a picture! At least no merchant traffics in my heart.'" While sympathizing with this painter, James knew that the craft of art required diligent practice: "The only thing that helps is to do something fine. There's no law in our glorious Constitution against that. Invent, create, achieve."

But where and how to start? A wide range of artists participate in one support group or another, but the majority are women between the ages of thirty and sixty. ("Women in their twenties may be just out of art school and don't know how isolated they are," said Karen Frostig, a teacher at the Massachusetts College of Art in Boston who has led several artist support groups.) Some groups may be women-only by design, such as the Women Artists Support Group in Florence, Massachusetts, whose founder, Rythea Lee Kaufman, noted a commonality of self-esteem issues for both women and artists. "Members let down their hair sooner, get genuine quicker, in a single-sex group than in one that's coed," she said. Other groups are often comprised exclusively or primarily of women by default, "because society stigmatizes men who ask for help," McCabe said. "Women are more likely to go to therapy or seek medical advice than men, and support groups follow that same pattern."

There are many ways in which an artists support group may be found. They may be listed on a bulletin board at an alternative or New Age bookstore, and some notices have been placed at food cooperatives, as well as at art supply stores. The alumni or career offices of art schools sometimes have information about them; on occasion, groups looking for new members advertise in an art magazine or they may be discovered through an Internet search engine. In certain instances, they come about spontaneously when one artist mentions the idea to another.

Within the support group itself a range of activities may take place. At the beginning of every meeting of the Women Artists Support Group, members engage in improvisational theater games, with the remainder of the meetings devoted to writing and sharing what they have written on the subject of isolation, creative blocks, or other specific issues. The creativity support groups run by Shawn McGivern at the Counseling Center for Artists in Arlington, Massachusetts, begins most sessions with visual relaxation exercises (based on Jungian principles), moving on to round-table discussions of members' "goals in their work and in their process of artmaking" and, occasionally, presentations by individual members of their work, which are followed by "feedback loops, which allow the person to articulate and others to make meaning," rather than critiques, "which cause fear," she said. Rivkah Lapidus's groups, on the other hand, sit in a circle and talk about the artwork individual members are pursuing (or want to create) and the struggles they have in accomplishing their artistic goals.

At A.R.T.S Anonymous, an organization with chapters around the United States, Europe, and Australia, there are weekly meetings following a regular pattern that is adapted for artists from the twelve-step model of Alcoholics Anonymous and focusing on "gaining control of the creative process," according to Claudia, regional facilitator for the Boulder, Colorado, chapter (last names are not used, similar to Alcoholics Anonymous). For the first week of the month, members may bring in artwork in progress and receive feedback if they wish. On the second week, members discuss the twelve steps of the program ("1. We admitted we were powerless over our creativity—that our lives had become unmanageable. 2. Came to believe that a Power greater than ourselves could restore us to sanity. 3. Made a decision to turn our will and our lives over to the care of God *as we understood Him* . . . ."). On subsequent weeks, individual members will describe what has been taking place in their lives creatively, or there may be a topic in which everyone may participate.

Artist's Way Groups

The largest network of artists support groups is The Artist's Way, which is also based on a twelve-step creativity recovery program formulated by Julia Cameron in her book (*The Artist's Way*) and workshops. Week One is "Recovering a Sense of Safety." Week Two is "Recovering a Sense of Identity." Week Three is "Recovering a Sense of Power." Individual groups, which are not licensed or sanctioned by Julia Cameron but have come into existence in order to follow her program in a group setting, pursue the twelve steps closely or with a wide degree of latitude, depending upon who has organized the group or its members. For instance, The Christian Artist's Way takes the basic structure of Julia Cameron's program but identifies the source of safety, identity, and power as God. (A second book by Cameron, published in 1996 and called *The Vein of Gold*, has also inspired a growing number of Vein of Gold groups, primarily composed of people who have been in Artist's Way groups.)

Support groups are usually defined as a number of people who congregate in order to talk about their experiences, assisting others as they describe their struggles with particular issues. However, in the electronic age, a growing number of groups communicate through e-groups and Web chat rooms, such as Artist's Way (*artistsway@yahoogroups.com*), Artist's Way Circle (*artistswaycircle@yahoogroups.com*), Artist's Way Discussion Group (*awdiscussion@yahoogroups.com*), Artist's Way graduates (*awgrads@yahoogroups.com*), The Artist's Way Recovery (*tawrecovery@yahoogroups.com*), The Christian Artist's Way (*tcaw@yahoogroups.com*) and The Well (*thewell@yahoogroups.com*). Some less Artist's Way–focused chat rooms may be found at Visual Artists Focus Group (*http://groups.yahoo.com/group/vafg*), Woman Made Gallery (*www.womanmade.org*), Art Women (*www.artwomen.org*) and Do While Studio (*www.dowhile.org*).

How a given support group is run depends on the consensus of its members or the person who is the designated leader. For some groups in a democratic art world, leadership can be problematic, while others find that a leader preserves focus. Artist's Way groups, which usually last twelve or thirteen weeks (new groups form after that), have a person in charge, but the overall format is determined by the teachings of Julia Cameron. There is no one leader of the Women Artists Support Group, and different members direct the activities at each meeting, whereas Rivkah Lapidus, Karen Frostig, and Linda Shanti McCabe all run their respective groups.

Because discussing emotional issues involving creativity (anxiety, creative blocks, fear, spontaneity) and related topics have brought everyone to the group, it is not uncommon that psychologists (or people who are quite interested in psychology) lead them. However, these psychologists are quick to claim that their role is not to run therapy sessions for artists. "When things come up, I'm there to offer psychotherapeutic frames," Lapidus said, "but I don't hit people over the head with overpsychologizing. I just want to lead the discussion."

Members of groups with specific leaders generally pay that leader a fee ($20 per one-and-a-half-hour session for Rivkah Lapidus, $195 for an eight-week group for McCabe), while leaderless groups may all chip in to rent a meeting room or simply meet at someone's home. "Groups that are led are safer, more focused, get to the issues, and translate the underlying issues more clearly than groups that are leaderless," said Karen Frostig. She noted that some members worry about revealing personal details, that individuals may go off on tangents that are extraneous to the group, and that hostility may arise within the group dynamic. "I try to monitor the safety of the group and keep people focused on why we all came together in the first place."

McCabe noted that charging members is beneficial in itself, since it ensures attendance and a positive approach to dealing with creativity issues. "If people don't pay, they don't show up," she said. "Or, they think, 'I didn't do anything important this week,' and they don't show up, but that's when they really should show up."

There is no requirement for Artist's Way group members to be visual artists, or composers, performers, writers, or involved in some other recognized art activity. One may be creative in every field, and "group members often include bankers, salesmen, teachers, housewives, lawyers, someone who runs a café," Cameron said. "The support you get is more diverse. It's better than a group of just painters, who may all agree that you can't show this-or-that kind of work. Someone in the group who isn't a painter and doesn't share the tribal assumptions of artists, may say, 'Well, why can't you show it, or show it somewhere else?' and that gets people to thinking about what they can do instead of what they can't."

Artist's Way groups are not franchised—run by teachers accredited by Julia Cameron or any institution—but are formed by people who have read and been moved by the book. Each group's makeup will be different, but they all follow the same basic tenets laid out in the book: There are "Morning Pages," in which one fills three pages with stream-of-consciousness writing in longhand (in order to overcome one's natural "censor" or "critic"); group members look for and assess their personal strengths and passions (to discover the type of creative work they individually seek to accomplish); and there is a "reframing" of past failures into current strengths (in order to learn from one's mistakes and "minimize one's aversion to risk").

While many Artist's Way groups are "peer-run," some are led by therapists and others who may charge a fee for running the sessions. Who leads the group, how it is led, and the fact of paying someone to lead may change in subtle or unsubtle ways the nature of the experience for group members. Mark Bryan, who cofounded the Artist's Way workshops with Cameron, noted that "groups that are led rather than convened are acceptable as long as they adhere to the principles outlined in the book. However, one should ask of everyone who teaches the Artist's Way groups, 'Have you been through the process and gained something from it?' and 'Are you currently involved in some creative endeavor?' The Artist's Way is supposed to be about a group dynamic that is nonhierarchical."

Bryan and others stress that there is a significant difference between Artist's Way and psychotherapy groups as the focus of the Artist's Way is on solutions rather than an airing of problems. "In psychotherapy groups, you are verbally processing thoughts and feelings," said Terrell Smith, a massage therapist in Boulder, Colorado, who has run Artist's Way groups since 1993. "In Artist's Way groups, we celebrate creativity together." Carol Floyd, a bookseller in Akron, Ohio, who has run Artist's Way groups intermittently since 1995, noted that there is less advice offered in an Artist's Way group than in therapeutic groups. "No one says, 'You ought to leave your husband,' or something like that," she said. "People offer each other options, saying something like, 'I know how you feel. My husband used to do that, and here's what I did.'" Some of the same issues may come up at an Artist's Way group as at a therapeutic group, Mark Bryan added. "An Artist's Way group won't solve a history of child abuse, but it may give one a voice in order to express it. The focus is how do you turn a complaint into a creative work."

As groups are not under the control of an organization, there is no one place to find an existing Artist's Way group. Some people who form groups take out advertisements in alternative newspapers or put up a notice at a bookstore where *The Artist's Way* is sold. One may write for information about how to form an Artist's Way group to Cameron's office—Power & Light, P.O. Box 1349, Taos, NM 87571, (505) 751–2156 or (505) 758–5424. There is an Artist's Way bulletin board on America Online, which may be found through the keyword "Exchange," then click on "Home/Health/Careers" and then "Support Groups," scrolling down for "Artist's

Way" (much of the information consists of Julia Cameron's schedule of workshops). One may also make a Web site search, using keywords "Artist's Way" or "Arts" or "Julia Cameron." Some Artist's Way groups on the Internet discuss individuals' problems and solutions, following the program as much as possible.

A.R.T.S. Anonymous

Before writing her book, Julia Cameron attended meetings of A.R.T.S. Anonymous, a group founded in 1984 that similarly focuses on overcoming mental blocks and other reasons that artists' lives are out of balance. A.R.T.S. Anonymous—P.O. Box 230175, New York, NY 10023, (212) 873–7075, *www.pagehost.com/arts*—modeled specifically after Alcoholics Anonymous and other twelve-step programs, is designed to help artists who are "addicted to avoiding their art" for one reason or another, according to Jill F. (the last names of twelve-step program members are always limited to an initial), the organization's executive director. "Basically, the person's relationship with art is not as they would wish. They may avoid their art—we refer to the 'anorexia of avoidance,' in which people martyr themselves to their art—while some people do art night and day, neglecting their jobs and families. Some people who come to our meetings simply have no community in the art world, and others want to be involved in a spiritual program."

There are between eighty and a hundred meetings of A.R.T.S. Anonymous in existence at any one time; they may be found in most major cities in the United States. Just as with the Artist's Way, A.R.T.S. Anonymous offers members a "safe" place to discuss their desire to create art, free from critiques and other judgments and with no promises of fame or fortune as artists. Members are "encouraged to create art on a daily basis—that's our road to sobriety," said Abigail B., the founder of A.R.T.S. Anonymous, who describes herself as a painter/sculptor/writer. "I have talents in many areas. We all have a basket of gifts."

Many A.R.T.S. Anonymous members also have a basket of problems, as the majority of them previously have been through other twelve-step programs, Abigail B. noted. Jill F., for instance, had attended Alcoholics Anonymous and Al-Anon meetings before joining this program, and others are veterans of programs to combat overeating, drug abuse, and more. "They have other problems," Abigail B. said, "and they come to A.R.T.S. Anonymous because they have found that twelve-step programs work."

Having a specific leader, or following Julia Cameron's book, or the catechism of A.R.T.S. Anonymous is useful for many peer groups, which "often fall apart in a short period of time when they have no guidelines for dealing with conflict between members," said Dale Schwartz, director of the New England Art Therapy Institute, where artists are treated individually and in guided support groups.

Support for Practical, Creative, and Personal Issues

"The primary reason that people come to us is because they are so isolated as artists," said Ivan Barnett, a Santa Fe, New Mexico, sculptor who, with two other people (a psychotherapist and a financial advisor), runs the support group Artist's Solutions, reachable at 2202 Camino Rancho Siringo, Santa Fe, NM 87505, (505) 471–1014.

"Someone may not have a burning problem or a question; they just want to be in a place where there's another artist. And, when you're in an artists' mecca like Santa Fe, that's really saying something about why we're needed." He noted that while some people talk about mental blocks at Artist's Solutions meetings, as they do at gatherings of Artist's Way and A.R.T.S. Anonymous, "that's not all we talk about. Some people want ideas on how to get their artwork into a gallery—very nuts-and-bolts stuff. Other people want to network and just make friends."

Barnett called the Artist's Way concept "too therapeutic in its approach," but noted that the reason Artist's Solutions has a psychotherapist codirector is because "some people's problems are of a psychological nature." Distinguishing between specifically creative problems (such as a mental block) and issues not peculiar to artists (a personality disorder, for instance) is not a simple matter. Perhaps, a mental block is the result of deep-seated trauma or the inability to overcome a reproving parent, and overcoming the block may be only the first step in resolving another problem. Treating the symptom is not the way to gain mental health, which may occur when personal problems are treated as artistic ones. One's background and how one generally deals with problems are what leads an individual to either a support group or to a therapist in the first place, and it may be just the treatment of a problem that differs from one to another. Artist support groups, such as Artist's Way, are about "creating the nurturing environment that makes it possible to be creative," Cameron said, but they won't cure personal trauma. In fact, Carol Floyd noted, someone in an Artist's Way group who describes a significant psychological problem "will be directed to get professional help outside the group."

A number of therapists around the United States work with artists of all disciplines and media, either in support groups or as individual clients, and one may find them through the associations to which they belong, such as the American Psychological Association—750 First Street N.E., Washington, DC 20002, (202) 336–5500, (800) 964–2000, for tie-line to state psychological associations—and the American Art Therapy Association, at 1202 Allanson Road, Mundelein, IL 60060, (847) 949–6064, *www.arttherapy.org*, for state chapter groups). A third organization whose members offer relevant help is the Performing Arts Medicine Association: c/o Dr. Ralph Manchester, 250 Crittenden Boulevard, Box 617, Rochester, NY 14642, (716) 275–2679. The association's resource directory includes mental health professionals who work with visual as well as performing artists. All of these associations provide lists of appropriate therapists in one's area.

Art therapy and therapy for artists are not synonymous. Art therapy uses artmaking activities as a way to help people describe their feelings when they may not be able to express them in words, and it has been frequently used for trauma victims and children. However, it is the understanding of both how images reflect an artist's feelings and the artistic process in general that leads artists of all media and disciplines to art therapists for counseling and support. The major drawback to art therapy as opposed to other mental-health practitioners is that most art therapists are not covered by insurance.

"Most art therapists have artist patients," said Beth Gonzalez-Delinko, an art therapist and president of the New York Art Therapy Association. "Some artists can't do purely verbal therapy and are more comfortable with their images than with words. Through examining their work—the use of space, the subject matter, color—you can discover the artists' personality." She added that, in general, artists come to therapy for the same reasons that most other people seek out a therapist—relationships and family issues.

Dale Schwartz noted that it is not important whether the people taking part in her creativity groups or in one-on-one sessions are professional or amateur artists, as "artmaking becomes a metaphor for increasing consciousness of our own patterns. The art activities we do allow participants to go deep within themselves for renewal and regeneration in their own expression." As in Artist's Way, creativity has a larger meaning than the completion of a work of art, and the approach is forward-looking, rather than at one's history or childhood. There are instances, however, when Schwartz works with artists on specifically art-related concerns, such as an art project that has become overwhelming to the individual "or how to regain their artistic inspiration."

Many other mental health practitioners who are not specifically art therapists also may examine artwork as part of their work with artists. "The biggest problem with artists is that they are nonverbal and, consequently, you don't see many of them as patients," said Hyman Weitzen, a psychiatrist in Miami, Florida, who has treated a number of artists over the years, frequently using their artwork in place of talking therapy. One of Jackson Pollock's psychiatrists, Joseph L. Henderson, also made artwork a substantial element of his sessions, writing later: "Since he was extremely unverbal, we had great trouble in finding a common language and I doubted I could do much to help him. Communication was, however, made possible by his bringing in a series of drawings illustrating the experiences he had been through. They seemed to demonstrate phases of his sickness."

Richard Rice, a psychiatrist in Northampton, Massachusetts, who also has a master of fine arts degree in sculpture, also noted that he encourages his patients to draw (or write a poem or a song), because "these images come from their feelings, which is what you're really trying to get at. I don't have to interpret the images too much but just let the patient talk about the images and see where it goes." The particular image itself may only be important in itself as a starting point for a discussion. "The patient and I are trying to tell a story, and the images are markers or signifiers in that story."

Many in the mental health field follow a psychological definition of art. According to Jay Harris, a New York psychiatrist, "art is a resolution of conflicts, and in a work of art we see both the conflict and the way in which it is resolved. When I look at my artist patients' work, I see how they resolve conflicts in their art and, by extension, in their lives."

Artists frequently worry that, through a therapists' tinkering with their personalities, their art will be significantly and irrevocably altered. Rice pointed out that "some artists are afraid that, if they resolve some conflicts, they won't have anything left to do their artwork with. I've generally found that getting some help for your problems has never hurt anyone and is usually helpful." Still, there is the famous example of German Expressionist Oskar Kokoschka, who, for the time he was a patient of Sigmund Freud, painted pictures of flowers. Jay Harris also noted that the colors of one of his patient's paintings began to reflect his office decor, which is beige. Looking around his office, he said, "I think it looks nice."

RESOURCES

Support Groups for Artists

A.R.T.S Anonymous
P.O. Box 230175
New York, NY 10023
www.pagehost.com/arts

For Information on Forming Artist's Way Groups

Julia Cameron
Power & Light
P.O. Box 1349
Taos, NM 87571
(505) 751–2156
(505) 758–5424

Artist's Solutions
2202 Camino Rancho Siringo
Santa Fe, NM 87505
(505) 471–1014

American Psychological Association
750 First Street N.E.
Washington, DC 20002
(202) 336–5500
(800) 964–2000 for tie-line to state psychological associations

American Art Therapy Association
1202 Allanson Road
Mundelein, IL 60060
(847) 949–6064
www.arttherapy.org

Performing Arts Medicine Association
c/o Dr. Ralph Manchester
250 Crittenden Boulevard, Box 617
Rochester, NY 14642
(716) 275–2679

CHAPTER TWELVE

Artist Societies and Artist Communities

Many artists look for others with whom they can create art. "Most of our members join for the 'paint-outs,' when people get together once a week and paint," Maxine White of the Delta Watercolor Society of Stockton, California, said, adding that ten members on the average are on hand for the weekly "paint-out" sessions. The approximately seventy-five members of the society get together for the five annual business meetings, which usually include painting demonstrations by outside professional artists, as well as for the three annual member exhibitions that take place at a local bank.

At the New Rochelle (New York) Art Association, the Iowa Watercolor Society, and the Shenandoah Valley Watercolor Society, the emphasis is less on creating together than on talking about one's work with other artists. "People are pretty isolated out here," Jo Myers-Walker, a past president of the Iowa Watercolor Society, said, "and we exist so that people don't feel they're completely alone. When I was president, I was contacted by members who called up to say 'I've done a really good painting today.' They just needed someone they could talk to about it."

Both the Iowa Watercolor Society and the New Rochelle Art Association provide newsletters to their members in order to keep them abreast of news in the field, such as which member is having an exhibit where and providing tips on techniques. Once a month, the New Rochelle group holds meetings that give its 150 members a chance to talk about their own work as well as watch a demonstration by a professional artist. The group's four members' shows and large annual juried competition provide additional opportunities for members to discuss what they and others are currently doing. For its part, the Iowa Watercolor Society schedules a week-long workshop during its annual juried exhibit for members to learn from a professional artist.

The monthly meetings of the Shenandoah Valley Watercolor Society are intended to provide support and technical advice to artists in the group, according to Mary Ann Baugher, a past officer of the group. Members often bring in their paintings for group critiques; those who have recently attended a workshop will discuss what they learned; and, on occasion, an art professor will be invited to speak to members. Baugher noted that she also belongs to the Virginia Watercolor Society. "They have an annual juried show, which is very good, but there really is no opportunity to meet fellow members," she said. "Meeting other members and talking about their work is what a lot of us need and want."

Most clubs and societies hold at least one exhibition per year, perhaps featuring the work of members or juried competitively, and this is another compelling reason for someone to join. Singly, an artist may not find a venue in which to exhibit his or her work but, in a group that sponsors its own shows, there is a chance for personal recognition and the prestige that may be attached to the particular society. Eligibility and membership costs for artist clubs and societies vary widely. The New Jersey Watercolor Society is an older organization (founded in 1940) and generally has stricter guidelines for jurying work into its exhibitions than the Garden State Watercolor Society (began in 1969) but, according to Elizabeth Roedell, past president of the Garden State group, the greater opportunity for artists to show their work is its main attraction to members. Some societies allow all comers, while others require jurying in or a different kind of admissions process. The Shenandoah Valley and Delta watercolor societies, for instance, permit anyone to join, requiring only the annual dues of $25 and $18, respectively. Membership in the Suffield, Connecticut–based Academic Artists Association, on the other hand, requires acceptance into two of the group's juried exhibitions within a four-year period as well as the $15 annual fee.

There are three levels of membership to the Florida Watercolor Society, starting at associate membership, "which can be anyone who is a Florida resident and wants to pay $20 to be a member," James Koevenig, a past president of the organization, said. A participating member, who is allowed to vote for officers, policies, and venues for the society's annual juried exhibition, must have had one painting in a juried show. A signature member, one allowed to use the society's initials (FWS) after his or her name, must have been accepted into three juried exhibits. Signature membership in the Kentuckiana Artists Pastel Society, on the other hand, requires artists to earn at least ten points, and these may be earned retroactively: Inclusion in a local fine art exhibit is one point, two points for a regional art show, three for a national art exhibition, and four for an international show (none of these are necessarily Kentuckiana shows); additionally, one may earn one point for being an active member in the society, two points for being an officer.

The use of the signature letters after one's name is more likely to carry weight for those artists who are members of recognized national, as opposed to regional or local, societies. The National Sculpture Society, for example, is a well-recognized association of artists from all over the United States who work in a variety of styles and materials, while the Cowboy Artists of America and the National Academy of Western Art—both of which offer signature letters to members—are more regional in focus and specific in content.

Both the American Watercolor Society and National Watercolor Society divide their members into two levels. The National Watercolor Society has both associates and signature members—the first group may join without jurying, paying $30 a year and receiving the society's newsletter, the second ($40 a year) requiring acceptance into the society's annual exhibition and then an additional jurying of three more paintings—while the American Watercolor Society has sustaining associates and active members. At the highest levels, members are permitted to include AWS or NWS after their names for professional purposes.

The National Academy of Design also has two levels of membership, both of which include signature privileges: The first is an associate member (ANA), who is proposed by a current associate and approved in an election by at least 60 percent of the entire associate membership; the second is an academician (NA), who is chosen from the associates and elected by 60 percent of the academicians. Unlike the national watercolor societies, no jurying of individual works of art or acceptance into past or current annual exhibitions is part of the entry process.

Members of the major regional and national groups claim that signature initials confer stature upon an artist and may help advance one's career. "The National Watercolor Society is a very prestigious organization, and the jurying in is so strict that to be able to put NWS after one's name is really a feather in one's cap," Meg Huntington Cajero, a past president of the society, said. "The letters NWS matter to dealers who would be more inclined to represent an artist with them, knowing that the artist has been seen as having attained a very high level of skill and accomplishment, and dealers would point out the 'NWS' to potential collectors." Ed Gallagher, director of the National Academy of Design, also stated that "it is worthwhile for an artist to let others know how he is esteemed by others."

The degree to which signature letters appended to one's name aids an artist's career is not fully clear. James Koevenig noted that a juror for a watercolor competition is often selected on the basis of that person being a member of either the American Watercolor Society or the National Watercolor Society, but many art dealers have little reason to believe that signature letters help a sale. "We've shown artists, some of whom put the letters AWS after their names, and we've shown other artists who didn't put those letters in or may not even have been members of an organization or society, and it never seems to have made a bit of difference," Jo Chapman, owner of the Chapman Gallery in Santa Fe, New Mexico, said. "Someone may look at the signature letters and ask, 'What does that mean?' and then I explain it to him, but with most collectors, if they like something, they like something."

Lawrence diCarlo, director of the Fischbach Gallery in New York City, stated that signature letters don't mean anything to his collectors or to himself, and Frank Bernarducci, director of Tatistcheff and Company, another New York art gallery that represents artists who work in watercolor, claimed that all the signature letters may do for artists is "help keep their egos under control, perhaps." Painter Will Barnet, who is a national academician as well as a member of the American Academy of Arts and Letters and the Century Club but does not use any of these signature letters after his name, said that the letters "have more of a human value than they are a benefit to one's career. It means something to me personally that other artists have accepted my work, but it doesn't matter to people who buy my work."

The larger regional and national societies do attract more people to their annual juried exhibitions, and they contain a higher percentage of professional artists—including those who live off the sale of their artwork as well as full-time art instructors—than smaller and more local groups and clubs. The larger societies offer little to no social interaction among members, however, unless one happens to meet at the annual shows. Artists seeking more support and camaraderie would be better off looking closer to home.

The only problem in this is that one may more easily find out about the larger regional and national groups than the smaller, more local ones. *American Artist's* annual spring and fall watercolor issues contains an up-to-date listing of the major watercolor societies in the United States and Canada, along with contact information and upcoming exhibitions. Yet more information on watercolor and other painting associations is available through various Web sites, such as World of Watercolor (*www.worldofwatercolor.com/artassoc.htm*) and makART (*http://makart.com/artlink/stwcs.html*). The International Sculpture Center—1050 Potomac Street N.W., Washington, DC 20007, (202) 965–6066—a service organization for sculptors as well as craftspeople, performance artists, and video artists, has an 11,000-member mailing list that includes local and regional sculpture societies in the United States and around the world—the center will provide information on applicable societies for free. There are no specific sources about societies devoted to oil painting, printmaking, or other art media.

Local, state, and federal arts agencies can provide information on art clubs and societies in one's area; for names, addresses, and telephone numbers of these agencies, contact Americans for the Arts, 927 15th Street N.W., Washington, DC 20005, (202) 371–2830, or the National Assembly of State Arts Agencies, 1010 Vermont Avenue N.W., Washington, DC 20005, (202) 347–6352, *www.arts-usa.org*. However, arts funding agencies are most likely to have information on groups that have previously applied for funding rather than general lists of all the clubs and societies in their domain. It is worthwhile noting that, although some of these organizations have post office box addresses, most are located at the home of the current president, and that job is usually rotated annually. One may have to make a few telephone calls before ascertaining the group's current headquarters.

Since most of these clubs and societies do eventually hold member or juried exhibitions, the venues for these shows—banks, arts centers and galleries, museums—will be able to provide contact people for the organizations. One may find out where these shows take place from editors of local newspapers that list such events. Of course, one would not wish to join any group blindly; those who are interested in being part of an artist club or society should visit the organization during a meeting or view a show that it has organized to determine whether or not one feels comfortable with the kind of work being done and the people in the group.

Artists societies fulfill a number of roles for their members. The juried exhibitions themselves establish and maintain a level of quality that acts as a goad to members, especially since full membership is often dependent upon being accepted in a certain number of shows. Certainly, the opportunity to meet other artists is valuable, although (as noted above) get-togethers are more customary with local art groups than with statewide, regional, or national organizations. The Florida Watercolor Society's annual weekend convention is "the only chance for members to meet," said another past president, Margaret Mills. Meeting other members is even less likely in societies that specialize in certain subject matter (marine art, equine art, or portraiture, for instance) or media, since members may be scattered all over North America. In these groups, the Web site, newsletter and other mailings, as well as the annual show, may be the principal link between members.

Joining such a group may be comparable to taking part in a cause—the cause, in this case, is increasing the visibility of the artwork or medium. "I wouldn't be where

I am today if it hadn't been for the Colored Pencil Society," said Janie Gildow, who lives in Arizona and has been a member of the Illinois-based society for years. "I felt like the lone wolf out there. I didn't think anyone else used the colored pencil." She credited the society with heightening the art world's acceptance of the medium. Another society and former board member, Bernard Pulin of Ottawa, Canada, stressed the group's role in advocating for "more lightfast, more professionally oriented" materials to manufacturers. "When you're selling a product," he said, "you want it to last for years and years. Because of research that the Colored Pencil Society conducted, which helped create a standard for manufacturers of colored pencils, pencils now do last longer than they did in the past."

For listings of national and regional watercolor and pastel societies, see the Resources section at the end of this chapter.

Miniature-Art Societies

Most art clubs and societies have rather loose rules for membership. Academic Artists Association of Springfield, Massachusetts, for instance, clearly looks for traditional realists, while other groups may specify the medium, such as sculpture or watercolor painting. Their aim is to bring in as many people as possible rather than be exclusive—with the exception of selecting people who meet a certain level of artistic quality. Some groups, however, such as the miniature-art societies, have very strict guidelines.

There are several societies of miniature artists in the United States—in Florida, Georgia, New Mexico, Pennsylvania, and the District of Columbia—and these groups establish the rules of what a miniature is. They define miniature art, specifying the image size of a two-dimensional work to be no greater than twenty-five square inches and the largest dimension of a sculpture eight inches. They also all have a "one-sixth" rule: The image—say, a man's head—must be one-sixth the actual size of the object; larger than that disqualifies the image as a miniature. There is also an "outside-the-frame" rule for two-dimensional works—the size of the total work, including the mat and frame—that varies from one society to the next. The Washington, D.C., group only permits the entire work to be six-by-eight inches, while Florida increases that to eight-by-ten inches. In the somewhat fussy field of miniatures, the rules all have their ardent supporters and critics. The British Hilliard Society of Miniaturists' rules state that "a head (as in a human portrait) should not exceed 5 centimetres (2 inches). . . . One loose definition [of a miniature] is a painting that can be held in the hand. . . . The Hilliard Society constitution states that paintings as a rule should not be larger than 5 – 7 inches, and portrait heads no larger than 2."

The purpose of these societies is not only to bring like artists together and provide an opportunity for exhibiting a particular type of artwork, but to improve the reputation of the miniature. After the development of photography in 1839, when the camera began to produce the portraits that had been the miniature artist's major activity for over a thousand years, the field of miniatures became thought-of as an eccentric novelty.

As a result, the market for miniatures has been relatively small. Many collectors tend to see miniatures as fun and decorative but not necessarily as serious art for which they should pay serious art money. Margaret Wisdom, who is secretary of the Miniature Art Society of America, noted that most art galleries also show no interest in exhibiting these works. Among the reasons for this is the fact that they would have to raise prices—currently averaging between $35 and $100 per object—considerably, to cover their own commissions, and that would turn off potential customers. Affordability tends to be a major consideration, because no collector buys just one painting to hang on the wall—a wall of any size would swallow up a tiny picture. Buyers frequently purchase five, or ten, or more, grouping them together to fill up the space that a larger picture would cover. Affordability also tends to work against artists in the miniature field, as hardly any are able to make a living from selling only miniatures.

Most self-supporting artists who create miniatures, in fact, earn their livelihood from larger, more expensive artworks that may not sell as quickly but bring in far more money. "It's a challenge," said Connie Ward Woolard of Silver Springs, Maryland. "It's a whole different approach than what I otherwise do, which is very large. It appealed to me to try something very, very tiny." Her miniature acrylic-on-watercolors-paper scenes of barns, Victorian houses, small-town street scenes, and landscapes range in size from one-and-a-half-by-one-and-a-half inches to four-by-six inches, while a mural she orchestrated on Courthouse Square in Rockville, Maryland, measured ninety feet long and ten feet high. To Woolard, miniatures represent "a break from other, paying projects."

Art gallery owners have also expressed reluctance to handle miniatures because of the difficulty in providing adequate security for tiny objects. "Miniatures are also very easy to steal, and that also concerns dealers," Wisdom said. "You can put one into your pocket and walk right out the door. Dealer can solve that problem by wiring the work to the wall or putting the work under glass, but that is an additional problem that most normal-sized artwork doesn't face."

The larger art world has also not tended to take miniatures seriously because of the low prices and the fact that many miniature paintings are sold with little brass easels for display on coffee tables—more frequently sold by interior decorators than through art galleries. There are some art galleries around the country that handle miniatures, although most collectors tend to follow the arts-and-crafts shows that either specialize in or include miniatures as a special category. The miniature-art societies themselves have helped foster sales for members by sponsoring annual exhibitions, and many artists join these groups—frequently more than one society—simply in order to have a place to show these works to the public. Richard Haynes, who belongs to the miniature-art societies of Florida and Georgia, noted that "you get to put three works in a show if you're a member, as opposed to only one piece if you're a nonmember." Residency in a particular state is clearly not a factor in membership.

Prices tend to be higher at the shows than at most galleries, sometimes reaching several thousand dollars per work, because the best work by the nation's top miniaturists is there. There is no directory of galleries representing miniatures, or of arts-and-crafts shows featuring these works. The best way to find out where these galleries or shows are is by reading the newsletters of the various societies.

The most common forms of miniatures in the crafts field tend to be utilitarian objects—although, of course, they are too small to be actually used—such as ceramic vases, jewelry, painted cigarette and jewelry boxes, and wooden furniture. This utilitarian focus has meant that these objects are sought after for dollhouses and, in fact, the main market for miniature crafts has been at dollhouse shows, which take place at various venues around the country. (Among the best sources of information for upcoming dollhouse shows are the monthly publications *Art Calendar* and *Sunshine Artists.*)

An added benefit of belonging to one of the miniaturist societies is having a group of fellow artists with whom to compare notes on such matters as which materials are best for painstakingly small work and how to handle some of the physical discomforts of miniature work. For instance, some artists use jewelers' caps, which contain a magnifying lens and a lamp, to enable them to see what they are doing; as it is an unwritten rule of miniature societies that the object must look as highly detailed under a microscope as to the naked eye, the ability to work with great precision is essential. Obviously, a miniature painter must forget about broad brushstrokes and have a delicate hand with a firm wrist. The traditional techniques of working small in paint are hatching (using fine lines to indicate shading), pointillism (dots), and stippling (dots, in a more generic sense), and this requires rather small brushes with tiny, fine points. Jane Mihalik, a painter in Basye, Virginia, needs an ongoing supply of new brushes with few bristles, while Louis Stern of Washington, D.C., prefers "small watercolor or acrylic brushes," even though he paints in oils, "because you can't get that much of a point in an oil brush."

Artists who create miniatures in other media must simply be careful or inventive. Bob Best of Great Falls, Virginia, whose miniature collages are three by five inches, has a "drawerful of tiny scissors" and otherwise makes use of tweezers to hold the image he is cutting out or pasting down. Margaret Wisdom, who fashions miniature animal motif sculptures in ceramics and wood, has used dental tools or whittled twigs in order to fashion her own tools for carving and shaping.

Working small may be more physically taxing than working large. Get-togethers of miniaturists frequently lead to conversations about work-related ailments and methods to relieve them. "Working this small gives me headaches," said Richard Haynes of Fairfield, New Jersey, whose oil and watercolor paintings average three-by-three-and-a-half inches in size. "After a long day of painting—and I put in some very long days—I can't focus on the TV in the evening. I listen to it and watch the colors. By morning, everything is back in focus again, thank God." Jane Mihalik agreed, noting that "it's very tough on the back. You have to be very still, sort of scrunched over. After a little while of this, I need a heating pad, or my husband will have to give me a back massage."

Nature and Wildlife Art

There are many different genres in the art world, all with their own societies, rules, and venues. As with the miniature-art societies, acceptance into juried exhibitions enables one to apply for membership, and membership confers a broader recognition among would-be collectors. To apply for associate membership into the American Academy of Equine Art, for instance, "you must have been accepted into three shows," said Werner Rentsch, president of the group. "For full membership, you must be a full-time practicing artist who paints horses, not just a landscape painter who includes a horse now and then." Other organizations, such as the Cowboy Artists of America and the Society of Animal Artists, make no requirements of having been in previous shows but make their decisions on the basis of the strength of the applicant's submitted slides as well as, in the case of the Cowboy Artists, history of earnings from selling western art in the realistic style of Frederic Remington and Charles Marion Russell.

Acceptance into one of these societies does not make an artist's career, but they reflect the place that one has earned in the eyes of his or her peers, which may bolster an artist's standing with the buying public. These groups also have newsletters, meetings, and other ways of keeping members abreast of opportunities and events in their fields. Magazines, such as *The Equine Image*, *Southwest Art*, *U.S.Art*, and *Wildlife Art*, are also devoted to these genres and frequently include the main galleries in the United States where these types of work are sold to the public, while R. R. Bowker's *Official Museum Directory* lists the institutions that specialize in showing these works.

The main societies of specialty artists in the United States are listed in this chapter's Resources section.

Artists' Communities

Over the centuries, the reputation of artists as a group has gone up and down. Plato looked down on them for creating inferior representations of the higher world, while Renaissance popes sought out their company. Artists have been adored as the antidote to the industrial world and scorned as nihilistic, self-absorbed bohemians. Their stock seems to be on the rise these days, however, as more and more individuals, groups, and institutions have been offering artists places to live and work at a growing number of artists' communities.

These communities, or colonies, invite artists—sometimes of one type, such as writers, or a multidisciplinary mix of fine artists, composers, writers, choreographers, and architects—to spend a period of time (weeks, months, years) devoted exclusively to pursuing their art. Artists' communities usually are located in a rural setting, removed from the distractions and unrelated concerns that keep artists from being fully productive.

"It's always a puzzle how to support artistic creativity," said David Macy, director of the MacDowell artists' colony in Peterborough, New Hampshire, one of the oldest artists' communities in the United States. "With the termination of National Endowment for the Arts fellowships to individuals"—in the mid–1990s, a result of political controversy over some of the fine artists to which the federal agency gave awards—"there has been a yearning on the part of many people to become involved in the support of creativity, beyond just writing a check to some organization and volunteering."

Some of the people who have founded new communities are artists themselves, making available land, studio facilities, and housing for other artists to use. Ann Sam, a painter in Millboro, Virginia, for example, is in the process of turning a three-hundred-acre dude ranch into a summertime artists' community called "RoundTop," starting in 2002, in part "because the landscape and quiet has always inspired me" and "because I really like to be around other artists." Similarly, Helen Chellin, who noted that "my own background is in art," opened Red Cinders Creativity Center in Hawaii in 2001, because "I have always been interested in communities."

Elsewhere, a Scandinavian-born painter, sculptor, and writer who goes by only one name, Neltje, and lives in Banner, Wyoming, opened a colony—the Jentel Artist Residency Program—in 2001, where (in 2003, when it becomes fully operational) six artists at a time come for one-month stays during six months of the year. The heirs of Lillian E. Smith, a writer who operated a longtime summer arts camp for girls in Clayton, Georgia, turned her residence and grounds into an artists' community in 1999. "We didn't want the land to be sold and developed into a Swiss Chalet or housing development," said Nancy Smith Fichter, director of the colony and niece of Lillian E. Smith. "All of the branches of the family agreed that we would be serving her memory best by turning this into a place where artists can get away from day-to-day responsibilities. The one short commodity for artists is peace and quiet, where they can do their work."

The new artists' communities have expanded the notion of what these places are and do. Some communities invite a group of artists, while others may bring in just one at a time. Some communities subsidize the artists' residency in full or in part, while others are run as full-priced bed-and-breakfasts that also welcome artists. There are communities that focus on professional artists, and others that largely operate workshops for serious amateurs. Most communities require artists to apply (fill out an application form, submit slides of work, references, and a statement of what they are working on and how they would benefit from the opportunity), but not all have outside jurying committees to evaluate the applicants' work and needs (Ann Sam said, "I'll pick from the applications").

The Alliance of Artists' Communities (255 South Main Street, Providence, RI 02903, *www.artistcommunities.org*), a membership organization of art colonies, used to have more specific guidelines for its member communities but, in the past few years, has "broadened our membership criteria to accept and include any organization that supports creativity," according to Cheryl Young, chair of the Alliance. "It just seemed ridiculous to split hairs. If people can go somewhere and just be artists, does it really matter that the setting is a bed-and-breakfast instead of a MacDowell-type colony?"

Colony Life

Opened in 1906, MacDowell is one of the longest-lived continuously operating artists' communities, and it has long set the benchmark for what an art colony is and does. Set in rural New Hampshire, far removed from urban distractions, fine, literary, and performing artists live and work together for three months at a time. It's actually difficult to get in touch with someone at The MacDowell Colony, since none of the artists' rooms or studios have telephones, and colony rules prohibit anyone from entering an artist's studio uninvited during the main 9:00 a.m.–5:00 p.m. work period. Literary readings, performances, exhibitions, and just talk itself tend to happen on an ad hoc basis, arising from the mix of people who happen to be in residence at any one time. In addition to the rule about visiting other artists, residents are also not permitted to come and go as they please. They may ask permission to leave the compound for a few days, if there is a notable holiday, family emergency, or some other problem, but otherwise the artists in residence are expected to willingly cut themselves off from the outside world.

Artists pay a $20 application fee, but otherwise their stay at MacDowell (room, board, studio space) is free; they are responsible for providing their own working materials, but even the cost of getting to and fro Peterborough may be covered by the colony's foundation if they apply and are approved for financial assistance. MacDowell's annual budget is $1.8 million—half of which is derived from income on its endowment and the other half is raised annually from grants and contributions—and the total cost of housing, feeding, and maintaining the facilities for the 225 artists who come to the colony each year is $220 per artist per day.

The approach of other artists' communities varies slightly or widely from the MacDowell model. The Millay Colony in Austerlitz, New York, and Djerassi Resident Artists Program in Woodside, California, both invite fine, literary, and performing artists for expense-paid residencies, but the residencies are only one month long. A distinguishing element at Millay is that there are no application fees. The Stonehouse Residency Program at Miramonte, California, which gives preferences to applicants who are visual arts faculty members at colleges and universities, also offers month-long residencies with free living and studio space but requires a $300 payment to cover the cost of food.

The Fine Arts Work Center in Provincetown, Massachusetts, provides seven-month-long residencies, which include free apartments and studios, but food is the responsibility of each resident. However, artists are given a monthly stipend of between $450 and $650 (the amount dependent upon how much money the colony has raised) for food, supplies, and personal items. A distinguishing characteristic of the Center is the fact that, whereas other artists' communities select fine artist residents based solely on slides of their work, this colony arranges a time for finalists to bring in their actual work to the site (either New York City or Provincetown) where the jurors will make the selection. Also, while the Fine Arts Work Center does not permit residents to leave for more than a few days, with the exception of the holiday season, artists may take jobs in the area in order to earn more money. Some artists, for instance, work as substitute teachers at the elementary school, noted Hunter O'Hanian, executive director of the Center. "There's not a lot of employment in the Provincetown area, but we understand that seven months is a long time, and people need to get out of the studio." Additionally, he added, residents might need more money to pay their student loans or "the rent on the apartment they left behind."

Seven months is also a long time for artists with families to be away, and the Center permits residents' families to live at the colony as well. The MacDowell Colony does not allow family members, and neither does the Alden B. Dow

Creativity Center of Northwood University in Midland, Michigan, which also prohibits pets during its ten-week summer residency term: "We want them to concentrate on their projects during their ten weeks, without the distraction of family, job, whatever," said Liz Drake, assistant director. One of the more generous colonies, Alden B. Dow provides each of its four residents with a one-time $750 stipend while there (to cover the costs of a project), another $350 every two weeks (for food and personal items), a two-bedroom apartment, studio space, and up to $500 for round-trip travel.

Artists' communities without sizeable endowments or foundations are more likely to ask residents to pay a higher percentage of their costs. The suggested daily fee at the Virginia Center for the Arts in Sweet Briar is between $30 and $75, while the Contemporary Artists Center in North Adams, Massachusetts, charges $400 per week ($200 for accommodations, $200 for use of a studio), and residents are responsible for their own food. Perhaps the costs involved are the reason that residencies at these colonies are usually shorter than at MacDowell, Alden B. Dow, or the Fine Arts Work Center.

Moving more into the bed-and-breakfast side of the artists' communities realm, one finds costs of $149 or $199 per night, depending upon the room, at Vitosha Guest Haus in Ann Arbor, Michigan, and either $491.20 or $691.40 per week at The Writers Retreat in Florence, Colorado. Working space is provided for residents, but artists are on their own for lunches and dinners.

The Alliance of Artists' Communities estimates that approximately 4,000 artists attend an art colony annually, a small fraction of all of the people who would like to go. Between 550 and 600 artists apply every year to Djerassi, of which only 60 or 65 are selected. While only four are picked out of the 200 applicants to the Roswell Artist-in-Residence Program in Roswell, New Mexico, the Atlantic Center for the Arts in New Smyrna, Florida, has a 30 percent acceptance rate. Nearly 1,000 artists seek a residency at Yaddo in Saratoga Springs, New York, and between 190 and 200 are chosen—the number fluctuates, because, while the average stay is five weeks, there is no set residency period, and artists may stay for between two weeks and two months at a time. At most artists' communities, the selecting jurors change from one year to the next, which may give hope to artists who are rejected one year that they might be picked the next.

There are a variety of benefits (and a few negatives) of these communities to artists. On the most basic level, artists are afforded the time and space to work, unimpeded by other concerns. Steve Levin, a painter and instructor at Williams College in Williamstown, Massachusetts, noted that he completed twelve works while at Roswell in 1998–99, more than double the number he would normally create while balancing his teaching responsibilities and home life. Within a community, artists are surrounded by like-minded peers with whom they can discuss ideas and their work, and many artists report becoming stimulated to work more productively in that environment—"it's a competitive quality in the best sense," David Macy said. There is also a network value to being around other artists, many of whom are otherwise employed by colleges and universities, since the friendships made at an artists' community may lead to a job. Steve Levin championed an artist that he met at Roswell for a teaching position at Williams College, and now the two are working together.

While offering the chance to work without distractions is the aim of all artists' communities, none keep tabs on anyone to ensure that work is being done. Different artists respond to this freedom in different ways, most taking the opportunity to work hard. Some people find the pressure to be productive quite intense, and they work too hard and burn out within a month.

Other artists find the secluded colony locations and the lack of diversions to be claustrophobic. "Some people are very much city types, thriving on things to do and phone calls," writer Peter Viereck, who has had residencies at MacDowell, Millay, and the Virginia Center for the Creative Arts, said. "Hart Crane needed loud jazz music to write his poetry; that would drive me crazy. But you do get people coming to these colonies who spend their time playing cards or ping-pong, maybe talking about their art but not doing anything. They come here and think, 'Golly, now I've got to be creative. What do I do?' For some people, that could be the kiss of death."

He added that there are also "colony bums" who go from one colony to the next, less for the desire to have the time and space in which to work than because they are professors on sabbatical who "line up one colony after another" to fill up the year. These people, he stated, tend not to do very much work and "by the second or third colony have lost their freshness."

Artist communities also get their share of repeaters who are invited back year after year—almost 40 percent of those who go to Yaddo, for instance, have been there before—although an increasing tendency is to bring in new faces, representing more women, minorities, and a geographical mix. The Fine Arts Work Center has a reputation of inviting "emerging" artists, while past credentials play a larger part of the selection process at MacDowell and some others. A valuable general source of information about these communities may be found in the directory *Artist's Communities*, published by Allworth Press.

There are many reasons, however, why artists' communities are not for everyone. Often, artists spend a week trying to get used to their surroundings and the freedom before getting down to work. Colony staff members also try to spot people who seem lost and to help them get on track. Most do, but some don't, or not completely. Those people generally leave early.

Both sculptor Mary Frank and painter Jules Olitski left Yaddo before their respective residencies were up; she because "it was a difficult time in my life and I found it hard to settle down to work, especially since I didn't know what kind of work I wanted to do," and he because "it was not my studio. It was not my air, not my choice of whom I was talking with or listening to. It wasn't a problem with Yaddo—Yaddo was fine, it was a lovely setting and everything was taken care of—but a personal thing at that time in my life. I did a little painting there, but it didn't really work for me. I found myself doing more writing than painting, writing a short novel about a lesbian witch."

When sculptor and installation artist Allyn Massey took up residence at Jentel during March 2001, she found the waist-deep snow and how far away she was from everything a drawback, because of the difficulty in obtaining materials she needed for her customary work. "It was the remoteness that had been appealing to me," she said, "but it did make it hard for me to work." She lasted the full month, creating watercolors. "I learned a lot about constellations while I was there; I learned a lot about birds, too. I saw cows calving. All night long, you could hear the bellowing of cows."

The kind of person who may benefit from an artists' community is someone who has something specific to do or who simply needs unfettered time to pursue ideas. "It takes about a week to adjust from what you came from to having everything done for you, but then your work really gets going," Benny Andrews, a painter, said. "People serving you food, leaving you alone when you want. Man, I could get used to that."

Resources

National and Regional Watercolor Societies

American Watercolor Society
47 Fifth Avenue
New York, NY 10003

Mid-Southern Watercolorists
6219 Cantrell Road
Little Rock, AR 72207

Midwest Watercolor Society
126 East Wing Street
Box 253
Arlington Heights, IL 60004
www.watercolors.org

National Society of Painters in Casein and Acrylic
969 Catasaugua Road
Whitehall, PA 18052

National Watercolor Society
915 South Pacific Avenue
San Pedro, CA 90731

New England Watercolor Society
146 Benvenue Street
Wellesley, MA 02482

Northeast Watercolor Society
Box 10582
Newburgh, NY 12553

Northern Plains Watercolor Society
P.O. Box 9724
Rapid City, SD 57709
www.npwatercolors.com

Northwest Watercolor Society
2224 S.W. 150th Street
Seattle, WA 98166

Rocky Mountain National Watermedia Society
c/o The Foothills Art Center
809 15th Street
Golden, CO 80401

Society of Watercolor Artists
P.O. Box 9504
Fort Worth, TX 76147

Southwestern Watercolor Society
3813 Indian Trail
Destin, FL 32541

Watercolor West
P.O. Box 213
Redlands, CA 92373

Western Federation of Watercolor Societies
6020 East Territory Drive
Tucson, AZ 85750

State and Local Watercolor Societies

Alabama
Watercolor Society of Alabama
P.O. Box 43011
Birmingham, AL 35243

Alaska
Alaska Watercolor Society
P.O. Box 90714
Anchorage, KA 99509
(907) 346–2712

Arizona

Arizona Watercolor Association
P.O. Box 37071
Phoenix, AZ 85069
(602) 943–6265
www.watercolor.org

Contemporary Watercolorists of Arizona
4010 East San Juan Avenue
Phoenix, AZ 85018

Northern Arizona Watercolor Society
30 East Vista Road
Sedona, AZ 85252

Southern Arizona Watercolor Guild
P.O. Box 145
Tucson, AZ 85752
www.watercolor-sawg.org

California

California Gold Coast Watercolor Society
P.O. Box 6485
Ventura, CA 93006

California Watercolor Association
P.O. Box 4631
Walnut Creek, CA 94596
http://californiawatercolor.org

Central Coast Watercolor Society
349 Zogata Way
Arroyo Grande, CA 93420

Coachella Valley Watercolor Society
71–225 Aerie Road
Palm Desert, CA 92260

Los Padres Watercolor Society
5441 Palace Court
Santa Barbara, CA 93111

Marin County Watercolor Society
364 Via Casitas
Greenbrae, CA 94904

Monterey Peninsula Watercolor Society
4059 Sunset Lane
Pebble Beach, CA 93953

Santa Clara Valley Watercolor Society
713 Gail Avenue
Sunnyvale, CA 94086

San Diego Watercolor Society
2400 Kettner Boulevard
San Diego, CA 92101
(619) 338–0502
www.sdws.org

Santa Cruz County Watercolor Society
1605 38th Avenue
Capitola, CA 95010

Stanislaus Watercolor Society
1409 Entrada Way
Modesta, CA 95355

Valley Watercolor Society
P.O. Box 8584
Calabasas, CA 91372

Watercolor Artists of Sacramento
Horizons, Inc.
Sacramento Fine Arts Center
5330-B Gibbons Drive
Carmichael, CA 95608

Colorado

Clear Creek Watercolor Society
P.O. Box 205
Empire, CO 80438

Colorado Watercolor Society
10467 West Arkansas Place
Lakewood, CO 80232

Pikes Peak Watercolor Society
P.O. Box 62693
Colorado Springs, CO 80962

Western Colorado Watercolor Society
P.O. Box 3584
Grand Junction, CO 81502

Connecticut

Connecticut Watercolor Society
P.O. Box 1313
Farmington, CT 06034

District of Columbia

Potomac Valley Watercolorists
6650 Barnaby Street
Washington, DC 20015

Washington Watercolor Association
2401 Jackson Parkway
Vienna, VA 22180

Florida

Florida Keys Watercolor Society
8042 Porpoise Drive
Marathon, FL 33050

Florida Suncoast Watercolor Society
3406 Wilderness Boulevard East
Parrish, FL 34219

Florida Watercolor Society
18104 Havenswood
Brooksville, FL 34610

Gold Coast Watercolor Society
2795 Hackney Road
Weston, FL 33331

Jacksonville Watercolor Society
10 10th Street
Atlantic Beach, FL 32233

Miami Watercolor Society
13626 S.W. 1
Miami, FL 33186

Palm Beach Watercolor Society
P.O. Box 1916
Boca Raton, FL 33429
(561) 496–0707

Tallahassee Watercolor Society
P.O. Box 38502
Tallahassee, FL 32315
www.freenet.tlh.fl.us/Watercolor/

Georgia

Georgia Watercolor Society
420 Walmart Way
Dahlonega, GA 30533
(770) 889–3713

Hawaii

Hawaii Watercolor Society
P.O. Box 22404
Honolulu, HI 96823

Idaho

Idaho Watercolor Society
HCR 1 Box 393
Tensed, ID 83861

Illinois

Great River Watercolor Society
1515 Jersey Street
Quincy, IL 62301

Illinois Watercolor Society
P.O. Box 482
Glenview, IL 60025

Lakes Region Watercolor Guild
5740 Regency Court
Gurnee, IL 60031

Indiana

St. Joe Valley Watercolor Society
P.O. Box 54763
Merrifield, IN 46544

Wabash Valley Watercolor Society
Wells Community Cultural Center
P.O. Box 57
Dayton, IN 47941
(765) 423-WVWS
http://dcwi.com/~wvws/

Watercolor Society of Indiana
11054 Spring Mill Lane
Carmel, IN 46032

Iowa

Iowa Watercolor Society
5509 Forrest Drive
Des Moines, IA 50311
or
822 East Williams
Ottumwa, IA 52501
(515) 684–6997

Kansas

Kansas Watercolor Society
P.O. Box 1796
Hutchinson, KS 67504

Kentucky

Kentucky Watercolor Society
P.O. Box 7125
Louisville, KY 40257
www.kentuckyartists.com/kws/index.html

Northern Kentucky Watercolor Society
1324 Old State
Park Hills, KY 41011

Louisiana

The Hoover Watercolor Society
530 Atkins Street
Shreveport, LA 71104

Louisiana Watercolor Society
P.O. Box 850287
New Orleans, LA 70185
E-mail: *lawatercolor@insideneworleans.com*

New Iberia Watercolor Society
143 West Main Street
New Iberia, LA 70560

Maryland

Annapolis Watercolor Club
202 Sharon Drive
Pasadena, MD 21122

Baltimore Watercolor Society
713 Stoney Spring Drive
Baltimore, MD 21210

Michigan

Michigan Water Color Society
240 West Maplehurst
Ferndale, MI 48220

South Western Michigan Watercolor Society
167 Dunham Drive
Battle Creek, MI 49015

Minnesota

Central Minnesota Watercolorists
7012 43rd Avenue S.E.
St. Cloud, MN 56304

Minnesota Watercolor Society
4011 Chicago Avenue South
Minneapolis, MN 55407

Northstar Watercolor Society
2610 Valley View Drive
White Bear Lake, MN 55110

Mississippi

Mississippi Watercolor Society
1336 Rice Road
Madison, MS 39110
www.mississippiwatercolor.org

Missouri

St. Louis Watercolor Society
P.O. Box 158
St. Louis, MO 63026
www.stlws.org

Missouri Watercolor Society
1406 Kenwood Drive
Fulton, MO 65251
(573) 642–6410
www.mowsart.com

Montana

Montana Watercolor Society
2517 Briggs
Missoula, MT 59803

Nevada

Nevada Watercolor Society
P.O. Box 27224
Las Vegas, NV 89124
(702) 393–6192
www.watercolorsociety.com

New Jersey

Essex WaterColor Club
41 Ellers Drive
Chatham, NJ 07928

Garden State Watercolor Society
6 Queens Lane
Pennington, NJ 08534
(732) 329–8232

New Jersey Water Color Society
Contact: Dot Ganek
125 Rynda Road
South Orange, NJ 07079
E-mail: *NJWCS@aol.com*

New Mexico

New Mexico Watercolor Society
P.O. Box 26084
Albuquerque, NM 87125
www.flash.net/~nmws

Taos Society of Watercolorists
P.O. Box 1872
Taos, NM 87571

New York

Aquerelle Club
41 Highfield
Glen Cove, NY 11542

Brooklyn Watercolor Society
1551 East 29th Street
Brooklyn, NY 11205
(718) 789–2545
www.bws.org

Cazenovia Watercolor Society
8933 Syracuse Road
Cazenovia, NY 13035

Central New York Watercolor Society
114 Juneway Road
Syracuse, NY 13215

Niagara Frontier Watercolor Society
25 Marvin Court
Hamburg, NY 14075
www.nfws.org

Upper Hudson Valley Watercolor Society
P.O. 70
Corinth, NY 12822

North Carolina

Blue Ridge Watermedia Society
P.O. Box 223
Lake Junaluska, NC 28745

High Country Watermedia Society
P.O. Box 1177
Newland, NC 28657

Watercolor Society of North Carolina
P.O. Box 163
Louisberg, NC 27549
(252) 975–1555
www.ncneighbors.com/954/

North Dakota

Red River Watercolor Society
4419 Oak Creek Drive
Fargo, ND 58104

Ohio

Central Ohio Watercolor Society
307 West Granville Road
Worthington, OH 43085

Mahoning Valley Watercolor Society
5025 Lockwood Boulevard
Youngstown, OH 44511

Northwestern Ohio Watercolor Society
1018 Brookley Boulevard
Toledo, OH 43607

Ohio Watercolor Society
1537 Briarwood Circle
Cuyahoga Falls, OH 44221

South Eastern Ohio Watermedia Society
817 Shinmek Street
Zanesville, OH 43701

Western Ohio Watercolor Society
3207 Annabelle Drive
Dayton, OH 45429

Oklahoma

Oklahoma Watercolor Association
11 South Broadway Drive
Edmond, OK 73034

Oregon

Watercolor Society of Oregon
9841 S.E. King Way
Portland, OR 97226

Pennsylvania

Pennsylvania Watercolor Society
379 Sandhill Road
Hershey, PA 17033

Philadelpha Water Color Club International
P.O. Box 1639
Media, PA 19063

Pittsburgh Watercolor Society
Center for the Arts
6300 Fifth Avenue
Pittsburgh, PA 15232

Rhode Island

Rhode Island Watercolor Society
Armistice Boulevard
Pawtucket, RI 02861
(401) 726–1876

South Carolina

South Carolina Watercolor Society
712 North Pittsburgh Street
Kennewick, WA 99336
(509) 783–3055

Tennessee
Tennessee Watercolor Society
7413 Huntland Drive
Knoxville, TN 37919

Texas
Central Texas Watercolor Society
P.O. Box 21686
Waco, TX 76702

El Paso Watercolorists
10526 Townwood Avenue
El Paso, TX 79932

San Antonio Watercolor Group
P.O. Box 17383
San Antonio, TX 78217

Society of Watercolor Artists
P.O. Box 9504
Fort Worth, TX 76147
(888) 273–2999

Southwestern Watercolor Society
74523 Wellesley Avenue
Garland, TX 75044
(972) 495–0579

Texas Watercolor Society
318 Twisted Wood
San Antonio, TX 78216
(210) 496–9249

Watercolor Art Society
601 West Alabama
Houston, TX 77006
(713) 942–9966

Watercolor East Texas
219 Parker Road
Nacog, TX 75961

Watercolor Society of South Texas
8102 Greenslope Drive
Austin, TX 78759

West Texas Watercolor Society
Box 370
Slaton, TX 79364

Utah
Utah Watercolor Society
P.O. Box 581005
Salt Lake City, UT 84158
(801) 266–1006
www.utwatercolor.com

Virginia
Central Virginia Watercolor Guild
500 Court Square
Charlottesville, VA 22902

Chesapeake Bay Watercolorists
7206 Newport Avenue
Norfolk, VA 23505

Shenandoah Valley Watercolor Society
Box 942
Bridgewater, VA 22812

Virginia Watercolor Society
P.O. Box 403
Roanoke, VA 24003

Washington
Eastern Washington Watercolor Society
P.O. Box 1701
Richland, WA 99352
www.cbvcp.com/ewws

Southwest Washington Watercolor Society
Box 2876
Vancouver, WA 98668

Spokane Watercolor Society
3419 South Saxon Court
Spokane, WA 99203

Wenatchee Watercolor Society
1122 Foothills Lane
Wenatchee, WA 98801

West Virginia
West Virginia Watercolor Society
560 Old Fairmont Pike
Wheeling, WV 26003

Wisconsin
Oriental Watercolor Society of Wisconsin
9919 West Green Tree Road
Milwaukee, WI 53224
(414) 353–9187

Wisconsin Watercolor Society
2025 East Newberry Boulevard
Milwaukee, WI 53211
(414) 964–7581

Wyoming
Scotch and Watercolor Society
P.O. Box 9551
Casper, WY 82609

Wyoming Watercolor Society
615 South 5th Street
Lander, WY 82520

Pastel Societies

Alabama
Alabama Pastel Society
1943 Brewster Road
Birmingham, AL 35235
(205) 856–8770

Arizona
Arizona Pastel Artists Association
President: Mr. Kerry Hughes
5755 N. 3rd Avenue
Phoenix, AZ 85013

California
North San Diego County Pastel Society
www.pastelsociety.com/index.htm

Pastel Society of San Diego
Box 80523
Central Post Office
San Diego, CA 92138

Sierra Pastel Society
P.O. Box 1557
6130 Lynx Trail
Pollack Pines, CA 95726

Colorado
Boulder Pastel Painters Association
P.O. Box 20185
Boulder, CO 80308
www.copaintersalliance.com

Pastel Society of Colorado
P.O. Box 3145
Grand Junction, CO 81502
www.pastelinternational.com/showcase/pscol/

Pikes Peak Pastel Society
P.O. Box 2443
Colorado Springs, CO 80901

Connecticut
Connecticut Pastel Society
Box 3006
Holland, MA 01521
www.pastelinternational.com/showcase/connps/

Florida
Pastel Society of North Florida
9620 Sunnybrook Drive
Navarre, FL 32566
www.pcola.gulf.net/~jimfew/psnf.htm

Georgia
Southeastern Pastel Society
6525 A.C. Smith Road
Dawsonville, GA 30334

Illinois
Midwest Pastel Society
6343 D.N. Claremont
Chicago, IL 60659

Kansas
MidAmerica Pastel Society
7503 West 54th Terrace
Overland Park, KS 66202
www.midamericapastel.org

Kentucky
Kentuckiana Pastel Society
2775 Big Bend Road
Battletown, KY 40104
(270) 497–4637
www.oneway.com/kaps

Louisiana
Degas Pastel Society
1202 Main Street, Apt. A
Madisonville, LA 70447

Maryland
Maryland Pastel Society
P.O. Box 54
Riderwood, MD 21139
www.marylandpastelsociety.com

Massachusetts

Pastel Painters Society of Cape Cod
P.O. Box 489
Barnstable, MA 02630
(508) 362–1256
www.capecodpastelsociety.com

Michigan

Great Lakes Pastel Society
P.O. Box 16775
Grand Rapids, MI 49516
www.glps.org
www.pastelinternational.com/showcase/glps

Minnesota

Lake Country Pastel Society
2192 1st Street
White Bear Lake, MN 55110

Missouri

Gateway Pastel Artists
9400 Banyon Tree Court
St. Louis, MO 63126

Ozark Pastel Society
535 South Chicago
Bolivar, MO 65613

Nevada

The Nevada Pastel Society
1775 Montessouri Street
Las Vegas, NV 89117
www.pastelinternational.com/showcase/nps/

New Jersey

Associated Pastelists on the Web
473 Marvin Drive
Long Branch, NJ 07740
www.artshow.com

Oil Pastel Association/United Pastelists of America
P.O. Box 374
Stockholm, NJ 07460

New Mexico

Pastel Society of New Mexico
P.O. Box 3571
Albuquerque, NM 87190
www.swcp.com/psnm
www.pastelsocietynm.org/psnm

New York

The Pastel Artists Group
P.O. Box 397
Skaneateles, NY 13152

Pastel Society of America
15 Gramercy Park South
New York, NY 10003
(212) 533–6931
www.pastelsocietyofamerica.org

North Carolina

Pastel Society of North Carolina
c/o UniqueOrn Enterprises
111 Roberts Street
Carrboro, MC 27510
(919) 933–9312
http://pastelsocietyofnc.com

Oregon

Pastel Society of Oregon
P.O. Box 105
Roseberg, OR 97470
www.pastelinternational.com/showcase/pso/

Texas

Austin Pastel Society
P.O. Box 26768
Austin, TX 78755

Central Texas Pastel Society
P.O. Box 3448
Temple, TX 76505
(254) 773–2286

Lone Star Pastel Society
P.O. Box 30294
Amarillo, TX 79120
www.pastelinternational.com/show case/lonestar/

Pastel Society of El Paso
5959 Sixta Drive
El Paso, TX 79932

Pastel Society of the Southwest
P.O. Box 670689
Dallas, TX 75367

Pastel Society of the West Coast
1016 Grand Avenue
San Francisco, CA 94080

Utah
Pastel Society of Utah
4300 So. 3760 West
West Valley, Utah 84120

Vermont
Vermont Pastel Society
681 Willow Brook Lane
St. George, VT 05495

Virginia
International Association of Pastel Society
P.O. Box 2057
Falls Church, VA 22042
(703) 241–2826
www.pastelinternational.com

Washington
Northwest Pastel Society
6619 132nd Avenue, N.E.
Kirkland, WA 98033
or
1420 N.W. Gilman Boulevard
Issaquah, WA 98027
www.nwps.org

Canada
Pastel Society of Canada
P.O. Box 3396 Stn D
Laurier Avenue West
Ottawa, Ontario K1P 6H8
Canada

Pastel Society of Eastern Canada
56 Ainslie Road
Montreal, Quebec H4W 1X6
Canada
(450) 667–9508
www.pastelinternational.com/showcase/psec/

Pastel Artists of Ontario Canada
3019 Britannia Road
RR#2
Milton, Ontario L9T2X6
Canada
www.pastelartists.com
www.pastelinternational.com/showcase/pao

Miniature Art Societies

United States
Cider Painters of America
35 Main Street
Dallas, PA 18612

Miniature Art Society of Florida
Jeanne Boyers
P.O. Box 867
Dunedin, FL 34698
www.miniature-art.com

Miniature Art Society of Georgia
P.O. Box 75
Marietta, GA 30061

New Mexico Miniature Arts Society
Betty Morgan
P.O. Box 2928
Roswell, NM 88201
(505) 625–5665
(505) 623–3213
(505) 624–9793
(505) 624–2755
www.zianet.com/snm/rosart.htm

Miniature Art Society of America
1595 North Peaceful Lane
Clearwater, FL 33676
(727) 584–3883

Miniature Painters, Sculptors, Gravers Society of Washington, DC
Margaret Wisdom
5812 Massachusetts Avenue
Bethesda, MD 20816
(301) 229–2463

West Coast Society of Miniature Art
P.O. Box 6734
Santa Barbara, CA 93160
E-mail: *rillabell@aol.com*

World Federation of Miniaturists
1595 North Peaceful Lane
Clearwater, FL 33676
(727) 584–3883

Canada

Canadian Society of Miniature Painters, Sculptors and Gravers
Societe Canadienne des Miniatures
84 Queensline Drive
Nepean, Ohtario K2H 7JS
Canada

Oceanside Miniature Art Society
P.O. Box 1662
133 MacMillan Street
Parksville, British Columbia V9P 2H5
Canada

Additionally, sources of information about creating and exhibiting miniatures may be found through the Hilliard Society of Miniaturists—11 Portway, Wells, Somerset BA5 2BA, United Kingdom, *www.art-in-miniature.org*—and Miniart Supply, at 7419 East 14th Street, Indianapolis, IN 46219, (317) 375–9359, as well as the Joan Cornish Willies Miniature Club— 1726 St. Croix Drive, Clearwater, FL 33759, (727) 797–4461, *www.tampaus.com/studios/pages/club.html*—and the Yahoo chat room The Miniature Canvas (*http://clubs.yahoo.com/clubs/theminiaturecanvas*).

Nature and Wildlife Art Societies

American Academy of Equine Art
P.O. Box 1315
Middleburg, VA 22117
(540) 687–6701
E-mail: *WadeAAEA@AOL.com*
www.horseworld.com/IMH/AAEA/Home.html

American Society of Marine Artists
P.O. Box 369
Ambler, PA 19002
(215) 283–0888
www.marineartists.org

Arundel Carvers Club
7826 Harle Road
Pasadena, MD 21122
(410) 255–7041

Audubon Artists
32 Union Square East
Room 1214
New York, NY 10003
(212) 260–5706

Chattahoochee Woodcarvers Club
4880 Lakeland Drive
Marietta, GA 30068

Cowboy Artists of America
P.O. Box 396
Blue Springs, MO 64013
(816) 224–2244

Decoy and Wildfowl Carvers Association
P.O. Box 5135
Hemet, CA 92544

Guild of National and Scientific Illustrators
P.O. Box 652
Ben Franklin Station
Washington, DC 20044
(301) 762–0189

Nashua Carving Club
23 Gendron Street
Nashua, NH 03062
(603) 883–5635

National Sculptors Guild
2683 North Taft Avenue
Loveland, CO 80538
(907) 667–2015

Northwest Carvers Association
P.O. Box 6092
Federal Way, WA 98063

Rio Grande Valley of Texas Woodcarvers
1419 Quamasia
McAllen, TX 78504

Savannah River Carving Club
Aiken, SC
E-mail: *jmack@groupz.net*

Smoky Mountain Woodcarvers Association
944 St. Johns Drive
Maryville, TN 37801
(423) 981–9070

Society of Animal Artists
47 Fifth Avenue
New York, NY 10003
(212) 741–2880

Western Academy of Women Artists
1550 North Stapley Drive
Mesa, AZ 85203
(602) 834–1201

Western Woodcarvers Association
4033 S.W. Canyon Road
Portland, OR 97221
(503) 228–1367

Wildlife Artisans Association
P.O. Box 2335
Rockport, MA 01966
(978) 768–7218

Wildlife Artist Association
5042 Casitas Pass Road
Ventura, CA 93001
(805) 649–3914

Women Artists of the West
15455 Glenoaks Boulevard
Sylmar, CA 91342
(818) 362–4941
or
31061 Via Limon
San Juan Capistrano, CA 92975
(714) 496–2628

World Wide Nature Artists' Group
P.O. Box 200
Clayton, Ontario K0A 1P0
Canada
(800) 397–6527
www.natureartists.com

Societies of Printmakers

California

Graphic Arts Workshop
2565 Third Street
San Francisco, CA 94107
(415) 285–5660
www.zpub.com/gaw

International Association
of Fine Art Digital Printmakers
570 Higuera Street #120
San Luis Obispo, CA 93401
(888) 239–9099
(805) 593–0200
(805) 781–3150
www.iafadp.org

Los Angeles Printmaking Society
24912 Via Santa Cruz
Mission Viejo, CA 92692

Florida

Florida Printmakers
10091 McGregor Boulevard
Ft. Myers FL 33919

Georgia

Southern Graphics Council
Lamar Dodd School of Art
Visual Arts Building
University of Georgia
Athens, GA 30602

Hawaii

Honolulu Printmakers
1111 Victoria Street
Honolulu, HI 96814
or
188 Aikahi Loop
Kailua HI 96734

Indiana

Mid America Print Council
c/o Brian Jones
School of Arts & Letters
Indiana University Southeast
New Albany, IN 47150
(715) 824–5403
(715) 346–2701

Maryland

Maryland Printmakers
P.O. Box 540
Savage, MD 20763
or
9214 Lawnview Lane
Laurel, MD 20708
(301) 953–2798

Massachusetts
Boston Printmakers
c/o Emmanuel College
400 The Fenway
Boston, MA 02115
or
34 Center Ave
Belmont, MA 02478

Monotype Guild of New England
110 Homestead Lane
Teaticket, MA 02536
(509) 495–0870

New Jersey
Printmaking Council of New Jersey
440 River Road
Somerville, NJ 08876
(908) 725–2110
(908) 725–2484

New York
New York Society of Etchers
Suite 7A
120 West 86th Street
New York, NY 10024

Oregon
Northwest Print Council
922 S.W. Main Street
Portland OR 97205
(503) 525–9259
or
17002 N.E. 50th Avenue
Vancouver WA 98686
(360) 574–3730

Pennsylvania
Pittsburgh Print Group
c/o Pittsburgh Council for the Arts
6300 Fifth Avenue
Pittsburgh PA 15232

The Print Center
1614 Latimer Street
Philadelphia, PA 19103
(215) 735–6090

Canada
Conseil québécois de l'estampe
811 rue Ontario Street East
Montreal, Quebec H2L 1P1
Canada
or
28 67th Avenue
LaSalle, Quebec H8P 3G5
Canada

Manitoba Printmakers Association
c/o Mary Krieger
845 Downing Street
Winnipeg, Manitoba R3G 2P6
Canada

Nova Scotia Printmakers Association
1688 Brow of Mountain Road
R.R. 3
Centreville Nova Scotia B0P 1J0
Canada

Printmakers Council of Prince Edward Island
RR#4 Breadalbane
Prince Edward Island
Canada C0A 1E0
(902) 621–0361

CHAPTER THIRTEEN

Artists' Membership Organizations

Besides co-ops (see chapter 8) and the various societies that focus on a particular medium (noted in chapter 12), artists may also join membership service organizations, which are largely volunteer, nonprofit groups that act as advocates for artist and generally assist artists in career- and work-related areas. The Chicago Artists' Coalition, for instance, provides a monthly newsletter of news and information for members (who pay $30 a year), discounts at art supply stores in the Chicago area, a no-interest emergency loan fund, monthly seminars on such subjects as taxes and record-keeping, a slide registry of member's artwork, a resource center of books for developing one's career, and group-rate insurance for one's health and artwork. The NOVA in Cleveland, Ohio, Boston Visual Artists Union in Massachusetts, and National Artists Equity Association in Washington, D.C., also provide similar kinds of assistance to their artist members.

Opportunities are sometimes available for members to meet, such as at the Artist Dialogue Series that NOVA developed, in which practical concerns (for instance, consignment agreements between artists and their dealers) or technical matters (such as advances in print media) are discussed. The International Sculpture Center also holds periodic conferences and symposia on subjects that range from the aesthetic and philosophical to business and technical issues.

Other, more specialized service groups provide help to particular segments of the artist population across the country, such as the Asian-American Arts Alliance (in New York City), Chicano Humanities and Arts Council in Denver, Colorado, ATLATL (aiding Native American artists) in Phoenix, Arizona, National Conference of Artists (aiding African-American artists) in Washington, D.C., Association of Hispanic Arts in New York City, and Women's Art Registry of Minnesota in Minneapolis. Separate organizations exist for artists working in various media, such as crafts, film and video, performance art, and sculpture. (Again, for more information on arts service and artist membership groups, contact the National Association of Artists Organizations at the address listed in Resources, below.)

In addition to the specific services to the field, an important element that these groups provide is advocacy. Power in our society exists in numbers, and organizations that can draw upon a sizable constituency may help to overturn laws that adversely affect artists or apply pressure on legislators and agencies to create new regulations and statutes that protect or assist them. In addition, studies that are conducted about artists—who they are and what they need—generally rely on artists' organizations, as these groups are the fastest and easiest resource for this kind of information. Many local, state, and regional arts councils also look for artist members for their boards, which allows artists to have an important say in establishing policies concerning such areas as funding, arts festivals, and public art. Historically, artist clubs and societies have become permanent fixtures in the art realm. For instance, the black artist Edward M. Bannister (1828–1901), while suffering slurs such as what was printed in a New York newspaper—"while the Negro may harbor an appreciation of art, he is unable to produce it"—founded the Art Club in Providence, Rhode Island, which later became the Rhode Island School of Design. The French Royal Academy of Painting and Sculpture was organized by the seventeenth-century painter Charles LeBrun in 1648 in order to elevate the status of independent artists and ensure that they would be selected for royal commissions in France. It was, in turn, because of the conservative policies of this academy that artists from the Impressionists on chose to band together in their own groups for the purpose of exhibiting their more modern styles of painting.

Similarly, in the United States, artists broke away from the conservative American Academy of Fine Arts (which had also been founded by artists, in 1802) to form the National Academy of Design in 1826. That group, in turn, was seen as overly restrictive by other artists, such as Robert Henri and the American Impressionists, who created their own respective organizations to display new work in independent exhibits. Henri's group was called The Eight; the Impressionists were referred to as The Ten. Yet another short-lived group of National Academy dissidents, the Association of American Painters and Sculptors, was formed in 1911 to hold regular shows of contemporary art. That association's greatest achievement was the 1913 Armory Show, which traveled to Boston, Chicago, and New York City, and brought the work of Brancusi, Cezanne, Duchamp, Matisse, Picasso, and other advanced European artists before the American public for the first time and forever changed the (somewhat stodgy) tenor of American art.

Banding together in groups may give artists far greater visibility than they may ever achieve individually. All clubs, societies, co-op galleries, artist-run spaces, and service organizations to which artists may belong take away a certain amount of the solitude that creators cultivate for their artmaking, but the return on this investment of time may be far greater than anything lost.

Below is a listing of associations of artists, as well as organizations that provide services to artists, such as newsletters, opportunities for exhibitions, conferences and space for meetings, workshops, and discounts on art supplies.

United States

Alabama

American Society of Portrait Artists
2781 Zelda Road
Montgomery, AL 36106
(800) 62-ASOPA
www.asopa.com

Alaska

Institute of Alaskan Native Art
P.O. Box 583
Fairbanks, AK 99708
(907) 465–7491

Shotridge Studios Cultural Center & Museum
407 Stedman Street
Ketchikan, AK 99901
(907) 225–0407

Arizona

ATLATL
2302 North Central Avenue
Phoenix, AZ 85004
(602) 253–2731

The Authors & Artists Resource Center
4001 East Fort Lowell Road
Tucson, AZ 85712
(602) 325–4733

Knifemakers' Guild
7148 West Country Gables
Peoria, AZ 85381
(602) 878–3064

Tucson/Pima Arts Council
240 North Stone Avenue
Tucson, AZ 85701
(602) 624–0595
www.tpacaz.org

Womankraft Corp./ Community Artists Project
388 South Stone Street
Tucson, AZ 85701
(602) 624–6441

California

Action Arts, Inc.
P.O. Box 253
Pasadena, CA 91102
(818) 584–6368

Alliance of California Artists
P.O. Box 821
Clovis, CA 93612
www.art-alliance.org

American Indian Art and Gift Shop
241 F Street
Eureka, CA 95501
(707) 445–8451
www.americanindianonline.org

Arts, Incorporated
315 West Ninth Street
Suite 201
Los Angeles, CA 90015
(213) 627–9276

Association of Clay and Glass Artists of California
839 Cole Street
San Francisco, CA 94117
(415) 566–0340
www.acga.net/index.html

Bay Area Video Coalition
111 17th Street
San Francisco, CA 94107
(415) 861–3282
www.bavc.org

Bead Society of Los Angeles
P.O. Box 241874
Los Angeles, CA 90024

Belize Caribbean Connection
1941 West 23rd Street
Los Angeles, CA 90018
(213) 732–9742
www.indians.org/color/84.htm

Black Photographers of California
107 Santa Barbara Place
Los Angeles, CA 90008
(213) 294–9024
www.blackphotographers.org

California Carvers Guild
250 San Simeon Avenue
San Simeon, CA 93452
(805) 927–4718
www.carversguild.com

California Community Foundation
606 South Olive Street
Los Angeles, CA 90014
(213) 413–4042

Foundation for Arts Resources
P.O. Box 38145
Los Angeles, CA 90038
(213) 744–0389

Humboldt Arts Council
214 E Street
Eureka, CA 95501
(707) 442–0278

Japanese American Cultural
and Community Center
244 South San Pedro Street
Suite 505
Los Angeles, CA 90012
(213) 628–2725

Metal Arts Society of Southern California
Box 37–1311
Reseda, CA 91337

Multicultural Arts, Inc.
1237 Masselin Avenue
Los Angeles, CA 90019
(213) 933–3447

Multicultural Studies
11110 Alondra Boulevard
Norwalk, CA 90650
(310) 860–2451

National Alliance of Media Arts and
Culture
346 Ninth Street
San Francisco, CA 94103
(415) 431–1391
www.igc.org.namac

National Latino Communications Center
3171 Los Feliz Boulevard
Suite 201
Los Angeles, CA 90039
(213) 663–8294

Portrait Art Society
San Jose, CA
(408) 956–8234
www.portraitartsociety.com

Pro Arts
461 Ninth Street
Oakland, CA 94607
(510) 763–4361

San Francisco State University
Extended Education
425 Market Street
San Francisco, CA 94105
(415) 904–7700

Sculptors' Guild of San Diego
Studio 36, Spanish Village
Balboa Park, CA 92101
(619) 238–0522

Self-Help Graphics & Art
3802 Cesar Chavez Avenue
Los Angeles, CA 90063
(213) 881–6444

Stanislaus Arts Council
1014 A Scenic Drive
Modesto, CA 95350
(209) 558–8628

Surface Design Association
P.O. Box 20799
Oakland, CA 94620
(707) 829–3110

Visual Communications
South California Asian American Studies Center
263 South Los Angeles
Suite 307
Los Angeles, CA 90012
(213) 680–4462

Colorado

Chicano Humanities and Arts Council, Inc.
4136 Tejon, Denver, CO 80201
(303) 477–7733

Colorado Center for Contemporary Art & Craft
513 Manitou Avenue
Manitou Springs, CO 80829
(719) 685–1861

Connecticut

Artists Collective
35 Clark Street
Hartford, CT 06120
(203) 527–3205

Arts & Crafts Association of Meriden
53 Colony Street
Meriden, CT 06450
(203) 235–5347

Brookfield Crafts Center
P.O. Box 122
Brookfield, CT 06804
(203) 775–4526

Connecticut Alliance of Black & Hispanic
Visual Artists
981 Winchester Avenue
Hamden, CT 06517
(203) 776–9912

Connecticut Guild of Craftsmen
P.O. Box 155
New Britain, CT 06050
(860) 225–8875

Creative Arts Workshop
80 Audubon Street
New Haven, CT 06510
(203) 562–4927

Handweavers Guild of America
120 Mountain Avenue
Bloomfield, CT 06002

Institute for Visual Artists
c/o Silvermine Guild Arts Center
1037 Silvermine Road
New Canaan, CT 06840
(203) 966–9700
www.silverminearts.org

Latino Youth Development
154 Minor Street
New Haven, CT 06519
(203) 776–3649

Office of Cultural Affairs
25 Stonington Street
Hartford, CT 06106
(203) 722–6488

Society for Connecticut Crafts
P.O. Box 615
Hartford, CT 06142
(860) 423–5532

Society of Connecticut Sculptors
211 Williams Street
Meriden, CT 06450
www.sculpting.com/Society/drive.htm

Washington Art Association
P.O. Box 173
Washington Depot, CT 06794
(860) 868–2878

Wesleyan Potters
350 South Main Street
Middletown, CT 06457
(860) 347–5925

Delaware

Council of Delaware Artists
1034 Oldfield Point Road
Elkton, MD 21921
(410) 392–7803

Delaware Foundation for the Visual Arts
P.O. Box 298
Rockland, DE 19732
(302) 475–8796

Dover Art League
21 Loockerman Street
Dover, DE 19904
(302) 674–0402
www.doverart.org

Ladybug Chapter for the National Quilting Association
156 East Second Street
New Castle, DE 19720
(302) 322–5813

Millsboro Art League
P.O. Box 1043
Millsboro, DE 19966
(302) 934–6440
www.angelfire.com/de2/millsboroartleague

Sussex County Arts Council
P.O. Box 221
Georgetown, DE 19947
(302) 856–5721

District of Columbia

American Institute of Architects
1735 New York Avenue N.W.
Washington, DC 20006
(202) 626–7300

Americans for the Arts
927 15 Street N.W.
Washington, DC 20005
(202) 371–2830
www.artsusa.org

Coalition of Washington Artists
P.O. Box 21584
Washington, DC 20009
(202) 362–0745

The Crafts Center
1001 Connecticut Avenue N.W.
Suite 1138
Washington, DC 20036
(202) 728–9603
E-mail: *craftsdc@erols.com*

Cultural Alliance of Greater Washington
410 Eighth Street N.W.
Suite 600
Washington, DC 20004
(202) 638–2406

Evans-Tibbs Collection
1910 Vermont Avenue N.W.
Washington, DC 20001
(202) 234–8164

Hand Papermaking, Inc.
Box 77027
Washington, DC 20013
(301) 220–2393
(800) 821–6604
E-mail: *handpapermaking@bookarts.com*

Indian Arts and Crafts Board
Room 4004 MIB
U.S. Department of Interior
Washington, DC 20240
(202) 208–3773

National Artists Equity Association*
P.O. Box 28068
Washington, DC 28028
(202) 628–9633
www.retronet.com/artview/docs/equity.htm

*Artist Equity chapters are located in:

Central California
(408) 375–6165

Northern California
(415) 626–6806
(415) 648–7908

San Diego
(619) 721–8909

Maryland
(301) 995–6298

New York
(212) 226–0581
(212) 966–7096

Philadelphia
(215) 287–7086

Pittsburgh
(412) 481–7544

Virginia
(703) 684–6318

Washington
(206) 547–4552

National Association of Artists' Organizations
918 F Street N.W.
Washington, DC 20004
(202) 347–6350
www.artswire.org/Artswire/naao/index.html

National Center on Arts and the Aging
600 Maryland Avenue S.W.
Washington, DC 20024
(212) 479–6990
(800) 424–9046

National Conference of Artists
409 Seventh Street N.W.
Washington, DC 20004
(202) 393–3116

National Endowment for the Arts
1100 Pennsylvania Avenue N.W.
Washington, DC 20506
(202) 682–5570
http://arts.endow.gov
Web site includes *arts.community*, a monthly online magazine on the nonprofit arts with news about the arts endowment and links to other Web sites, and an Arts Resource Center that offers information on arts service organizations and current research in the arts.

Washington Sculptors Group
P.O. Box 42534
Washington, DC 20015
(202) 686–8696
www.washingtonsculptors.org

Florida

Alliance Film & Video Cooperative
924 Lincoln Road
Suite 214
Miami Beach, FL 33139
(305) 538–8242

Florida Craftsmen
501 Central Avenue
St. Petersburg, FL 33701
(813) 821–7291

Koubek Memorial Center
University of Miami
2705 S.W. Third Street
Miami, FL 33135
(305) 649–6000

Portrait Society of America, Inc.
P.O. Box 11272
Tallahassee, FL 32302
(877) 772–4321
www.portraitsociety.org

Professional Association of Visual Artists
P.O. Box 2665
Dunedin, FL 34698
www.pava.cftnet.com

Society of North American Goldsmiths
5009 Londonderry Drive
Tampa, FL 36647
(813) 977–5326

Society for Photographic Education
P.O. Box 2811
Daytona Beach, FL 32120
(904) 255–8131

Society of North American Goldsmiths
5009 Londonderry Drive
Tampa, FL 33647
(813) 977–5326

Women in the Visual Arts
5030 Champion Boulevard
Boca Raton, FL 33496
www.artscape.com/orgs/witva

Georgia

Alternate Roots
1083 Austin Avenue
Atlanta, GA 30307
(404) 577–1079

The Arts Exchange
750 Kalb Street, S.E.
Atlanta, GA 30312
(404) 624–4211

Atlanta Bureau of Cultural Affairs
887 West Marietta
Atlanta, GA 30318
(404) 853–3261
(404) 817–6823

Handweavers Guild of America, Inc.
Two Executive Concourse
Suite 201
3327 Duluth Highway
Duluth, GA 30136
(770) 495–7702

Southeast Community Cultural Center
750 Kalb Street, S.E.
Atlanta, GA 30312
(404) 624–4211

Video Data Bank
675 Ponce de Leon Avenue, N.E.
Atlanta, GA 30308
(404) 817–6815

Guam

Isla Center for the Arts
University of Guam
P.O. Box 5203
Mangilao, Guam 96923

Hawaii

Arts Council of Hawaii
P.O. Box 38000
Honolulu, HI 96837
(808) 524–7120

Honolulu Academy of Arts
900 South Beretania Street
Honolulu, HI 96814
(808) 532–8714

Illinois

American Society of Artists
P.O. Box 1326
Palatine, IL 60078
(312) 751–2500
(312) 991–4748

Beacon Street Gallery & Theatre
4520 North Beacon Street
129 1/2 West State Street
Chicago, IL 60640
(708) 232–2728

Chicago Artists' Coalition
11 East Hubbard
Chicago, IL 60611
(312) 670–2060

Destin Asian
5945 North Lakewood
Suite 2
Chicago, IL 60660
(312) 275–7101

International Sculpture Center
401 North Michigan Avenue
Chicago, IL 60611
(312) 527–6634
E-mail: *isc@sba.com*

National Association of Independent Artists
P.O. Box 334
Dundee, IL 60118
(847) 426–8532

National Council for Education in the Ceramic Arts
1411 West Farragut Street
Chicago, IL 60640
(312) 784–7057

Near Northwest Arts Council
1579 North Milwaukee
Room 300
Chicago, IL 60622
(312) 278–7677

Professional Photographers of America, Inc.
1090 Executive Way
Des Plaines, IL 60018
(708) 299–8161

Sun Foundation
RR 2
P.O. Box 156E
Washburn, IL 61570
(309) 246–8403

Video Data Bank
Columbus at Jackson Boulevard
Chicago, IL 60603
(312) 899–5172

Indiana

Indianapolis Art Center
820 East 67th Street
Indianapolis, IN 46220
(317) 255–2464
www.indplsartcenter.org/inartctr

Iowa

Des Moines Woodworkers Association, Inc.
(515) 967–7686

Iowa Basketweavers Guild
1974 Middle Assian Road
Decorah, IA 52001
(319) 532–9774

Iowa Designer Crafts Association
2501 33rd Street
Des Moines, IA 50310

Iowa Federation of Handweavers and Spinners
3101 Raven Street
Iowa City, IA 52245
(319) 338–4361

Iowa Quilters Guild
621 Sixth Street
Nevada, IA 50201
(515) 382–6181

Kentucky

American Quilter's Society
Box 3290
Paducah, KY 42002
(502) 898–7903

Enamelist Society
Box 310
Newport, KY 41072
(606) 291–3800
E-mail: *klinedl@ucbeh.san.uc.edu*

Louisville Visual Artists
3005 River Road
Louisville, KY 40207
www.louisvillevisualart.org

North Fork Media, Inc.
307 Fifth Street
Whitesburg, KY 41858
(606) 633–4252

Louisiana

Arcadiana Arts Council
P.O. Box 53762
Lafayette, LA 70505
(318) 233–7060

Artists Alliance
125 Main Street
Lafayette, LA 70502
(318) 233–7518

Arts Council of Greater Baton Rouge
427 Laurel Street
Baton Rouge, LA 70801
(504) 344–8558

Arts Council of New Orleans
821 Gravier Street
Suite 600
New Orleans, LA 70112
(504) 523–1465

Commission on the Arts
P.O. Box 828
Slidell, LA 70459
(504) 646–4375

New Orleans Video Access Center
2010 Magazine Street
New Orleans, LA 70130
(504) 524–8626

Red River Sculpture Society
10 Springlake Way
Shreveport, LA 71106
(318) 868–9422
www.ArtTRUST.net

Maine

American Art Pottery Association
P.O. Box 710
York Harbor, ME 03911

Crown of Maine Quilters
29 Dyer Street
Presque Isle, ME 04769
(207) 764–4213

L/A Arts
49 Lisbon Street
Lewiston, ME 04240
(800) 639–2919
www.laarts.org/

Maine Arts
582 Congress Street
Portland, ME 04101
(207) 772–9012

Maine Artists Space
20–36 Danforth Street
Portland, ME 04101
(207) 773–6245
www.maineartistspace.org

Maine Arts Sponsors Association
P.O. Box 2352
Augusta, ME 04338
(207) 626–3277
E-mail: *masa@mint.net*

Maine Crafts Association
15 Walton Street
Portland, ME 04103
(207) 780–1807
E-mail: *gael_mckibben@onf.com*

Maine Writers and Publishers Alliance
190 Mason Street
Brunswick, ME 04011
(207) 729–6333

Mainely Weavers
92 Underwood Road
Falmouth, ME 04105
(207) 781–2396

New England Artisans Guild
44 Leighton Road
Pownal, ME 04069
(207) 688–4483
www.burrows.com/guild.html

South Maine Guild of Spinners & Weavers
254 Diamond Hill Road
North Berwick, ME 03906
(207) 698–1684

Union of Maine Visual Artists
836 Begaduce Road
Brookville, ME 04617
(207) 326–8459

United Maine Craftsmen
R.R. 2
P.O. Box 1920B
Manchester, ME 04351
(207) 621–2818
E-mail: *umc@mainecraftsmen.org*
www.mainecraftsmen.org

Upcountry Artists
15 Anson Street
Farmington, ME 04935
(207) 778–4764

Yankee Artisan
56 Front Street
Bath, ME 04530
(207) 443–6215
www.javanet.com/~psedge

Maryland

Bead Society of Greater Washington
P.O. Box 70036
Chevy Chase, MD 20813
(301) 277–6830
E-mail: *bsgw@erols.com*

Ceramics Guild
12532 Woodridge Lane
Highland, MD 20777

National Council for the Traditional Arts
1320 Fenwick Lane
Suite 200
Silver Spring, MD 20910
(301) 565–0654

Pyramid Atlantic
6001 66th Avenue
Riverdale, MD 20737
(301) 459–7154

Visual Arts Resource Center
218 West Saratoga Street
Baltimore, MD 21201
(410) 962–8565
www.mdartplace.org/

Massachusetts

ArtistSupport
Career Services
Women's Educational and Industrial Union
356 Boylston Street
Boston, MA 02116
(617) 536–5657

Arts Extension Service
604 Goodell
University of Massachusetts
Amherst, MA 01003
(413) 545–2360

Asparagus Valley Potter's Guild
R.R. 2
Amherst, MA 01002
(413) 256–8691
E-mail: *mcohen@javanet.com*

Boston Arts Organization
P.O. Box 6061, JFK Station
Boston, MA 02114

Boston Film and Video Foundation
1126 Boylston Street
Boston, MA 02215
(617) 536–1540
www.actwin.com/BFVF

Boston Visual Artists Union
P.O. Box 399
Newtonville, MA 02160
(617) 695–1266

Chesterwood Seminars for Professional Sculptors
Chesterwood Estate & Museum
Stockbridge, MA 01262
(413) 298–3579

International Guild of Glass Artists, Inc.
54 Cherry Street
Box 1809
North Adams, MA 01247
(413) 663–5512
E-mail: *alewis@vgernet.net*

Lexington Arts and Crafts Society
130 Walthern Street
Lexington, MA 02173
(617) 862–9696

New England Sculptors Association
44 Fuller Street
Waban, MA 02468
www.nesculptors.com

New England Wood Carvers
P.O. Box 561
Lexington, MA 02173
www.pair.com/rtrudel

Photographic Resource Center
602 Commonwealth Avenue
Boston, MA 02215
(617) 353–0700

Research Institute of African Diaspora
12 Morley Street
Roxbury, MA 02119
(617) 427–8325

Society of Arts and Crafts
175 Newbury Street
Boston, MA 02116
(617) 266–1810
www.societyofcrafts.org

United South End Settlements
566 Columbus Avenue
Boston, MA 02118
(617) 375–8132

Michigan
Ann Arbor Art Association
117 West Liberty
Ann Arbor, MI 48104
(313) 994–8004

The Arts & Crafts Society
1194 Bandera Drive
Ann Arbor, MI 48103
(745) 665–4729
www.arts-crafts.com

Artists Club
22923 Ravenscroft
Farmington Hills, MI 48331
(248) 661–4863

Artists Equity Association—Michigan Chapter
23191 Stewart Avenue
Warren, MI 48089

Concerned Citizens for the Arts in Michigan
230 East Grand River
Suite 201
Detroit, MI 48226
(313) 961–1776

Copper Country Associated Artists
307 Sixth Street
Calumet, MI 49913
(906) 482–1790

Detroit Society of Women Painters and Sculptors
418 Barclay Road
Grosse Pointe Farms, MI 48236
(313) 885–2368

Farmington Area Artists Club
20414 Shadyside
Livonia, MI 48152

Grand Valley Artists
4 Jeffereson, S.E.
Grand Rapids, MI 49503
(616) 458–0315

Grosse Pointe Artists Association
P.O. Box 36125
Grosse Pointe Farms, MI 48236

International Chaldean Association of Professional Visual Artists
800 Livernois
Ferndale, MI 48220
(248) 882–6664

International Guild of Fine Artists
1555 Tannahill Lane
Bloomfield Hills, MI 48304
(248) 334–4158
(800) 762–4271
www.igfa.com

Michigan Traditional Arts Program
Michigan State University
East Lansing, MI 48824
(517) 355–2370

Midland Artists Guild
P.O. Box 1892
Midland, MI 48641

National Conference of Artists—Michigan Chapter
3011 West Grand Boulevard
Detroit, MI 48202
(313) 875–0923
www.ncamich.org

Oakland County Cultural Affairs
1200 North Telegraph Road
Pontiac, MI 48053
(313) 858–0415

Oil Painters of America
316 Birney Street
Essexville, MI 48732

United Black Artists, USA, Inc.
7661 LaSalle Boulevard
Detroit, MI 48206
(313) 898–5574

Working Women Artists
2697 Heather Drive
East Lansing, MI 48823
(517) 332–6205

Minnesota

American Association of Woodturners
3200 Lexington Avenue
Shoreview, MN 55126
(612) 484–9094
E-mail: *aaw@compuserve.com*

American Society of Classical Realism
1313 Fifth Street, S.E.
Minneapolis, MN 55414
(612) 379–3908
www.classicalrealism.com

Compas
308 Landmark Center
75 West Fifth Street
Room 304
St. Paul, MN 55102
(612) 292–3287

Lake Region Arts Council
P.O. Box 661
112 West Washington Avenue
Fergus Falls, MN 56537
(218) 739–4617

Native American Arts Initiative
Region 2 Arts Council
426 Bemdji Avenue
Bemdji, MN 56601
(218) 751–5447

Northfield Arts Guild
304 Division Street
Northfield, MN 55057
(507) 645–8877

Pillsbury Neighborhood Service Center for Cultural Arts
3501 Chicago Avenue South
Minneapolis, MN 55407
(612) 824–0708

Resources and Counseling for the Arts
308 Prince Street
St. Paul, MN 55101
(651) 292–4381

Missouri

Artists Blacksmith's Association of North America
P.O. Box 206
Washington, MO 63090
(314) 390–2133
www.wuarchive.wustl.edu/edu/arts/black-smithing/ABANA

Columbia Art League
1013 East Walnut Street
Columbia, MO 65201
(573) 443–8838

Craft Alliance
6640 Delmar Boulevard
St. Louis, MO 63130
(314) 725–1177
www.craftalliance.org

Greater Kansas City National Hispanic Heritage Commission
10430 Askew Avenue
Kansas City, MO 64137
(816) 765–1992

Heart of America Indian Center
1340 East Admiral Boulevard
Kansas City, MO 64106
(816) 421–0039

Kansas City Artists Coalition
201 Wyandotte
Kansas City, MO 64105
(816) 421–5222

Missouri Artisans Business Development Association
2101 West Broadway
Box 322
Columbia, MO 65203
(660) 829–0009

Missouri New Art Association
7714 Summit Street
Kansas City, MO 64114

National Oil & Acrylic Painter Society
The Painters Society
P.O. Box 676
Osage Beach, MO 65065

Sedalia Visual Art Association
816 La Grand Drive
Sedalia, MO 65301

St. Charles Artists Guild
130 Prairie Haute Drive
St. Charles, MO 63301
(314) 946–9933

St. Louis Artists Guild
2 Oak Knoll Park
Clayton, MO 63105
(314) 727–6266

Stained Glass Association of America
P.O. Box 22642
Kansas City, MO 64113
(816) 361–9173
E-mail: *sgaofa@aol.com*

Montana

Flathead Valley Community College
777 Grandview Drive
Kalispell, MT 59901
(406) 756–3945

Professional Knifemakers Association, Inc.
2905 North Montana Avenue
Helena, MT 59601

Salish Kootenai College
Box 117
Pablo, MT 59855
(406) 675–4800

Nebraska

Metro Arts
P.O. Box 1077
Omaha, NE 68101
(402) 341–7910

Mexican American Commission
P.O. Box 94965
Lincoln, NE 68509
(402) 471–2791

Nee-shoch-ha-chee Community Development Corporation
P.O. Box 748
Winnebago, NE 68071
(402) 878–2972

United Association of Crafters
5219 North 64th Street
Omaha, NE 68104
(712) 527–3678

Nevada

Allied Arts Council of Southern Nevada
3135 Industrial Road
Suite 224
Las Vegas, NV 89109
(702) 731–5419

New Hampshire

Amherst Arts Association
Box 435
Amherst, NH 03031

Laconia Arts Association
333 Mechanic St
Laconia, NH 03246

Manchester Artists Association
PO Box 636
Manchester, NH 03105
(603) 485–9012

Mt. Washington Valley Arts Association
P.O. Box 1603
North Conway, NH 03860
(603) 367–4764

Academy of American Dolls
73 N Spring Street
Concord, NH 03301

Artisan's Workshop
P.O. Box 124
New London, NH 03257
(603) 526–4227

League of NH Craftsmen
205 N. Main St
Concord, NH 03301
(603) 224–3375

Meredith-Laconia Arts & Crafts
Rte. 3
Meredith, NH 03253
(603) 279–7920

New Hampshire Weavers Guild
P.O. Box 241
Deerfield, NH 03037
(603) 352–2638

North Country Studio Conference
P.O. Box 875
Hanover, NH 03755
(603) 795–2889

New Hampshire Professional Photographers Association
23 Depot St
Pittsfield, NH 03263
(603) 435–8063

Peterborough Community Film Society
P.O. Box 126
Dublin, NH 03444

The Drum
P.O. Box 353
Raymod, NH 03077
(603) 895–1459

Metalhead Society
3 Harwood Road
Mount Vernon, NH 03057
(603) 672–9648

New Hampshire Potters Guild
Box 762
Durham, NH 03824
(603) 659–2698

Studio Potter Network
69 High Street
Exeter, NH 03833
(603) 772–6323

Woodworking Association of North America
P.O. Box 478
Depot Road
Tamworth, NH 03886
(603) 323–7500

New Jersey

Aljira, Inc.
2 Washington Place
Newark, NJ 07042
(201) 643–6877

Arts Alliance for Contemporary Glass
1501 Glasstown Road
Millville, NJ 08332
(609) 825–6800
www.ContempGlass.org/index.html

International Sculpture Center
14 Fairgrounds Road
Hamilton, NJ 08619
(609) 689–1051
www.sculpture.org

Passaic County Cultural and Heritage Council
One College Boulevard
Paleston, NJ 07505
(201) 684–6555

Visual Arts League
1007 Old Bridge Turnpike
East Brunswick, NJ 08816
(732) 254–7611
www.valweb.org

New Mexico

American Bladesmith Society
Box 977
Peralta, NM 87042
E-mail: *abs@rt66.com*

American Indian Arts and Crafts Association
122 La Veta, N.E.
Albuquerque, NM 87108
(505) 265–9149
E-mail: *iaca@ix.netcom.com*

Hispanic Culture Foundation
P.O. Box 7279
Albuquerque, NM 87194
(505) 831–8360

Indian Arts & Crafts Association
122 La Veta, N.E.
Albuquerque, NM 87108
(505) 265–9149
E-mail: *iaca@ix.netcom.com*
www.hogan1.atin.com/iaca

School of American Research
Indian Arts Research
P.O. Box 2188
Santa Fe, NM 87504
(505) 982–3584

Senior Arts
P.O. Box 4679
Albuquerque, NM 87196
(505) 877–4430

New York

Americans for the Arts
1 East 53 Street
New York, NY 10022
(212) 223–2787

American Craft Council
72 Spring Street
New York, NY 10012
(212) 274–0630
(800) 724–0859
E-mail: *amcraft@mindspring.com*

American Institute of Graphic Arts
1059 Third Avenue
New York, NY 10021
(800) 548–1634

American Society of Media Photographers
419 Park Avenue South
New York, NY 10016
(212) 889–9144
www.asmp.org

Art Table
270 Lafayette Street
New York, NY 10012
(212) 343–1735
www.arttable.org
Resource center for women

Artists Space
38 Greene Street
New York, NY 10013
(212) 226–3970

Arts Council at Freeport
P.O. Box 97
130 East Merrick Road
Freeport, NY 11520
(516) 223–2522

Arts Council for Wyoming County
P.O. Box 249
63 South Main Street
Perry, NY 14530
(716) 237–3517

Arts for Greater Rochester
335 East Main Street
Suite 200
Rochester, NY 14604
(716) 546–5602

Asian American Arts Alliance
339 Lafayette Street
New York, NY 10012
(212) 979–6734

Association of Hispanic Arts
173 East 116th Street
New York, NY 10029
(212) 860–5445
www.artswire.org/aha/aha.htm

Association of Independent Video and Filmmakers
625 Broadway
Ninth Floor
New York, NY 10012
(212) 473–3400
www.aivf.org

Authors Guild
330 West 42nd Street
29th Floor
New York, NY 10036
(212) 398–0838

Bead Society of Greater New York
P.O. Box 427
New York, NY 10116

Brooklyn Arts Council
200 Eastern Parkway
Brooklyn, NY 11238
(718) 783–4469

Brooklyn Working Artists Coalition
P.O. Box 020072
Brooklyn, NY 11202
(718) 596–2507
www.bwac.org

Center for Book Arts
626 Broadway
New York, NY 10012
(212) 460–9768
E-mail: *bookarts@pipeline.com*

Center for Safety in the Arts
155 Avenue of the Americas
New York, NY 10013
(212) 366–6900

College Art Association
275 Seventh Avenue
New York, NY 10001
(212) 691–1051
www.collegeart.org

Creative Coalition
1100 Avenue of the Americas
New York, NY 10036
(212) 512–5515

El Museo del Barrio
1230 Fifth Avenue
New York, NY 10029
(212) 831–7272

En Foco, Inc.
32 East Kingsbridge Road
Bronx, NY 10468
(718) 584–7718

The Field
161 Avenue of the Americas
New York, NY 10013
(212) 691–6969

Graphic Artists Guild
91 John Street
New York, NY 10011
(212) 791–3400
E-mail: *pbasista@NAC.net*

Guild chapters are located in Albany, NY: (518) 251–3015;
Atlanta, GA: (404) 297–8435;
Boston, MA: (781) 455–0363;
Chicago, IL: (773) 761–7292;
Washington, DC: (301) 530–6971
Indianapolis, IN: (317) 925–3275;
New York, NY: (212) 791–0334;
Portland, OR: (503) 245–9832;
San Francisco, CA: (510) 839–4236;
Seattle, WA: (206) 471–0820

Grupo de Artistas Latino Americanos, Inc.
21 West 112th Street
New York, NY 10026
(212) 369–3401

Hatch-Billops Collection
491 Broadway
New York, NY 10012

Heresies
P.O. Box 1306
Canal Street Station
New York, NY 10013
(212) 227–2108

Hispanic Academy of Media Arts and Sciences
P.O. Box 3268
New York, NY 10163
(212) 686–7030

International Agency for Minority Artist Affairs
163 West 125th Street
New York, NY 10027
(212) 749–5298
(212) 873–5040

International Society of Copier Artists
759 President Street
Suite 2H
Brooklyn, NY 11215
(718) 638–3264

Ken Keleba House
214 East Second Street
New York, NY 10009
(212) 674–3939

Latino Collaborative
280 Broadway
Suite 412
New York, NY 10007
(212) 732–1121

Long Island Arts Council
130 East Merrick Road
Freeport, NY 11520
(516) 223–2522

Media Alliance
c/o Thirteen/WNET
356 West 58th Street
New York, NY 10019
(212) 560–2919

Midmarch Associates
Box 3304 Grand Central Station
New York, NY 10163
(212) 666–6990

Molly Olga Neighborhood Art Classes
139 Locust Street
Buffalo, NY 14204
(716) 885–1388

National Association of Women Artists
41 Union Square West
New York, NY 10003
(212) 675–1616

National Crafts Association
1945 East Ridge Road
Rochester, NY 14622
(716) 266–5472
(800) 715–9594

National Institute of American Doll Artists
Box 656693
Fresh Meadows, NY 11365
(970) 824–8407

National Sculpture Society
Dept. AA, 1177 Avenue of the Americas
New York, NY 10036
(212) 764–5645
www.sculptor.org/NSS/

New York Artists Equity Association
498 Broome Street
New York, NY 10013
(212) 941–0130

New York City Department of Cultural Affairs
2 Columbus Circle
New York, NY 10019
(212) 841–4100

New York Foundation for the Arts
155 Avenue of the Americas
New York, NY 10013
www.nyfa.org
(212) 366–6900
(800) 232–2789

Ollantay Art Heritage Center
P.O. Box 720636
Jackson Heights, NY 11372
(718) 565–6499

Organization of Independent Artists
19 Hudson Street
Suite 402
New York, NY 10013
(212) 219–9213

Poets and Writers
72 Spring Street
New York, NY 10012
(212) 226–3586

Small Studio Alliance
Crary Mills Potters
R.R. 4
P.O. Box 252
Canton, NY 13617
(315) 386–4721

Society of Photographer and Artist Representatives, Inc.
60 East 42 Street
New York, NY 10165
(212) 779–7464

Squeaky Wheel/Buffalo Media Resources
P.O. Box 251 Ellicott Station
Buffalo, NY 14205
(716) 884–7172

Visual Artists and Galleries Association
521 Fifth Avenue
New York, NY 10017
(212) 808–0616

Womens Studio Workshop
P.O. Box 489
Rosendale, NY 12472
(845) 658–9133
www.wsworkshop.org

North Carolina

ArtMetal Project
505 Luther Road
Apex, NC 27502

Black Artists Guild
P.O. Box 2162
400 North Queens Street
Kinston, NC 28501
(919) 523–0003

City of Raleigh Arts Commission
311 South Blount Street
Raleigh, NC 27601
(919) 831–6234

Guilford Native American Art Gallery & Association
P.O. Box 5623
Greensboro, NC 27435
(910) 273–6605

HandMade in America
P.O. Box 2089
Asheville, NC 28802
(828) 252–0121
www.wnccrafts.org

Tri-State Sculptors
4916 Liles Road
Raleigh, NC 27606
(919) 859–3698
www.greensboro.com
or
95 Cumberland Circle
Asheville, NC 28801
(828) 258–2742

Winston-Salem Delta Fine Arts
1511 East Third Street
Winston-Salem, NC 27101
(910) 722–2625

YMI Cultural Center
39 South Market Street
Asheville, NC 28802
(704) 252–4614

North Dakota

North Dakota Indian Arts Association
Mandan Train Depot
401 West Main Street
Mandan, ND 58554
(701) 663–1263

Ohio

American Ceramics Society
P.O. Box 6136
Westerville, OH 43806
(614) 890–4700
www.acers.org

Art for Community Expression
772 North High
Suite 102
Columbus, OH 43215
(614) 294–4200

Miami Valley Arts Company
P.O. Box 95
Dayton, OH 45402
(513) 228–0737

National Needlework Association
Box 2188
Zanesville, OH 43702
(614) 455–6773
E-mail: *tnna.info@offinger.com*

National Woodcarvers Association
7424 Miami Avenue
Cincinnati, OH 45243
(513) 561–0627
www.chipchats.org

NOVA/New Organization for the Visual Arts
4614 Prospect Avenue
Cleveland, OH 44103
(216) 431–7500

Professional Artists Services
Peaceworks Gallery
703 Bryden Road
Columbus, OH 43205
(614) 464–4648

Sculpture Center
12206 Euclid Avenue
Cleveland, OH 44106
(216) 229–6527
www.sculpturecenter.org

Society of Craft Designers
Box 3388
Zanesville, OH 43702
(740) 452–4541
E-mail: *scd@offinger.com*

Women of Color Quilter's Network
556 Bessinger Drive
Cincinnati, OH 45240
(513) 825–9707

Oklahoma

Oklahoma Indian Arts & Crafts Cooperative
P.O. Box 966
Aadarko, OK 73005
(405) 247–3486

Oklahoma Sculpture Society
3612 N.W. 19th Street
Oklahoma City, OK 73107
(405) 942–6887
http://oktechmasters.org
www.searchok.com/~oss/

Oklahoma Visual Arts Coalition
P.O. Box 54416
Oklahoma City, OK 73154
(405) 842–6991
E-mail: *ovac@telepath.com*

Red Earth, Inc.
2100 N.E. 52 Street
Oklahoma City, OK 73111
(405) 427–5228

Oregon

Alliance of Artists' Communities
2311 E. Burnside Street
Suite 300
Portland, OR 97214
(503) 797–6988
E-mail: *aac@artistcommunities.org*
www.artistcommunities.org

American Sewing Guild
P.O. Box 8476
Medford, OR 97504

Guild of Oregon Woodworkers
Box 1866
Portland, OR 97207
(503) 492–1515

Interstate Firehouse Culture Center
5340 North Interstate
Portland, OR 97217
(503) 823–2000

Mid-Valley Quilt Guild
Box 621
Salem, OR 97308

National Council for Education
for Ceramic Arts
P.O. Box 158
Bandon, OR 97411
(503) 347–4394
(800) 99-NCECA

Oregon Potters Association
19855 N.E. Trunk Road
Dundee, OR 97115

Quintana Galleries
139 N.W. Second Avenue
Portland, OR 97209
(503) 223–1729

Pennsylvania

Creative Artists Network
P.O. Box 30027
Philadelphia, PA 19103
(215) 546–7775

Greater Philadelphia Cultural Alliance
320 Walnut Street
Suite 500
Philadelphia, PA 19106
(215) 440–8100

International Arts-Medicine Association
3600 Market Street
Philadelphia, PA 19104
(215) 525–3784

Manchester Craftsmen's Guild
1815 Metropolitan Street
Pittsburgh, PA 15233
(412) 322–1773
www.artsnet.heinz.cmu.edu/mcg/

Nexus/Foundation for Today's Art
137 North Second Street
Philadelphia, PA 19106
(215) 629–1103

Philadelphia Sculptors Society
www.philasculptors.com

Pittsburgh Filmmakers
477 Melwood Avenue
Pittsburgh, PA 15213
(412) 681–5449

Pittsburgh Trust for Cultural Resources
209 Ninth Street
Fifth floor
Pittsburgh, PA 15222
(412) 471–6070

Taller Puertorrigueno
2721 North Fifth Street
Philadelphia, PA 19133
(215) 426–3311

Women's Caucus for Art
Moore College of Art
1920 Race Street
Philadelphia, PA 19103
(215) 854–0922

Rhode Island
New England Artists Trust
P.O. Box 1481
Providence, RI 02908
(617) 361–7876

Society of American Silversmiths
P.O. Box 3599
Cranston, RI 02910
(401) 461–3156
www.silversmithing.com

South Carolina
Artists of Color
South Carolina State University
Stanback Museum
Orangeburg, SC 29115
(803) 536–7013

Clay Arts Society
1932 Calhoun Street
Columbia, SC 29201
(803) 733–8331

South Dakota
Dakota Artists Guild
Dahl Fine Arts Center
713 7th Street
Rapid City, SD 57701
(605) 394–4108
(605) 342–1584

Mitchell Area Arts Council
119 West Third Avenue
Mitchell, SD 57301
(605) 996–4111

Mobridge Artists Association
PO Box 851
Mobridge, SD 57601
(605) 845–7639

NE Artists' Network
1116 North Broadway
Watertown, SD 57201
(605) 882–1780

Oscar Howe Memorial Association
College of Fine Arts
414 East Clark
Vermillion, SD 57069
(605) 677–5481
(605) 665–3368

Sioux Empire Gem & Mineral Society
26684 Apple Lane
Hartford, SD 57033
(605) 367–7058
(605) 526–4356

Tennessee
Africa in April Cultural Awareness Festival
P.O. Box 111261
Memphis, TN 38111
(901) 785–2542

African American Cultural Alliance
P.O. Box 22173
Nashville, TN 37218
(615) 256–7720

Memphis Black Arts Alliance
Shelby State Community College
P.O. Box 40854
Memphis, TN 38174
(901) 458–3400

Native American Indian Association
211 Union Street
Suite 932
Nashville, TN 37221
(615) 726–0806

Rose Center
P.O. Box 1976
Morristown, TN 37816
(615) 581–4330

Texas

Alliance for American Quilts
7660 Woodway
Houston, TX 77063

Art League of Houston
1953 Montrose Boulevard
Houston, TX 77006
(713) 523–9530

American Society of Furniture Artists
P.O. Box 35339
Houston, TX 77235
(713) 721–7600
www.asofa.org

Art Tile Alliance
806 Rosedale Terrace
Austin, TX 78704
(512) 447–2575

The Association of American Cultures
1703 West Kingshighway
San Antonio, TX 78201
(210) 736–9272

Austin Artists' Harvest
P.O. Box 80546
Austin, TX 78708
(512) 473–5866

Austin League of Minority Artists
3010 Govalle Avenue
Austin, TX 78702
(512) 926–8339

Austin Visual Arts Association
P.O. Box 13313
Austin, TX 78711
(512) 457–0075
www.txarts.net/avaa

Black Arts Alliance
1157 Nauasota
Austin, TX 78702

Centro Cultural Aztlan
803 Castroville Road
Suite 402
San Antonio, TX 78237
(210) 432–1896

Community Artists' Collective
1501 Elgin Avenue
Houston, TX 77004
(713) 523–1616

Country Corner
Box 727
Van Horn, TX 79855
(915) 283–2788

Cultural Arts Council of Houston
1964 West Gray
Suite 224
Houston, TX 77109
(713) 527–9330

D-Art Visual Arts Center
2917 Swiss Avenue
Dallas, TX 75204
(214) 821–2522

Dallas Office of Cultural Affairs
1925 Elm Street
Dallas, TX 75201
(214) 670–3687

Houston Women's Caucus for Art
1413 Westheimer
Houston, TX 77006
(409) 295–3006

National Association of Latino Arts and Culture
3618 Cesar Chavez
San Antonio, TX 78207
(210) 432–3482

Society for Photographic Education
P.O. Box 222116
Dallas, TX 75222
(817) 273–2845

Texas Fine Arts Association
700 Congress
Austin, TX 78701
(512) 453–5312
www.main.org/tfr

Texas Sculpture Association
P.O. Box 830529
Richardson, TX 75083
(972) 437–3250
www.txsculpture.com

Texas Society of Sculptors
P.O. Box 49291
Austin, TX 78765
(512) 321–2737
www.flash.net/~tsos

Virginia
Arts Services Network
1812 West Main Street
Richmond, VA 23220
(804) 359–9488

Branches of the Arts
P.O. Box 26034
Richmond, VA 23260
(804) 355–3586

Furniture Society
Box 18
Free Union, VA 22940
(804) 973–1488
E-mail: *FurnSoc@aol.com*

Harrison Museum of African American Culture
P.O. Box 12544
Roanoke, VA 24026
(703) 345–4818

National Art Education Association
1916 Association Drive
Reston, VA 22091
(703) 860–8000

National Polymer Clay Guild
1350 Beverly Road
McLean, VA 22101
(202) 895–5212

Southeastern Virginia Arts Association
P.O. Box 1673
Norfolk, VA 23501
(804) 683–8714

Washington
Allied Arts of Seattle
105 South Main
Room 201
Seattle, WA 98104
(206) 624–0432

Artist Trust
1402 Third Avenue
Suite 415
Seattle, WA 98101
(206) 467–8734

Association of Pacific Northwest Quilters
Box 22073
Seattle, WA 98122
(206) 622–2826

Glass Art Society
1305 4th Avenue
Suite 711
Seattle, WA 98101
(206) 382–1305
www.glassart.org

Northwest Carvers Guild
P.O. Box 6092
Federal Way, WA 98063
http://members@aol.com/WeRCarvers/index.htm

Northwest Polymer Clay Guild
604 17th Avenue West
Kirkland, WA 98033
(425) 822–4107

Reflex
105 South Main
Suite 204
Seattle, WA 98104
(206) 682–7688

Washington Potters Association
P.O. Box 84255
Seattle, WA 98124

Wisconsin

Milwaukee Inner City Arts
642 West North Avenue
Milwaukee, WI 53212
(414) 265–5050

No Limits for Women Arts
1001 Kedzie Madison, WI 53704
(608) 249–6013

Wisconsin Alliance of Artists and Craftspeople
P.O. Box 185
Cross Plains, WI 53528
(608) 798–4811
www.artcraftwis.org

Wisconsin Artists, Inc.
Box 121
Bancroft, WI 54921

Wisconsin Fine Arts Association
West 62 North 718 Riveredge Drive
Cedarburg, WI 53012
(414) 377–8230

Wisconsin Folk Museum
100 South Second Street
Mt. Horeb, WI 53572
(608) 437–4742

Wisconsin Painters and Sculptors, Inc.
341 North Milwaukee Street
Milwaukee, WI 53202
(414) 276–0605

Wisconsin Regional Artists Associations
610 Langdon Street
Madison, WI 53703
(715) 356–6470

Women's Caucus for Artist—Central Wisconsin Chapter
P.O. Box 8161
Madison, WI 53708
(608) 286–0251
www.nationalwca.com

Wisconsin Women in the Arts
8700 South 15th Street
Oak Creek, WI 53154
(414) 762–0270

Canada

Alberta

Alberta Craft Council
10106 124th Street
Edmonton, Alberta T5N 1P6
(403) 488–6611

Alberta Handicrafts Guild
11 Mayfair Road, S.W.
Calgary, Alberta T2V 1Y5

Alberta Potters Association
400, 119 14th Street, N.W.
Calgary, Alberta T2M 1Z6
(403) 270–3759

Alberta Printmakers Society
P.O. Box 6821, Station D
Calgary, Alberta T2P 2E7
Canada
(403) 287–1056
http://members.nbci.com/printmakers

Alberta Society of Artists
5151 Third Street, S.E.
Calgary, Alberta T2H 2X6
Canada
(403) 640–4542

Film and Video Arts Society of Alberta
9722–102nd Street
Edmonton, Alberta T5X 0X4
Canada
(403) 429–1671

British Columbia

Embroiderers Association of Canada, Inc.
4424 Rangemont Place
Victoria, British Columbia V8N 5L6
Canada
(604) 477–1583

Federation of Canadian Artists
1241 Cartwright Street
Vancouver, British Columbia V6H 4B7
Canada
(604) 681–8534
www.artists.ca

Crafts Association of British Columbia
1386 Cartwright Street
Granville Island
Vancouver, British Columbia V6H 3R8
Canada
(604) 687–6511

Manitoba

Craft Guild of Manitoba
183 Kennedy Street
Winnipeg, Manitoba R36 1S6
Canada
(204) 943–1190

Manitoba Crafts Council
3–100 Arthur Street
Winnipeg, Manitoba R3B 1H3
Canada
(204) 942–1816

Mentoring Artists for Women's Art
2A–290 McDermot Avenue
Winnipeg, Manitoba R3B 0T2
Canada
(204) 949–9490

New Brunswick

Association des artistes acadiens professionnelles du Nouveau-Brunswick
Aberdeen Cultural Centre
140 Botsford Street
Suite 10
Moncton, New Brunswick E1C 4X4
Canada
(506) 852–3313

New Brunswick Crafts Council
P.O. Box 1231
Fredericton, New Brunswick E3B 5C8
Canada
(506) 450–8989

New Brunswick Filmmakers Cooperative
P.O. Box 1537, Station A
Fredericton, New Brunswick E3B 4Y1
Canada
(506) 455–1632

Newfoundland and Labrador

Newfoundland Independent Filmmakers Cooperative
40 Kings Road
St. John's, Newfoundland A1C 3P5
Canada
(709) 753–6121

Visual Arts–Newfoundland and Labrador
Devon House
59 Duckworth Street
St. John's, Newfoundland A1C 1E6
Canada
(709) 738–7303

Nova Scotia

Metal Arts Guild of Nova Scotia
153 Frenchman's Road
Oakfield, Nova Scotia B2T 1A9
Canada
(902) 454–0994

Nova Scotia Designer Crafts Council
1809 Barring Street
Suite 901
Halifax, Nova Scotia B3J 3K8
Canada
(902) 423–3837

Photographic Guild of Nova Scotia
122 Flagstone Drive
Dartmouth, Nova Scotia B2V 1Z8
Canada

Visual Arts–Nova Scotia
1113 Marginal Road
Halifax, Nova Scotia B3H 4P7
Canada
(902) 423–4694
http://vans.ednet.ns.ca

Ontario

Artist-Run Network
183 Baathurst Street
Toronto, Ontario M5T 2R7
Canada
(416) 703–1275

Artists in Stained Glass
c/o Ontario Crafts Council
35 McCaul Street
Suite 220
Toronto, Ontario M5T 1V7
Canada
(416) 581–1072

Arts Biz
33 North Oval
Hamilton, Ontario L8S 3YZ
Canada
(905) 526–9560
www.artsbusiness.com

Association for Native Development in the Performing and Visual Arts
39 Spadina Road
Toronto, Ontario M5R 2S9
Canada
(416) 972–0871

Association of National Nonprofit Artists Centers (ANNPAC)
183 Bathurst Street
Toronto, Ontario M5T 2R7
Canada
(416) 869–1275

Canadian Artists Network: Black Artists in Action
54 Wolseley Street
Toronto, Ontario M5T 1A5
Canada
(416) 703–9040

Canadian Artists' Representation/Le Front des Artistes Canadiens (CAR/FAC)
100 Gloucester Street
Suite B1
Ottawa, Ontario K2P 0A4
Canada
(613) 231–6277
or
221–100 Arthur Street
Winnipeg, Manitoba R3B 1G4
Canada
(204) 943–7211
or
497 Robinson Street
Moncton, New Brunswick E1C 5E7
Canada
(506) 855–0746
or
401 Richmond Street West
Suite 440
Toronto, Ontario M5V 3A8
Canada
(416) 340–8850
or
210–1808 Smith Street
Regina, Saskatchewan S4N 0N7
Canada
(306) 565–8916
or
21 Forest Drive
Aylmer, Quebec J9H 4E3
(819) 682–4183

Canadian Conference of the Arts
189 Laurent Avenue Eaast
Ottawa, Ontario K1N 6P1
Canada
(613) 238–3561

Canadian Crafts Council
189 Laurier Avenue East
Ottawa, Ontario K1N 6P1
Canada
(613) 235–8200

Canadian Native Arts Foundation
77 Mowat Avenue
Suite 508
Toronto, Ontario M6K 3E3
Canada
(416) 588–3328

Canadian Society of Painters in Water Colour
258 Wallace Street
Suite 102, Toronto, Ontario M6P 3M9
Canada
(416) 533–5100

Fusion: The Ontario Clay and Glass Association
225 Confederation Drive
Scarborough, Ontario M1G 1B2
Canada
(416) 438–8946

Inuit Art Foundation
Country Place
2081 Merivale Road
Nepean, Ontario K2G 1G9
Canada
(613) 224–8189

Native Arts and Crafts Corporation
1186 Memorial Avenue
Thunder Bay, Ontario P7B 5K5
Canada
(807) 622–5731

Ontario Crafts Council
35 McCaul Street
Toronto, Ontario M5T 1V7
Canada
(416) 977–3551

Ontario Handweavers and Spinners
35 McCaul Street
Toronto, Ontario M5T 1V7
Canada
(416) 971–9641

Pastel Society of Canada
P.O. Box 3396
Station D
Ottawa, Ontario K1P 6H8
Canada
(613) 825–4577

The Print and Drawing Council of Canada
c/o Extension Gallery
80 Spadina Avenue
Suite 503
Toronto, Ontario M5V 2J6
Canada
(416) 977–5311, ext. 323

Sculptors' Society of Canada
P.O. Box 40
Suite 301
Toronto, Ontario M5X 1B5
Canada
(416) 214–0389
www.cansculpt.org

Visual Arts—Ontario
439 Wellington Street
Toronto, Ontario M5V 1E7
Canada
(416) 591–8883

Prince Edward Island

Prince Edward Island Crafts Council
156 Richmond Street
Charlottetown, Prince Edward Island C1A 1H9
Canada
(902) 892–5152

Quebec

Artexte
3375 Boulevard St. Laurent
Suite 103
Montreal, Quebec H2X 2T7
(514) 845–2759

Independent Film and Video Alliance
5505 St. Laurent Boulevard
Suite 3000
Montreal, Quebec H2T 1S6
Canada
(514) 277–0328

Regroupement des artistes en Arts Visuels due Quebec
460 St. Catherine Street West
Suite 412
Montreal, Quebec H3B 1A7
Canada
(514) 866–7101

Saskatchewan

Association des artistes de la Saskatchewan
514 Victoria Avenue East
Suite 218
Regina, Saskatchewan S4N 0N7
Canada
(306) 522–0940

Saskatchewan Craft Council
813 Broadway Avenue
Saskatoon, Saskatchewan S7N 1B5
Canada
(306) 653–3616

Saskatchewan Embroiderers Guild
P.O. Box 563
Cut Knife, Saskatchewan S0M 0N0
Canada

Saskatchewan Wildlife
Artists Association
P.O. Box 9513
Saskatoon, Saskatchewan S7K 7G1
Canada
http://swaa.hypermart.net/swaalink.htm

Selected Bibliography

There has been a growing quantity of information that has been compiled in various sources that may be of great help to artists. No one book can tell artists everything they need to know anymore; artists whose long-term goal is to support themselves solely through the sale of their art probably should begin to assemble a library of career-oriented books and other publications.

Sources of Public and Private Grants

American Art Directory. R. R. Bowker, 1999.

American Council for the Arts: *Money for Film and Video Artists*. American Council for the Arts, 1991.

American Council for the Arts: *Money for Performing Artists*. American Council for the Arts, 1991.

American Council for the Arts: *Money for Visual Artists*. American Council for the Arts and Allworth Press, 1991.

Annual Register of Grant Support. R. R. Bowker, 1994.

Brunner, Helen, ed.: *Money to Work*, Art Resources International, 1992.

Directory of Grants in the Humanities. Oryx Press, 1999.

Fandel, Nancy A., ed.: *A National Directory of Arts and Education Support by Business and Corporations*. Washington International Arts Letters, 1989.

Fandel, Nancy A., ed.: *A National Directory of Grants and Aid to Individuals in the Arts*. Washington International Arts Letters, 1993.

Gullong, Jane, Noreen Tomassi, and Anna Rubin: *Money for International Exchange in the Arts*. American Council for the Arts and Arts International, 1992.

Hale, Suzanne, ed.: *Foundation Grants to Individuals*. The Foundation Center, 1991.

Klein, Kim: *Fundraising for Social Change*. Chardon Press, 1996.

Oxenhorn, Douglas, ed.: *Money for Visual Artists*. American Council for the Arts, 1993.

Roosevelt, Rita K., Anita M. Granoff, and Karen P.K. Kennedy: *Money Business: Grants and Awards for Creative Artists*. The Artists Foundation, 1985.

White, Virginia P.: *Grants for the Arts*. Plenum Press, 1980.

Other Sources of Financial Support for Artists

ARTnews: *ARTnews' International Directory of Corporate Art Collections*. ARTnews, 1992.

Christensen, Warren, ed.: *National Directory of Arts Internships*. National Network for Artist Placement, 1998.

Jeffri, Joan: *ArtsMoney: Raising It, Saving It, and Earning It*. University of Minnesota Press, 1983.

Jeffri, Joan, ed.: *Artisthelp: The Artist's Guide to Human and Social Services.* Neal-Schuman, 1990.

Kartes, Cheryl: *Creating Space: A Guide to Real Estate Development for Artists.* American Council for the Arts and Allworth Press, 1993.

Kruikshank, Jeffrey L. and Pam Korza: *Going Public: A Field Guide to the Developments of Art.* Arts Extension Service, University of Massachusetts, 1989.

Porter, Robert, ed.: *Guide to Corporate Giving in the Arts.* American Council for the Arts, 1987.

Career Skills for Artists

Abbott, Robert J.: *Art & Reality: The New Standard Reference Guide and Business Plan for Actively Developing Your Career as an Artist.* Steven Locks Press, 1997.

Abbott, Susan: *Corporate Art Consulting.* Allworth Press, 1999.

Abbott, Susan and Barbara Webb: *Fine Art Publicity: The Complete Guide for Galleries and Artists.* Allworth Press, 1996.

ArtCalendar: *Making a Living as an Artist.* ArtCalendar, 1993.

Artists Communities: A Directory of Residencies in the United States that Offer Time and Space for Creativity. Alliance of Artists' Communities. Allworth Press, 2000.

Brabec, Barbara: *Handmade for Profit: Hundreds of Secrets to Success in Selling Arts & Crafts.* M. Evans & Co., 1996.

Brabec, Barbara: *The Crafts Business Answer Book & Resource Guide.* M. Evans & Co., 1998.

Caplan, Evan, Tom Power, Livingston Biddle, eds: *The Business of Art*, Prentice Hall, 1998.

Caputo, Kathryn: *How to Start Making Money with Your Crafts.* Betterway Publishing, 1995.

Cochrane, Diana: *This Business of Art.* Watson-Guptill, 1988.

Cummings, Paul: *Fine Arts Market Place.* R. R. Bowker, 1977.

Davis, Sally Prince: *The Fine Artist's Guide to Showing and Selling Your Work.* North Light Books, 1990.

Davis, Sally Prince: *Graphic Artists Guide to Marketing and Self-Promotion.* North Light Books, 1987.

Egan, Dorothy: *How to Start Making Money with Your Decorative Painting.* North Light Books, 1998.

Frascogna, Xavier M. and J. Lee Hetherington: *This Business of Artist Management.* Watson-Guptill, 1997.

Gerhard, Paul: *How to Sell What Your Make: The Business of Marketing Crafts.* Stackpole Books, 1996.

Goldfarb, Roz: *Careers by Design: A Headhunter's Secrets for Success and Survival in Graphic Design.* Allworth Press, 1997.

Goodman, Calvin J.: *Art Marketing Handbook.* GeePeeBee, 1985.

Gordon, Elliott, and Barbara Gordon: *How to Sell Your Photographs and Illustrations.* Allworth Press, 1990.

Grant, Daniel: *The Artist's Guide: Making It in New York City.* Allworth Press, 2001.

Grant, Daniel: *The Artist's Resource Handbook.* Allworth Press, 1997.

Grant, Daniel: *The Business of Being an Artist.* Allworth Press, 2000.

Grant, Daniel: *The Fine Artist's Career Guide*, Allworth Press, 1998.

Graphic Artists Guild Handbook: Pricing and Ethical Guidelines. Graphic Artists Guild, 1984.

Hadden, Peggy: *The Artist's Guide to New Markets.* Allworth Press, 1998.

Hill, Elizabeth, Catherine O'Sullivan and Terry O'Sullivan: *Creative Arts Marketing.* Butterworth-Heinemann, 1996.

Holden, Donald: *Art Career Guide.* Watson-Guptill, 1983.

Hoover, Deborah A.: *Supporting Yourself as an Artist.* Oxford University Press, 1989.

Indian Arts and Crafts Board: *Potential Marketing Outlets for Native American Artists and Craftspeople.* Indian Arts and Crafts Board (U.S. Department of the Interior, 1849 C Street N.W., MS–4004, Washington, DC 20240), 1993.

Janecek, Lenore: *Health Insurance: A Guide for Artists, Consultants, Entrepreneurs & Other Self-Employed.* American Council for the Arts, 1993.

Katchen, Carole: *How to Get Started Selling Your Art.* North Light Books, 1996.

Klayman, Toby and Cobbett Steinberg: *The Artist's Survival Manual.* Charles Scribner's Sons, 1987.

Landman, Sylvia: *Crafting for Dollars: Turn Your Hobby into Serious Cash.* Prima Publications, 1996.

Langley, Stephen, and James Abruzzo: *Jobs in Arts and Media Management.* New York: American Council for the Arts, 1992.

Manolis, Argie, ed: *Crafts Market Place: Where and How to Sell Your Crafts.* Betterway Publications, 1997.

MFA Programs in the Visual Arts: A Directory. College Art Association of America, 1987.

Michels, Caroll: *How to Survive & Prosper as an Artist.* Henry Holt and Company, 2001.

Muth, Marcia: *How to Paint and Sell Your Work.* Sunstone Press, 1984.

NAAO Directory. National Association of Artists Organizations, 1989.

Oberrecht, Kenn: *How to Start a Home-Based Crafts Business.* Globe Pequot Press, 1997.

Pratt, Nina: *How to Find Art Buyers.* Succotash Press, 1994.

Pratt, Nina: *How to Sell Art.* Succotash, 1992.

Ramsey, Dan: *The Crafter's Guide to Pricing Your Work.* Betterway Publications, 1997.

Rosen, Wendy: *Crafting as a Business.* Sterling Publications, 1998.

Sager, Susan Joy: *Sellling Your Crafts.* Allworth Press, 1998.

Shaw Associates: *The Guide to Arts & Crafts Workshops.* Shaw Associates, 1991.

Shaw Associates: *The Guide to Photography Workshops & Schools.* Shaw Associates, 1992.

Shaw Associates: *The Guide to Writers Conferences.* Shaw Associates, 1992.

Shipley, Lloyd W.: *Information Resources in the Arts.* Library of Congress, 1986.

Shiva, V.A.: *Arts and the Internet: A Guide to the Revolution.* Allworth Press, 1996.

Shiva, V.A.: *The Internet Publicity Guide: How to Maximize Your Marketing and Promotion in Cyberspace.* Allworth Press, 1997.

Stolper, Carolyn L., and Karen Brooks Hopkins: *Successful Fundraising for Arts and Cultural Organizations.* Oryx Press, 1989.

Viders, Sue: *Producing and Marketing Prints.* Color Q, Inc., 1992.

West, Janice: *Marketing Your Arts & Crafts: Creative Ways to Profit from Your Work.* Summit Publishing Group, 1994.

Art and the Law

Conner, Floyd, et al.: *The Artist's Friendly Legal Guide.* North Light Books, 1988.

Crawford, Tad and Susan Mellon: *The Artist-Gallery Partnership: A Practical Guide to Consigning Art.* Allworth Press, 1998.

Crawford, Tad: *Business and Legal Forms for Crafts.* Allworth Press, 1998.

Crawford, Tad: *Business and Legal Forms for Fine Artists.* Allworth Press, 1999.

Crawford, Tad: *Business and Legal Forms for Graphic Designers.* Allworth Press, 1999.

Crawford, Tad: *Business and Legal Forms for Illustrators.* Allworth Press, 1998.

Crawford, Tad: *Business and Legal Forms for Authors and Self-Publishers.* Allworth Press, 1996.

Crawford, Tad: *Legal Guide for the Visual Artist.* Allworth Press, 1999.

Crawford, Tad and Eva Doman Bruck: *Business and Legal Forms for Graphic Designers.* Allworth Press, 1990.

Duboff, Leonard D.: *The Law (in Plain English) for Crafts.* Allworth Press, 1998.

Leland, Caryn: *Licensing Art and Design.* Allworth Press, 1995.

Messman, Carla: *The Artist's Tax Workbook.* Lyons & Burford, 1992.

Norwick, Kenneth P., and Jerry Simon Chasen: *The Rights of Authors, Artists, and Other Creative People.* Southern Illinois University Press, 1992.

Wilson, Lee: *Make It Legal.* Allworth Press, 1990.

Health and Safety in the Arts and Crafts

Enteen, Robert: *Health Insurance: How to Get It, Keep It, or Improve What You've Got.* Paragon House, 1992.

Mayer, Ralph: *The Artist's Handbook.* Viking, 1982.

Mayer, Ralph: *The Painter's Craft.* Penguin Books, 1977.

McCann, Michael: *Artist Beware.* Lyons & Burford, 1993.

Rossol, Monona: *The Artist's Complete Health and Safety Guide.* Allworth Press, 1994.

Shaw, Susan D., and Monona Rossol: *Overexposure: Health Hazards in Photography.* American Council for the Arts and Allworth Press, 1991.

Silver Lake Editors: *Hassle-Free Health Coverage: How to Buy the Right Medical Insurance Cheaply and Effectively.* Silver Lake Publishing, 1999.

Spandorfer, Merle: *Making Art Safely.* John Wiley & Sons, 1997.

Of Related Interest

Baumol, William J., and William G. Bowen: *Performing Arts: The Economic Dilemma.* MIT Press, 1966.

Benedict, Stephen, ed.: *Public Money and the Muse: Essays on Government Funding for the Arts.* W. W. Norton, 1991.

Cockcroft, Eva, John Weber, and James Cockcroft: *Toward a People's Art: The Contemporary Mural Movement.* E. P. Dutton, 1977.

Conrad, Barnaby III: *Absinthe: History in a Bottle.* Chronicle Books, 1988.

Dardis, Tom: *The Thirsty Muse: Alcohol and the American Writer.* Ticknor & Fields, 1989.

Feld, Alan L., Michael O'Hare, and J. Mark Davidson Schuster: *Patrons Despite Themselves: Taxpayers and Arts Policy.* New York University Press, 1983.

Jeffri, Joan: *The Emerging Arts: Management, Survival and Growth.* Praeger, 1980.

Misey, Johanna L., ed.: *National Directory of Multi-Cultural Arts Organizations.* National Assembly of State Arts Agencies, 1990.

Mitchell, W. J. T., ed.: *Art and the Public Sphere.* University of Chicago Press, 1992.

Naude, Virginia, and Glenn Wharton: *Guide to the Maintenance of Outdoor Sculpture.* American Institute for Conservation of Historic and Artistic Works, 1995.

Netzer, Dick: *The Subsidized Muse: Public Support for the Arts in the United States.* Cambridge University Press, 1978.

Shore, Irma, and Beatrice Jacinto: *Access to Art: A Museum Directory for Blind and*

Visually Impaired People. American Foundation for the Blind, 1989.

Snyder, Jill: *Caring for Your Art: A Guide for Artists, Collectors, Galleries, and Art Institutions.* Allworth Press, 1990.

Whitaker, Ben: *The Philanthropoids: Foundations and Society.* William Morrow, 1974.

Art Publications

A number of magazines and journals are published for artists. They include news in the field, trends and opinions, listings of upcoming juried art shows, art workshops, and other opportunities, technical information, and career advice as well as feature articles. Among these are:

ACTS Facts
Arts, Crafts, and Theater Safety
181 Thompson Street
Room 23
New York, NY 10012
(212) 777–0062
$10 a year

American Artist
One Color Court
Marion, OH 43305
(800) 347–6969
$24.95 a year

The Artist's Magazine
P.O. Box 2120
Harlan, IA 51593
(800) 333–0444
$24 a year

ArtJob
236 Montezuma Avenue
Santa Fe, NM 87501
(505) 988–1166
$24 a year

ARTnews
P.O. 2083
Knoxville, IA 50197
(800) 284–4625
$32.95 a year

Art Now Gallery Guide
Art Now, Inc.
P.O. Box 888
Vineland, NJ 08360
(201) 322–8333
$35 a year

The Chronicle of Philanthropy
1225 23rd Street N.W.
Washington, DC 20037
(202) 466–1200
$67.50 a year

Fairs and Festivals in the Northeast
Fairs and Festivals in the Southeast
Arts Extension Service
Division of Continuing Education
358 North Pleasant Street
University of Massachusetts
Amherst, MA 01003
(413) 545–2360
$7.50 each; $13 for both

Institute Items
Art & Craft Materials Institute
100 Boylston Street
Suite 1050
Boston, MA 02116
(617) 426–6400
$20 a year (for individual artists)
$50 a year (for companies)

New Art Examiner
1255 South Wabash
4th floor
Chicago, IL 60605
(312) 786–0200
$35 a year

Pen, Pencil & Paint
National Artists Equity Association
P.O. Box 28068
Washington, DC 20038
(800) 727–6232
$12 a year

Sunshine Artists USA
2600 Temple Drive
Winter Park,
FL 32789
(407) 539–1399
$22.50 a year

Index

D

E

F

G

H

I

J

K

L

M

N

BOOKS FROM ALLWORTH PRESS

The Quotable Artist
by Peggy Hadden (hardcover, $7\frac{1}{2} \times 7\frac{1}{2}$, 224 pages, 19.95)

The Artist's Complete Health and Safety Guide, Third Edition
by Monona Rossol (paperback, 6×9, 416 pages, $24.95)

The Business of Being an Artist, Third Edition
by Daniel Grant (paperback, 6×9, 352 pages, $19.95)

The Fine Artist's Career Guide
by Daniel Grant (paperback, 6×9, 304 pages, $18.95)

The Artist's Resource Handbook, Revised Edition
by Daniel Grant (paperback, 6×9, 248 pages, $18.95)

An Artist's Guide: Making It in New York City
by Daniel Grant (paperback, 6×9, 256 pages, $19.95)

The Artist's Quest for Inspiration
by Peggy Hadden (paperback, 6×9, 272 pages, $15.95)

The Artist's Guide to New Markets: Opportunities to Show and Sell Art Beyond Galleries
by Peggy Hadden (paperback, $5\frac{1}{2} \times 8\frac{1}{2}$, 252 pages, $18.95)

Caring for Your Art: A Guide for Artists, Collectors, Galleries, and Art Institutions, Third Edition
by Jill Snyder (paperback, 6×9, 256 pages, $19.95)

Artists Communities: A Directory of Residencies in the United States That Offer Time and Space for Creativity, Second Edition
by the Alliance of Artists' Communities (paperback, $6\frac{3}{4} \times 9\frac{7}{8}$, 256 pages, $18.95)

The Fine Artist's Guide to Marketing and Self-Promotion
by Julius Vitali (paperback, 6×9, 224 pages, $18.95)

Corporate Art Consulting
by Susan Abbott (paperback, $11 \times 8\frac{1}{2}$, 256 pages, $34.95)

Legal Guide for the Visual Artist, Fourth Edition
by Tad Crawford (paperback, $8\frac{1}{2} \times 11$, 272 pages, $19.95)

Business and Legal Forms for Fine Artists, Revised Edition with CD-ROM
by Tad Crawford (paperback, $8\frac{1}{2} \times 11$, 144 pages, $19.95)

Please write to request our free catalog. To order by credit card, call 1-800-491-2808 or send a check or money order to Allworth Press, 10 East 23rd Street, Suite 510, New York, NY 10010. Include $5 for shipping and handling for the first book ordered and $1 for each additional book. Ten dollars plus $1 for each additional book if ordering from Canada. New York State residents must add sales tax.

To see our complete catalog on the World Wide Web, or to order online, you can find us at www.allworth.com.